Everyday Vegan Eats

Everyday
Vegan Eats

*Family Favorites
from My Kitchen to Yours*

Zsu Dever

Vegan Heritage Press

Woodstock • Virginia

Everyday Vegan Eats: Family Favorites from My Kitchen to Yours by Zsu Dever
(Copyright © 2014 by Zsu Dever)

ISBN 13: 978-0-9854662-6-8

First Edition, May 2014
10 9 8 7 6 5 4 3 2 1

Vegan Heritage Press books are available at quantity discounts. For information, please visit our website at www.veganheritagepress.com or write the publisher at Vegan Heritage Press, P.O. Box 628, Woodstock, VA 22664-0628.

Library of Congress Cataloging-in-Publication Data

Dever, Zsu, 1972-
   Everyday vegan eats : family favorites from my kitchen to yours / Zsu Dever.
        pages cm
   Includes index.
   ISBN 978-0-9854662-6-8
   1. Vegan cooking. I. Title.
   TX837.Z78 2014
   641.5'636--dc23
                                    2014001821

Photo credits: Cover and interior photography by Zsu Dever. Photo of the author by Katelyn Dever.

Cover design: Dianne Wenz

Cover Photo: Front: Scampi Pasta with Asparagus and Walnuts (page 148); Back (from top) Arroz non Pollo (page 180) and Greek Gyros with Tzaziki Sauce (page 77).

Disclaimer: Allergies can be a serious threat to one's health. If you know you have food allergies, please take necessary cautions whenever you cook. If you require a medical diagnosis, or if you are contemplating any major dietary change, please consult a qualified health-care provider. You should always seek an expert medical opinion before making changes in your diet.

Distributed by Andrews McMeel Publishing/Simon & Schuster

Printed in the United States of America

Dedication

To my mother who somehow always found a way to fill the family table with love. You are so dearly missed!

Contents

10. Breakfast & Brunch

11. Desserts & Bakery

Introduction

I hail from a long line of restaurateurs and chefs and have trained under one of the best chefs I have ever known—my dad. He taught me how flavors can harmonize and sing, and, when my family became vegan thirteen years ago, I took that knowledge and applied it to vegan cookery in my own kitchen.

With *Everyday Vegan Eats,* I share my family's favorite recipes to show just how easy and delicious vegan cooking can be. Whether you're slowly moving into vegan options—or even going vegan over-night, like my family did—you are entering a world of surprisingly delicious and satisfying new flavors and textures, while still enjoying healthy versions of many of the same dishes you used to make with meat and dairy. This cookbook delivers what we all want: *Everyday Vegan Eats,* with delicious com-fort food recipes that everyone can enjoy.

As a longtime vegan, I know that eating a plant-based diet can be a challenge because we do not (yet) live in a vegan world. To help make eating vegan as easy as possible, I share information on how to establish a vegan pantry, how to shop for vegan ingredients, and provide other helpful tips for both the novice and long-time vegan.

This book shows you how cooking vegan can be a smooth transition that's easy on your budget. *Everyday Vegan Eats* features familiar homestyle recipes that you may have thought were out of reach now that you are eating vegan. The recipes are for good old-fashioned comfort foods re-imagined to suit a healthier, more compassionate lifestyle. In these pages, you'll find Tater Tot Casserole, Lasagna Americana, Chili Mac, Minestrone Soup, and other delicious family favorites. Many of the recipes are also quick to prepare, making them easy on your schedule as well. In addition, I have provided recipes for plant-strong proteins and vegan dairy alternatives, including homemade seitan and vegan mayonnaise, as well as instructions on how to properly prepare tofu and tempeh. I even include my recipe for making a fantastic vegan yogurt that beats commercial yogurts by a mile.

As you can tell from my website, www.zsusveganpantry.com, I am passionate about helping new vegans and those trying to eat more vegan meals succeed with this win-win way of cooking, eating, and living. *With Everyday Vegan Eats,* my goal is to help you become a happy vegan by making sure that your every meal is satisfying and delicious.

I begin by sharing some things you need to know as you pick out which recipes to try first, and move on to basic recipes for homemade ingredients that you can use in my dishes, although you can substitute with storebought items as indicated in the ingredient lists. I hope you enjoy my recipes as much as my family does. I'm proud to say we love every one of them at the Dever house!

CHAPTER 1

Vegan Everyday

Over time, certain foods become close to our hearts. These comfort foods evoke childhood memories or some precious moment from long ago. Some dishes might remind you of your mom or dad preparing an afternoon snack, such as a favorite soup and sandwich or a warm batch of chocolate chip cookies.

In this book, you'll discover that you can be vegan everyday with the recipes that have become comfort-food traditions in my family. Once you try them, they could very well become favorites for you and yours.

In this book, you will discover how easy it is to make vegan versions of your favorites by substituting certain ingredients, whether homemade or purchased in a store. I provide many vegan protein and dairy-free options in Recipe Basics. I call on those recipes throughout this book, but there is no need to use only my options. If you'd rather use a commercial vegan protein or dairy-free product, substitute as you wish.

In writing this book, it was important to me to create recipes that you can adjust to suit your own tastes. So, no matter what the dish, feel free to adapt my recipes to your own preferences. For example, if you grew up eating mac-and-cheese with broccoli florets, then you can enjoy my recipe for the same dish made vegan, but add some broccoli florets so it "tastes like home." If your mom made tuna salad with dill weed, then add dill to the Tempeh No-Tuna Salad recipe in this book. If your former egg salad was made without mustard but included chives, then by all means, omit the mustard from the Eggless Tofu Salad and add minced chives. In other words, make these comfort food dishes taste just the way you like them.

Menu Planning

Eating vegan is no different than eating any other way. The difference lies in the ingredients you choose, and for this you may find yourself exploring some new territory. The most cost-effective way to eat, is, of course, at home—cooking your own food. It is also a healthful way to eat and can be quite fun—except perhaps the cleaning-up part, but that is the case regardless of what you eat. In fact, it is easier to clean up burnt vegan cheese than burnt dairy cheese and much easier to scrub off day-old tofu than day-old eggs.

Have you ever heard the adage, "If you fail to plan, you plan to fail"? Planning your weekly menu in advance keeps you on the winning side. It also makes grocery shopping easier and avoids unnecessary spending. We can all use more cash in our wallets!

Menu planning can be as simple as jotting down what you plan to make for dinner on a piece of paper, or filling in a weekly menu template for every meal of the day, such as the ones provided on my website, www.zsusveganpantry.com. There you will find printable, diet-specific menu templates, including those that are gluten-free and soy-free. (Look under the Menu/Shopping tab.) Instructions on how to use the templates are provided there, where you will also find an efficient shopping list.

Once you have your weekly menu planned, it's time to make a shopping list. If you know the layout of your supermarket, organize your list according to where you'll find certain foods (such as produce, frozen foods, etc.) to help make shopping quicker and easier.

Menu planning and your grocery list go hand in hand, since you can refer to the recipes on your menu to check the ingredients you may need to buy to prepare the recipes. Make sure to double-check your pantry for ingredients you may already have. Once you have taken care of the weekly menu ingredients, add snack items to the list, including fresh fruits, vegetables, and nuts.

Remember, in order to eat vegan, you need to have vegan food available at home, which translates to a well-stocked refrigerator, freezer, and pantry.

Ingredients You'll Want to Know

Before moving on to the cooking, I'd like to introduce you to some ingredients that can be a vegan cook's best friends and are used in many of the recipes in this book. Have a look at these ingredients and try to pick some of them up over the next few grocery shopping trips so you have them on hand for when you dig into the recipes.

Almonds: These nuts are used in the form of nut milk and nut cream in many recipes in this book. When making nut milk or cream, use blanched almonds which have had the skins removed. If you need to blanch your own nuts, plunge them into boiling water for 30 seconds, then drain them and pop the skins off. Once blanched, the nuts and skins separate and make this process easy.

Applesauce: If you do not eat a whole jar of applesauce weekly, consider buying it in small single-serving containers. There is less waste even if they cost a little more. No longer will you have to open a whole jar of applesauce just to use two tablespoons.

Arrowroot or cornstarch: While the two are almost interchangeable, arrowroot is the more stable of the two and one I prefer to use as a thickener given the choice between the two. Arrowroot has been used to develop these recipes. When thickening sauces or soups with either one, however, it is important to note that once the starch is added (in the form of a slurry), the dish should only be cooked long enough to thicken. Cooking these starches too long will cause them to break, and your sauce will revert back to its original thin consistency.

Brown sugar: Regular brown sugar is simply white sugar with the molasses added back in. Light brown sugar has a higher moisture content than dark brown sugar and both have a place in the kitchen. Use either one in recipes that do not specify the variety to use.

Chickpea flour: Garbanzo beans are dried and ground to make chickpea flour, which I use in seitan recipes.

Chipotle in adobo: These canned, smoked jalapeños in a tomato sauce can be found in the international aisle or near the pickled jalapeños. Once opened, make Chipotle Adobo Purée with it (page 63).

Coconut milk: Thick and creamy, canned coconut milk is the milk that is first pressed from the ground meat of the coconut. This is not the same as coconut milk beverage (in quart or half-gallon containers) or the same as the water from young coconuts. The milk tends to separate if it has been in the can too long, so shake the can before opening it to mix the contents; the separation of the fat and water content is natural.

Corn flour: Finely ground corn flour is not interchangeable with regular cornmeal in this book. You can make corn flour by grinding cornmeal to a fine flour.

Dulse seaweed flakes: Sea vegetables are chock full of trace minerals. If you are new to culinary seaweed, dulse is the lightest tasting of the bunch and the easiest on newbie seaweed diners. There are several recipes in this book that use dulse deliciously. Check out Tempeh No-Tuna Sandwiches (page 84), Coco Loco Soba with Dulse and Kale (page 146), No-Fish Filet Sandwiches (page 74), and New England Chowder (page 56).

Granulated sugar: When choosing a granulated sugar, look for one that is not refined at all, one that is naturally refined, or one that is organic. Regular sugar is filtered using cow bone char, so organic sugar, by definition, is not filtered using bone char.

Golden flax seeds: This seed is high in omega-3 fatty acids and is a great binder in baked goods because of its high lecithin content. Buy whole flax seeds and grind them to a fine meal as needed using a personal blender. Otherwise you can purchase pre-ground flax seed meal, but keep it stored in the freezer. I use golden flax instead of brown flax because it looks prettier in dishes. You can use either one, as they both have the same thickening and nutritional properties.

Medium-grind cornmeal: Medium-grind stone-ground corn is great for making cornbread and polenta. This is the only kind of cornmeal used in this book.

Neutral-tasting oil: When I need a neutral-tasting oil for recipes, I buy sunflower, grapeseed, or safflower oil.

Nutritional yeast: This is deactivated yeast that is full of protein and vitamin B. It tastes "nutty" or "cheesy;" although I have never really associated it much with cheesiness, a lot of vegans have. It adds a complex flavor to foods and is the main ingredient in Savory Broth Mix (page 19). It is available as flakes and powder; all the recipes in this book use it in flake form, but if you have the powder version, just use half as much as the recipe calls for.

Olive oil: All the recipes in this book were developed using extra-virgin olive oil, but regular olive oil is a perfectly acceptable substitution.

Quinoa: This is a high-protein seed that is used as a grain in cooking. It has a very bitter outer coating that must be rinsed off very well.

Reduced-sodium tamari: High-quality tamari soy sauce contains no wheat (check the ingredients). I prefer the taste of tamari over regular soy sauce as it is richer and deeper. All the recipes in this book were developed using the reduced sodium version of tamari. If you use a full-sodium version of tamari or regular soy sauce, reduce the amount that is called for in the recipes as the final product might be too salty or overpowering.

Soy Curls: These are a meat substitute made of non-GMO whole soybeans. Unlike textured vegetable protein, Butler Soy Curls are not defatted and have no added chemicals or preservatives. They are available online through various outlets.

Tahini: Tahini can easily be made at home using sesame seeds. Grind 1 cup of sesame seeds with 3 tablespoons of neutral-tasting oil (page 4) in a personal blender or standard blender until the mixture is smooth.

Tapioca flour or starch: One and the same, tapioca starch or flour is the dried ground root of the cassava plant and is used to thicken liquids and bind ingredients.

Toasted sesame oil: This is a very deep, nutty, and distinct oil. It tends to be used in moderation as it has a strong flavor. There is only one recipe where I use it with a heavy hand, but it is a well-balanced dish: Chilled Sesame Soba Noodles (page 150).

Plain unsweetened vegan milk: With the numerous vegan milks now available, it is important to double-check which kind of milk you are using for cooking. When it comes to drinking, you can choose by flavor, but when it comes to cooking, "plain" and "unsweetened" is the only way to go — unless you enjoy a sweet, vanilla-tasting Stroganoff! In addition, be aware that different milks have different thickening abilities. All the recipes in this book were developed using plain, unsweetened almond milk and plain, unsweetened soy milk. If you are making dessert, feel free to use sweetened vanilla milk, where you feel it is appropriate; however, I specify "plain unsweetened" for the sake of consistency.

Vegan cheese: Vegan cheeses are as varied as their dairy counterparts. Some are made with soy; some are made with almonds, rice, or coconut. For this reason their melting points and textures also vary greatly. When making a dish with commercial cheese where the intention is to melt the cheese, it is best to use a mixture of different brands of vegan cheeses. This is especially true for lasagna, enchiladas, and other casseroles. In addition, vegan cheeses tend to melt better when the dish is covered.

Vital wheat gluten: When wheat flour is washed of its bran and starch, what is left is protein. This protein is dried and ground into flour. This is used to make seitan.

Ingredient Substitutions

Transforming favorite family recipes into vegan ones is all about using plant-based ingredients instead of animal ingredients. Here is a list of common ingredient substitutions.

- **Butter:** Earth Balance spread is the one I recommend, although there are other brands on the market. Look for one without hydrogenated vegetable oil.

- **Cow's milk:** Some substitutions are soy milk, nut milk, grain milk, seed milk, and coconut milk. I prefer almond milk as my go-to vegan milk. Some of my favorite brands are Califia Farms, Almond Breeze, and 365 Everyday Value Organic. For cooking, my preferences are almond milk and soy milk and any of the above as a beverage or cereal accompaniment.

- **Dairy cream:** Homemade nut milk makes the best cream to use for cooking. For your coffee, storebought brands are readily available by various manufacturers.

- **Buttermilk:** Add 2 teaspoons apple cider vinegar to 1 cup of soy milk, which will curdle and thicken it.

- **Dairy yogurt:** These vary greatly by brand and the kind of milk being cultured. For the best tasting yogurt, make your own.

- **Sour cream:** There are great brands of vegan sour cream on the market today.

- **Ice cream:** Storebought vegan ice cream comes in many varieties and is readily available. Many different flavors and brands exist, so search until you find one you like. There are also numerous cookbooks for making your own vegan ice cream at home. There are also non-dairy sherbets and popsicles, which are great alternatives to their dairy-based counterparts.

- **Eggs:** Eggs serve multiple purposes in the cooking world. If making scrambled eggs for breakfast, substitute mashed tofu, using my recipe (page 206) as a jumping-off point, or try the Vegan Omelet recipe on page 208. If you are missing sunny-side up eggs with the runny yolk, try The Vegg, available at www.theveggg.com. For replacing eggs in baking, it is best to use a vegan recipe that has been tested; however, common vegan substitutions for eggs in baked goods include commercial egg substitutes (such as Ener-G Egg Replacer), silken tofu, bananas, starches, nut butters, ground flax seed, and oil.

- **Honey:** Substitute maple syrup, agave nectar, or sugar mixed with a little water (at a ratio of 3 tablespoons water to 1 cup sugar) for honey.

- **Meat:** There are storebought meat substitutes galore! From vegan shrimp to vegan ground beef, choices abound. From a protein-substitution perspective, legumes, soy, tofu, tempeh, seitan, dark leafy greens, broccoli, nuts, and seeds are just some of the options. From a taste perspective, check out great vegan recipes (some in this very book) that mimic the flavor and texture of meat, without the cost to the animals.

- **Gelatin:** Gelatin is derived from bones, skin, ligaments, and tendons of animals. It is used as a thickener in gelatins and aspic. Vegan substitutions include seaweed-derived thickeners such as agar-agar and Irish moss.

Where to Shop

The following is a list of where to shop for the ingredients you will need. It may surprise you to discover that most of the ingredients used in this book can be found in a regular supermarket, so that's where we begin.

Regular grocery stores: Regular chain grocers have come a long way in the past decade. There are now natural food or health food aisles in these stores where more and more vegan and vegetarian products are showing up. Also check the produce section for tofu and vegan cheeses and check the international aisles for tamari, tahini, spring roll wrappers, and chipotle peppers, among other products.

Ethnic grocers: Hit up ethnic grocers whenever you can. Indian grocers will carry spices, black salt, dry legumes, flours, and rice. Mexican grocers will carry spices, various kinds of chiles, flours, and all kinds of corn products, including masa and husks. Asian grocers will carry seaweed, rice, soy products, yuba, spices, produce like oyster mushrooms, vegan fish sauce and vegan oyster sauce, potsticker wrappers, and rice flours.

Big-box health food stores: These stores get a bad rep as being too expensive and over-priced. In truth, if you are shopping for bulk ingredients or basic staples they are much cheaper than any chain grocery store. Their organic produce is inexpensive and their tofu and bulk items are priced below the competition. In addition, if you order a case of a single item, you get a discount.

Co-ops: These are not really stores in the sense that you can shop at one; instead, co-ops are food distribution outlets. Typically, a group of people team up to buy a certain quantity of food from the organization; the co-op delivers the food to a member and that member distributes the order to the other members. Some North American co-ops are Azure Standard (www.azurestandard.com) and Bulk Natural Foods (www.bulknaturalfoods.com). For a nationwide list of food co-ops, visit my website (www.zsusveganpantry.com). Other food co-ops are actual brick-and-mortar stores that are owned and operated by the employees. To find a cooperative grocer in your area, search the database at www.cooperativegrocer.coop.

Farmer's markets: Farmer's markets offer amazingly fresh produce and also limit the distance the food travels to you. You also have the chance to interact with the actual growers of your food and ask any pertinent questions. Find local farmer's markets in your area by searching the database at www.localharvest.org.

Community Supported Agriculture (CSA): CSAs are produce production and distribution systems that directly connect the consumers to the farmers. They are a group of farms that unite, harvesting and delivering their produce to the consumers. Typically, the consumers pay for the produce for the season in advance, and the produce is delivered to the consumers as it is harvested weekly or biweekly. Other CSAs offer the consumer the option to choose which produce to buy. To find a local CSA, search the database at www.localharvest.org.

Online Shopping: Many people prefer the ease and convenience of shopping online, especially for specialty items. Several online outlets offer free shipping and deep discounts, making shopping on-line hard to resist. In the Resources section, I've listed some of the best places to locate ingredients such as nutritional yeast and Soy Curls on the web.

Cooking Techniques

Some specific cooking techniques are called for in several of the recipes in this book, from blending nuts to grinding vegan proteins. Below is a list of these techniques and how to do them.

Roasting Peppers

Roasting peppers accomplishes two things: it cooks the pepper and imparts a smoky flavor, and it helps remove the skin of the pepper. There are multiple ways of roasting the pepper to char the skin, but they all have a few important things in common: the flesh of the pepper needs to cook; the skin needs to cook and char, but the pepper must not overcook, otherwise the skin will not peel off. It is not necessary that the entire pepper be charred; it is better to have most of it blistered than all of it blackened. The process:

1. **Cook the pepper:** To roast the pepper either (1) cook the pepper over high heat directly over a burner, turning as needed, (2) cook the pepper over high heat in a cast iron skillet, turning the pepper as needed (3) broil the pepper 8 inches from the heat source, turning as needed, for 15 to 20 minutes (4) cook the pepper in hot oil for 1 minute.
2. **Steam off the skin:** Once the pepper is roasted, it needs to steam. Transfer the roasted pepper to a large bowl and cover the bowl with a plastic wrap to trap the steam. Steam the pepper for 15 minutes. I prefer the bowl method over placing the peppers in paper bags because the bags let out some steam, while the bowl and wrap let out very little.
3. **Peel the pepper:** Once the pepper has steamed, it needs to be peeled, stemmed, and seeded. Remove the pepper from the bowl and place it on the plastic wrap that was covering the bowl. Using the plastic wrap or your hands, rub the charred skin from the flesh of the pepper; it will easily rub off if the pepper is cooked and the skin has steamed. After peeling, use a paring knife to stem and seed the pepper. Use as needed.

Blending Nuts

Some recipes require nuts to be ground into sauces, nut milks, or nut creams. Cashews are softer and will more readily grind into a fine powder. Blanched almonds are harder and more difficult to grind. In order to make the smoothest sauce possible, you can either grind the nuts first into a powder, blend the sauce long enough to achieve a smooth sauce, or soak the nuts in the recipe liquid overnight. A quick-soaking method is to first heat the liquid that the nuts will be soaking in. Another quick method is to blend the nuts and liquid, allow it to sit for 15 minutes and then blend again until smooth. If needed, strain the milk or cream through 8 layers of cheesecloth or a nut milk bag. Because of their distinct flavors, nuts are not interchangeable when a specific nut is called for in a recipe.

Pressing Tofu

When a recipe calls for pressed tofu, the tofu needs to have as much liquid pressed out as possible. Pressing tofu for 10 minutes presses out most of the liquid. Pressing for 30 minutes results in another half as much liquid being released as pressing for 10 minutes. Pressing the tofu for 1 hour will press out a few more tablespoons of liquid, and an overnight press will press out another few tablespoons of liquid. Tofu pressed overnight is best for tofu that will be marinated. A Tofu Xpress is the easiest way to press tofu, but if you do not have one, wrap the tofu in a flour sack towel and place in the refrigerator overnight. This method is much better than using objects to press the tofu, but is not quite as effective as the Tofu Xpress. It is, however, sufficient for most recipes that need pressed tofu.

Pan-Sautéing

To pan sauté seitan or marinated tofu slices, dredge the slices (on both sides) in flour or corn flour, shaking off the excess. Heat a few teaspoons of oil or melt vegan butter in a skillet over medium heat. Add the dredged slices to the hot pan and cook, undisturbed, until the seitan or tofu is golden brown, about 2 to 3 minutes. Flip and cook, undisturbed, until golden brown and crisp on the other side, another 2 minutes.

Pan-Frying

To pan fry ingredients, such as onions, seitan, tofu, or mushrooms, fill a large pot or large skillet with 1/2-inch-deep layer of oil (or as indicated in the recipe). Heat the oil over medium heat until hot. Below are a few ways to check if your oil is the correct temperature, none of them being to add water to the hot oil; that is far too dangerous.

1. Add a kernel of popcorn to the heating oil. When the oil is hot enough the kernel will pop.
2. Add a cube of white bread to the oil. If the bread browns in 1 minute, the oil is ready. If it browns faster, the oil is too hot.
3. Stick the handle of a wooden spoon into the oil. If the oil bubbles around the spoon, the oil is hot enough. If the oil bubbles too intensely, the oil is too hot.
4. Gauge the temperature with a heat-resistant thermometer, measuring at 350°F to 365°F
5. Do not crowd your pan. Fry in batches. If there are too many items in the hot oil all at once, the temperature drops drastically and you wind up with greasy and soggy food.

Grinding Protein

To grind Tender Soy Curls, Simple Seitan, or other vegan protein, pulse the chopped protein in a food processor until minced or ground.

Cutting Techniques

Aside from making food look prettier, cutting your ingredients into the right size and shape speeds cooking time and increases cooking efficiency. When pieces of the same ingredient are cut into different sizes, they cook at different rates and leave some pieces overcooked and others undercooked. In raw foods, such as salads, cutting the ingredients the proper size is appealing visually and texturally.

Below are the cutting techniques used in the recipes in this book:

Slicing: To cut completely through an ingredient. Think sliced bread.

Coarsely chopped: To chop something into small, 1/2-inch pieces, although they don't have to all be the exact same size.

Finely chopped: To chop something into smaller, 1/4-inch pieces fairly uniform in size.

Minced (very finely chopped): To chop into tiny pieces. This is mainly used for herbs, garlic and ginger. Accomplish this by running your knife back and forth through the ingredients to be very finely chopped.

Matchsticks: This cut is the same as julienning an ingredient. First cut the large piece into uniform slices about 2 inches long, then stack the slices and cut the stacks into 1/4-inch strips. If the ingredient to be julienned is round, such as a carrot, slice the carrot into elongated oblong slices by cutting it on a deep bias. Then stack the oblong slices and cut into thin strips.

Cubing or dicing: I specify this when it is important for an ingredient to be cut into a certain size cubes, such as when cubing tofu into 1/2-inch pieces or tempeh into 1-inch pieces.

Shredding: Use a grater to shred hard ingredients such as carrots or zucchini. Use a knife to shred cabbage or large leafy greens.

Half-moon slices: Just like the name of the cut, slice the round ingredient in half lengthwise and then slice the halves into 1/4-inch pieces.

Nutrition

It's a great decision choosing vegan, but it's important to be a healthy vegan. Vegan nutrition education goes beyond the scope of this book, but it is important to have some basic knowledge about the three issues that come up most often: protein, calcium, and vitamin B_{12}.

Proteins are the building blocks of body tissue, and amino acids are vital elements. Some amino acids are made in the body, while some aren't. Those that aren't need to be ingested, therefore they are called essential amino acids (EAA). All essential amino acids are made by plants. Some animals eat plants to ingest their essential amino acids. Some humans eat these animals, not realizing that the animals get their EAA the same place humans can—from plants. Eating a vegan diet skips the middle-animal. Can you get enough protein eating a vegan diet? Let's see... 100 calories of sirloin steak contain 5.5 grams of protein. 100 calories of broccoli contain 11 grams of protein. 100 calories of kale contain 9 grams of protein. 100 calories of black beans contain 7 grams of protein. (The largest land animals need more protein than a tiny human and they eat only plants.)

The dairy industry has been busy trying to convince us that without dairy we are in danger of becoming calcium deficient. This is simply untrue. For most of human history, people did not consume dairy. After weaning, humans tend to lose the enzyme the body uses to digest lactose. Humans who drink animal milk are the only creatures that drink the milk of another species. Being vegan and getting enough calcium is easy to do when you eat a varied diet, one rich in legumes and dark leafy greens. Eating fortified foods can also help ensure that you get the proper calcium intake.

Vitamin B_{12} is made by bacteria in the soil, and omnivores get it because the grazing animals pick it up from the soil. Vegans need a reliable supply of B_{12}, so it's a good idea to take a B_{12} supplement a few times a week. (See Resources under Nutrition.)

Recipe Flexibility Icons

The recipes feature helpful notations (icons) that indicate certain characteristics that may be of special interest to you. At a glance, the notations provide concise information that can help you with meal planning. (For a recipe list by icon, see page 15.) The icons include:

Gluten Free: These recipes are inherently gluten free, whether that is because all the ingredients themselves are gluten free or there is a choice between two items in the ingredients list, one being gluten free. Otherwise, the recipe itself needs no alterations or substitutions.

Soy Free: These recipes are inherently soy free, whether that is because all the ingredients themselves are soy free or there is a choice between two items in the ingredients list, one being soy free. Otherwise, the recipe itself needs no alterations or substitutions.

(continues on page 14)

The Perfect Pantry

Keeping a full and well-stocked pantry is the best way to get dinner on the table fast. Any dried goods can be stocked up over time and rotated to ensure freshness. Buy dry pantry goods as the super savers do—stock up when the prices are low. If tamari is $2 off, buy four bottles and keep them in your pantry. They will last a long time, and cost much less in the long run.

The same can't be done with refrigerated or frozen items, unless they have a long shelf life and you have the storage space. The most cost-efficient place to shop for pantry supplies is a big box natural food store, especially one with bulk bins and store-brand items available.

The following list does not include ingredients that are common to most kitchens, including ordinary seasonings such as salt, pepper, ground spices, and dried herbs; everyday condiments such as mustard and ketchup; or common baking needs such as baking soda, all-purpose flour, and baking powder.

Shelf-Stable Staples

- Reduced-sodium tamari
- Liquid smoke
- Vinegars (apple cider vinegar, brown rice vinegar, balsamic vinegar)
- Dulse seaweed flakes
- Soy Curls
- Nutritional yeast flakes
- Dry beans and legumes (split peas, chickpeas, kidney beans, navy beans, black-eyed peas, lentils, Lima beans, pinto beans, black beans, mung beans)
- Extra virgin olive oil or regular olive oil
- Neutral-tasting oil (sunflower, grapeseed, or safflower are best)
- Toasted sesame oil
- Roasted red peppers, jarred
- Dried pasta (spaghetti, angel hair, linguine, elbow, fusilli, lasagna, soba, rice noodles)
- Vegetable broth
- Flours: whole wheat flour, spelt flour, whole wheat pastry flour (optional), chickpea flour, vital wheat gluten, medium-ground cornmeal, corn flour
- Thickeners: arrowroot or cornstarch, tapioca flour or starch
- Grains: old-fashioned rolled oats, brown basmati rice, long-grain brown rice, arborio rice, pearl barley; quinoa
- Nuts and seeds: cashews; almonds, pecans, peanuts, walnuts, golden flax seeds, sesame seeds
- Nut butters and tahini

Baking/Sweets:

Maple syrup
Agave nectar (optional)
Applesauce
Pure vanilla extract (not imitation)
Natural granulated sugar
Cocoa powder (fair-trade; unsweetened or Dutch-processed)
Vegan chocolate chips (semi-sweet, fair-trade)

Canned:

Various beans: chickpea, pinto, kidney, cannellini, black
Tomatoes, whole and diced, San Marzano or Muir Glen
Tomato paste
Artichoke hearts
Pitted black, green, and Kalamata olives
Capers
Chipotle chiles in adobo
Coconut milk

Freezer:

Vegetables: spinach, corn kernels, peas
Fruit: blueberries, cherries, strawberries, peaches, mangos

Refrigerator:

Tofu: silken, soft, firm, and extra-firm
Earth Balance or other vegan non-hydrogenated margarine
Vegan milk, plain/unsweetened (almond or soy)
Vegan cheese
Vegan sour cream
Vegan cream cheese
Vegan mayonnaise
Vegan yogurt (plain/unsweetened)
Tempeh
Vegan sausage
Tortillas, (7-inch) flour and (5-inch) corn

Fresh Produce:

You should also stock a good variety of fresh produce, including basics such as onions, garlic, carrots, potatoes, and celery, as well as lemons, limes, and seasonal fruits and vegetables.

Include a variety of leafy greens such as kale, baby spinach, arugula, and fresh herbs. You'll also want to keep salad fixings on hand including romaine lettuce, cucumber, tomato, bell pepper, and avocado, and a rotation of asparagus, green beans, broccoli, cauliflower, summer and winter squash, corn, and mushrooms.

Gluten-Free Option: These recipes need some ingredient substitution and cooking alteration to make them gluten free, but all the information you need will be provided in the headnote of the recipe.

Soy-Free Option: These recipes need some ingredient substitution and, perhaps, cooking alteration to make them soy free, but all the information you need will be provided in the headnote of the recipe.

Quick & Easy: While most of the recipes in this book are easy to prepare, not all of them are quick, since some need longer prep or cooking times. If you're looking for recipes that are both easy and quick, look for the Quick & Easy icon notation or consult the handy list (opposite). These recipes can be complete in 30 minutes or less, including prep time and cooking time, given that you have all the ingredients called for handy. Naturally, the first time a recipe is made it takes more effort and attention than subsequently, but once you have some familiarity with the dish it can be prepared quickly and easily.

In the next chapter, I share my favorite recipes for some cooking basics, including pantry ingredients, and dairy and meat alternatives that will help you transition easily into a delicious, healthy, vegan lifestyle.

Guide to "Quick & Easy" Recipes

In addition to most of the basic recipes (pages 17-42), the recipes in the following list can be ready in 30 minutes or less.

Vegetable Broth (page 21)

CHAPTER 2

Recipe Basics

A chapter on basic recipes is included in most vegan cookbooks, and it's an important inclusion for two good reasons: flavor and economy. While there are vegan prepared foods available, they can be expensive and some might not be the healthiest options. While you may enlist the convenience of vegan prepared foods at certain times, you can save a lot of money by making these basic recipes and keeping them on hand.

The recipes in this chapter are divided into three groups: Pantry Basics, where you'll find recipes for broths, seasonings, and sauces that will add flavor to your recipes; Dairy-Free Basics, which provides easy recipes for homemade dairy-free staples such as mayonnaise, along with some tasty dairy-free sauces; and Vegan Protein Basics, featuring recipes for homemade seitan and bacon tofu and instructions on cooking beans and legumes.

Pantry Basics

Broth and sauces are among the most important basic pantry ingredients because they are instrumental in adding flavor and dimension to your meals. Being vegan does not mean compromising taste; it means enhancing it, much in the same way that omnivore recipes do—by adding flavor wherever possible. Broths and flavorings are essential to great recipes.

The simple and quick recipes in this section are utilized in other recipes in the book and will add extra layers of flavor. Some even freeze well for future use, allowing you to create a grocery store of staples right in your fridge and freezer.

If you prefer not to make these basics from scratch, you can always buy them ready-made at the store, but the trade-off is that storebought versions of these ingredients are generally more expensive than making them yourself. Some may also have added ingredients such as preservatives that you may not want.

If you make these basics in advance and keep them on hand, they can be as convenient to use as storebought versions—only better.

Savory Broth Mix

This is a low-salt, all-purpose broth mix featured in many recipes in this book because it adds depth, flavor, and dimension to dishes without a lot of extra work. This recipe successfully doubles and triples and keeps well when properly stored in a dark container at room temperature, out of direct sunlight. See page 4 for more information about nutritional yeast.

1 CUP NUTRITIONAL YEAST FLAKES

1 TABLESPOON ONION POWDER

1 TABLESPOON DRIED PARSLEY

2 TEASPOONS DRIED SAGE

2 TEASPOONS SEA SALT

2 TEASPOONS PAPRIKA

1 TEASPOON GARLIC POWDER

1 TEASPOON DRIED THYME

1 TEASPOON DRIED OREGANO

1 TEASPOON GRANULATED SUGAR

1/2 TEASPOON DRIED ROSEMARY

1/2 TEASPOON FRESH GROUND BLACK PEP-
PER

1/2 TEASPOON GROUND TURMERIC

1/2 TEASPOON GROUND CORIANDER SEED
(OPTIONAL)

1/4 TEASPOON GROUND CELERY SEED (OP-
TIONAL)

MAKES 1 CUP

QUICK & EASY
GLUTEN FREE
SOY FREE

In a dry blender, combine the yeast, onion, parsley, sage, salt, paprika, garlic powder, thyme, oregano, sugar, rosemary, black pepper, turmeric, and coriander and celery seeds, and blend to a powder. Allow the powder to settle before opening the blender top.

Transfer the mixture to an opaque container with a tight lid. Store at room temperature, away from direct sunlight. The broth mix will keep well for 6 months.

To use, mix 2 teaspoons of the broth mix with 1 cup of water or as directed in recipes.

CHEF'S TIP: It is helpful to measure an additional batch of the ingredients, minus the nutritional yeast, at the same time that you prepare a single recipe. In this way you have all the spices and herbs pre-measured for next time, and you merely have to blend them with the nutritional yeast for a fresh batch of Savory Broth Mix. Just be sure to label the container you store the extra mixture in.

Hearty Umami Flavoring

This umami-rich seasoning is reminiscent of Vegemite, the dark Australian condiment, albeit much thinner than the famous paste. While it is interesting as a spread on toast, it is quite useful to season seitan and tofu to achieve a deep, hearty flavor.

1 CUP NUTRITIONAL YEAST FLAKES

1/4 CUP INSTANT GRAIN COFFEE GRANULES OR INSTANT DECAFFEINATED COFFEE GRANULES

1/4 CUP TOMATO PASTE

1/4 CUP REDUCED SODIUM TAMARI

2 TABLESPOONS WATER

1 TEASPOON SEA SALT

1 TEASPOON GARLIC POWDER

1 TEASPOON ONION POWDER

MAKES 3/4 CUP

QUICK & EASY
GLUTEN FREE

Combine the yeast, coffee, tomato paste, tamari, water, sea salt, garlic powder, and onion powder in a small bowl. Stir well to combine.

Transfer the thickened mixture to a storage container. Use immediately in recipes or store in an airtight container in the refrigerator, where it will keep for 1 week.

Vegetable Broth

The time of buying canned vegetable broth or using commercial bouillon cubes can now come to an end. Make a batch of this and store it in the fridge or freezer. I promise, your wallet and taste buds will thank you for it. If, however, your time or space is limited, purchase storebought boxed vegetable broth that is rich and flavorful, such as Imagine brand. (See photo page 16.)

2 TABLESPOONS OLIVE OIL

8 SCALLIONS, COARSELY CHOPPED

3 MEDIUM ONIONS, WITH SKINS BUT ROOTS
    CUT OFF, COARSELY CHOPPED

3 MEDIUM CARROTS, SCRUBBED AND
    COARSELY CHOPPED

3 CELERY RIBS, COARSELY CHOPPED

1 MEDIUM PORTOBELLO MUSHROOM,
    GILLS SCRAPED OUT, OR 6 PORTOBELLO
    STEMS OR 6 CREMINIS, WIPED CLEAN AND
    COARSELY CHOPPED

4 GARLIC CLOVES, COARSELY CHOPPED

2 TABLESPOONS TOMATO PASTE

3 QUARTS WATER

2 TEASPOONS DRIED THYME

1 TEASPOON WHOLE PEPPERCORNS

1 TEASPOON SEA SALT

2 BAY LEAVES

1 BUNCH PARSLEY, STEMS ONLY

MAKES ABOUT 8 CUPS

GLUTEN FREE
SOY FREE

Heat the oil in a large pot over medium heat. Stir in the scallions, onions, carrots, celery, and mushrooms. Cook, stirring, until lightly browned, about 15 minutes.

Stir in the garlic and tomato paste and cook, stirring, until the tomato paste darkens, about 1 minute. Stir in the water, thyme, peppercorns, salt, bay leaves, and parsley. Bring the broth to a boil. Reduce it to a strong simmer and cook for 30 minutes or until the vegetables are tender.

Strain the broth into a large bowl through a colander or large strainer. Discard the vegetables.

Transfer the broth to quart-size mason jars or other airtight containers. Store the broth in the refrigerator, where it will keep for 7 days. The broth can also be frozen for up to 3 months.

VARIATION: Mild Seaweed Vegetable Stock. After straining the broth, transfer it to a large pot. Stir in 1/4 cup dulse seaweed flakes for every 8 cups of broth. Simmer the broth for 5 minutes. Strain the broth for very mild seaweed broth or use as is. You may also use kelp or kombu. If using kelp or kombu, use 3 tablespoons of whole leaves or 2 teaspoons of granules for every 8 cups of broth. Follow the cooking instructions for the dulse variation.

Quick Barbecue Sauce

Lightly smoky, sweet, and tangy, this sauce is a classic all-purpose barbecue sauce. The sauce reduces thick and sweet when roasting or grilling with it. The amount of smoke flavor is a personal taste, so adjust the amount of liquid smoke as desired, but no more than one teaspoon—a little goes a long way. For convenience, some great storebought barbecue sauces are made by Annie's Naturals and Organicville.

2 TABLESPOONS GRAPESEED OR SUNFLOWER OIL

1 SMALL ONION, FINELY CHOPPED

6 CLOVES GARLIC, FINELY CHOPPED

1/4 CUP DISTILLED WHITE VINEGAR

1/4 CUP PACKED BROWN SUGAR

2 TABLESPOONS NATURAL SUGAR

1 CUP KETCHUP

1/4 CUP WATER

1 TABLESPOON MOLASSES

1/4 TO 1 TEASPOON LIQUID SMOKE

1/4 TEASPOON SEA SALT

1/8 TEASPOON GROUND BLACK PEPPER

1/8 TEASPOON CAYENNE

MAKES 1 1/2 CUPS

QUICK & EASY
GLUTEN FREE
SOY FREE

Heat the oil in a medium saucepan over medium heat. Add the onion and cook, stirring, until the onion softens, about 3 minutes. Add the garlic. Cook, stirring, until golden, about 2 more minutes.

Stir in the vinegar and sugars and cook, stirring, until the sugar dissolves, about 1 minute.

Stir in the ketchup, water, molasses, liquid smoke, salt, black pepper, and cayenne. Bring to a boil, then reduce it to simmer and cook, partially covered, until the flavors meld, 10 minutes.

Blend the sauce for a smoother consistency, if desired. The sauce will keep for 7 days when stored in an airtight container in the refrigerator. It also freezes well for up to 3 months in an airtight container.

Salsa Fresca

Why shell out big bucks for fresh salsa when it is so easy and economical to make at home? If you're using a food processor, the salsa takes mere minutes to prepare. Bookmark this recipe and the next time you need a jar of salsa, make this instead. If you need a store brand salsa, my favorite is the freshly made one that is available in the produce section of Whole Foods or other grocers.

4 RIPE MEDIUM TOMATOES, CUT INTO 1/4-
    INCH DICE

1/4 SMALL RED ONION, FINELY CHOPPED

1/4 CUP FINELY CHOPPED CILANTRO LEAVES

2 GARLIC CLOVES, MINCED

2 TABLESPOONS FRESH LIME JUICE

1 SMALL JALAPEÑO, SEEDED AND MINCED

SEA SALT AND FRESH GROUND BLACK PEPPER

————————————

MAKES 2 1/2 CUPS

QUICK & EASY
GLUTEN FREE
SOY FREE

In a medium bowl, combine the tomatoes, onion, cilantro, garlic, lime juice, jalapeño, and salt and pepper to taste. Mix well. Alternatively, coarsely chop the tomato, onion, cilantro, and jalapeño and transfer them to a food processor. Pulse until finely chopped, then transfer the vegetables to a medium bowl and stir in the garlic, lime juice, and salt and pepper, to taste.

Set aside for 15 minutes to combine the flavors. Taste and adjust salt and pepper as needed. Store the salsa in the refrigerator in an airtight container for up to 3 days.

Timeless Tomato Sauce

Tomato sauce is so easy and quick to make at home. The kind of tomatoes you use really are important. The best Italian tomatoes will produce superior results, so don't just grab any old can. This recipe doubles well, just be sure to simmer the sauce five minutes longer. For storebought equivalents, lovely jarred tomato sauces are made by Whole Food's 365 Everyday Value Organic brand and Amy's line of vegan tomato sauces.

2 TABLESPOONS OLIVE OIL

1 MEDIUM CARROT, FINELY SHREDDED

4 GARLIC CLOVES, FINELY CHOPPED

1 SMALL BUNCH BASIL, STEMS ONLY, OR 1 TA-
BLESPOON FINELY CHOPPED BASIL LEAVES

1 (28-OUNCE) CAN WHOLE OR DICED TOMA-
TOES, LIGHTLY DRAINED (SAN MARZANO OR
MUIR GLEN)

SEA SALT AND FRESH GROUND BLACK PEPPER

1/2 TO 1 TEASPOON GRANULATED SUGAR, OP-
TIONAL

MAKES ABOUT 2 CUPS

QUICK & EASY

GLUTEN FREE

SOY FREE

Heat the oil in a large pot over medium heat. Stir in the carrot and cook, stirring, until softened, about 2 minutes. Stir in the garlic and the basil stems. Cook, stirring, until the garlic is golden, about 1 minute.

Stir in the tomatoes. If using whole tomatoes, break them up with your hand or a spoon as you add them. Bring the sauce to a boil. Lightly boil the sauce over medium heat until it thickens, about 10 to 12 minutes, stirring occasionally. Add salt and black pepper to taste and, if needed, add sugar, to taste. Remove the basil stems and discard.

If using basil leaves, stir them into the sauce 2 minutes before the sauce is ready.

If a smooth sauce is desired, blend the sauce with an immersion blender (or in a blender in batches).

Chef's Tips:

- The carrot in this recipe adds needed sweetness to the sauce without adding sugar.
- After using the leaves of basil to make soup or pesto, wrap the stems in plastic wrap and store them in the freezer. If you have some on hand, they do not need to be thawed before use. Basil stems have a lot of flavor.
- During out-of-season months, when fresh basil is unavailable, substitute 1/2 teaspoon dried basil for the fresh and add it along with the garlic.

Dairy-Free Basics

Right after meat, replacing dairy is the chief consideration for new vegans. The dairy industry would have you believe you need dairy products to get enough calcium. The fact is, calcium is abundantly available in leafy greens, tofu, nuts, and beans, as well as commercially available vegan milks, so there is no need for such a concern.

There are numerous milk alternatives on the market, including soy milk, nut milk, seed milk, and even grain milk. There are flavored variations on each of them, such as vanilla and chocolate. For the recipes in this book you will need a plain, unsweetened vegan milk, such as almond milk or soy milk.

Other dairy-free items such as mayo, sour cream, and cream cheese are available in well-stocked supermarkets. Even butter is easily replaced with great-tasting commercial vegan butter.

This chapter contains recipes for dairy alternatives that are either not so readily available at the grocers, are made easily at home, or taste better made at home. For example, I have not been able to find a delicious alternative for a cheese sauce on the market, but the recipe in this chapter will knock your socks off. Ditto for the Ranch Dressing. By the end of the chapter you'll be wondering why dairy is still even around.

Say (vegan) cheese!

Some people have great intentions when they decide go vegan, but have difficulty giving up cheese. When trying vegan cheese versions, they invariably compare them to dairy cheese. The fact is, dairy is dairy and it has a unique flavor. There are some amazing vegan cheeses out there, but don't expect an exact match to the flavor of dairy cheese. Even so, vegan cheeses have been evolving. Companies are now selling fermented and aged vegan cheese products, and people have begun making their own vegan cheese at home.

Have you ever watched a movie based on the glowing recommendations of friends who inform you that you will have a life-changing experience only to experience a discouraging let-down? The problem is too much hype. It's the same deal with vegan versus dairy cheese. Don't set yourself up for disappointment. Vegan cheese is fine, but it is not dairy cheese. If you are one of these cheese-loving folks, read on.

If you have trouble breaking the dairy cheese habit, I suggest you avoid both dairy and vegan cheese for 30 days. That's right, "The 30-day Cheese Cleanse." Habits take around 21 days to form – both good and bad. After 30 days, your taste buds and expectations are altered. After 30 days, try vegan cheese but keep your expectations realistic. During the 30 days feel free to enjoy the "Cheese Sauce" (page 27).

Other types of dairy are very easy to replace with nutritious alternatives. Check out the vegan substitutions of generally animal-derived foods, such as milk, butter, eggs, and yogurt.

Cheese Sauce

This is a basic cheese sauce suitable for adding to nachos or baked potatoes. It can also be made with a Tex-Mex flare. As a transplanted Texan, I know that Chile con Queso is on every table and at every event in that great state. Vegans shouldn't have to miss out!

1 CUP PLAIN UNSWEETENED VEGAN MILK

1/4 CUP VEGAN CREAM CHEESE

3 TABLESPOONS VEGAN MAYONNAISE

3 TABLESPOONS DICED JARRED PIMIENTOS
   OR ROASTED RED PEPPERS

2 TABLESPOONS NUTRITIONAL YEAST FLAKES

1/2 TEASPOON SEA SALT

1/4 TEASPOON ONION POWDER

1/4 TEASPOON PAPRIKA

1/8 TEASPOON GROUND TURMERIC

PINCH WHITE PEPPER

3 TABLESPOONS GRAPESEED OR SUNFLOWER
   OIL

4 TABLESPOONS UNBLEACHED ALL-PURPOSE
   FLOUR

1 TEASPOON APPLE CIDER VINEGAR

MAKES 2 CUPS

QUICK & EASY

Blend the milk, cream cheese, mayo, pimientos, nutritional yeast, salt, onion powder, paprika, turmeric, and white pepper in a blender until very smooth, scraping down the sides as needed. Set aside.

Heat the oil in a small saucepan over medium heat. Stir in the flour and mix with a whisk. Cook for 2 minutes, whisking continuously.

While still whisking, slowly add the cream cheese mixture to the flour mixture, whisking until the sauce is very smooth.

Bring the sauce to a boil and immediately reduce it to a simmer, still whisking. Simmer the sauce until it thickens and is heated through, about 5 minutes, stirring occasionally. Keep warm but do not boil, or it will break. Whisk in the vinegar, adjust the seasoning with salt, if needed, and serve immediately.

VARIATION: Chile con Queso. Stir in one (10-ounce) can of drained diced tomatoes with green chiles to the sauce along with the cream cheese mixture.

Gluten-Free Cheese Sauce

This gluten-free version of cheese sauce is thickened with tofu and is just as creamy and luscious as the original.

1 CUP MASHED SOFT OR FIRM TOFU

3/4 CUP PLAIN UNSWEETENED VEGAN MILK, DIVIDED

1/4 CUP VEGAN CREAM CHEESE

3 TABLESPOONS VEGAN MAYONNAISE, STORE-BOUGHT OR HOMEMADE (PAGE 31)

3 TABLESPOONS DICED JARRED PIMIENTOS OR ROASTED RED PEPPERS

1 TABLESPOON GRAPESEED OR SUNFLOWER OIL

2 TABLESPOONS NUTRITIONAL YEAST FLAKES

1/2 TEASPOON SEA SALT

1/4 TEASPOON ONION POWDER

1/4 TEASPOON PAPRIKA

1/8 TEASPOON GROUND TURMERIC

PINCH WHITE PEPPER

1 TABLESPOON ARROWROOT STARCH

1 TEASPOON APPLE CIDER VINEGAR

MAKES 2 CUPS

QUICK & EASY
GLUTEN FREE

In a blender, combine the tofu, 1/2 cup milk, cream cheese, mayo, pimientos, oil, nutritional yeast, salt, onion powder, paprika, turmeric, and white pepper and blend until very smooth, scraping down the sides as needed.

Whisk together the remaining 1/4 cup milk and arrowroot in a small bowl. Set aside.

Transfer the tofu mixture to a small saucepan and heat over medium heat. Bring to a boil and immediately reduce to a simmer. Stir in the arrowroot mixture. Cook, whisking as it simmers, until heated and thickened, about 30 seconds. Keep warm but do not boil, or it will break. Whisk in the vinegar, adjust seasoning using salt to taste, and serve immediately.

VARIATION: Gluten-Free Chile con Queso. Stir in one (10-ounce) can of drained diced tomatoes with green chiles to the sauce along with the cream cheese mixture.

Ranch Dressing

Oh, yeah. You've been waiting for this. No vegan, and I mean no vegan, will ever have to endure life without ranch dressing ever again.

1/4 CUP VEGAN MAYONNAISE, STOREBOUGHT
 OR HOMEMADE (PAGE 31)

1/4 CUP VEGAN SOUR CREAM

2 TABLESPOONS PLAIN UNSWEETENED VEGAN
 MILK

2 TEASPOONS RICE VINEGAR

1/2 TEASPOON SEA SALT

1/2 TEASPOON NATURAL SUGAR

1/4 TEASPOON ONION POWDER

1/4 TEASPOON GARLIC POWDER

1/4 TEASPOON WHITE PEPPER

1/8 TEASPOON DRIED THYME

1/8 TEASPOON DRY MUSTARD

1 TEASPOON DRIED CHIVES

1/2 TEASPOON DRIED PARSLEY

MAKES ABOUT 1 CUP

QUICK & EASY
GLUTEN FREE

Combine the mayo, sour cream, milk, vinegar, salt, sugar, onion powder, garlic powder, pepper, thyme, and mustard in a personal blender or a container wide enough to utilize an immersion blender. Blend until well-combined, about 30 seconds.

Stir in the chives and parsley. Pulse the blender a few times to break up the herbs.

Store the dressing in the refrigerator in an airtight container for about a week.

Tartar Sauce

There is cocktail sauce, made with ketchup and horseradish, and then there is tartar sauce, made with mayo and relish—a red and white sauce rivalry. Slather this creamy sauce on the Seafood Tofu (see the Marinated Tofu variation on page 34) or No-Fish Filet Sandwiches (page 74). Don't miss the Thousand Island Dressing variation at the end. Some people call it "special sauce."

2/3 CUP VEGAN MAYONNAISE, STOREBOUGHT
   OR HOMEMADE (PAGE 31)

3 TABLESPOONS MINCED ONION

2 TABLESPOONS SWEET RELISH

1 TABLESPOON FRESH LEMON JUICE

SEA SALT AND FRESH GROUND BLACK PEPPER

———————————————

MAKES ABOUT 1 CUP

QUICK & EASY
GLUTEN FREE

In a small bowl, combine the mayo, onion, relish, and lemon juice. Stir to mix well. Season with salt and pepper, to taste.

Store in an airtight container in the refrigerator for up to a week.

VARIATION: Thousand Island Dressing. Omit the lemon juice. Stir 3 tablespoons of ketchup into the sauce.

Vegan Mayo Two Ways

The Full-Fat version uses xanthan gum and guar gum to stabilize the mixture. Without them, the mayo would separate and break over time or when heated. The Lower-Fat version uses silken tofu as a stabilizer and contains half the oil. The trade-off is that it is thinner than the Full-Fat version.

Full-Fat Mayo:

1/2 CUP PLAIN UNSWEETENED SOY MILK, CHILLED

1 TABLESPOON DIJON MUSTARD

1 TABLESPOON BETTER THAN SOYMILK ORIGINAL POWDER

2 TEASPOONS TAPIOCA STARCH

1/2 TEASPOON GUAR GUM

1/2 TEASPOON XANTHAN GUM

2/3 CUP GRAPESEED OIL, CHILLED

1 TABLESPOON OLIVE OIL, CHILLED

1 TABLESPOON FRESH LEMON JUICE

1 TEASPOON APPLE CIDER VINEGAR

1/2 TEASPOON SEA SALT

1/4 TEASPOON AGAVE NECTAR

Lower-Fat Mayo:

1/2 CUP SILKEN TOFU

1/4 CUP PLAIN UNSWEETENED SOY MILK, CHILLED

2 TEASPOONS DIJON MUSTARD

1 TEASPOON TAPIOCA STARCH

1/3 CUP GRAPESEED OIL, CHILLED

1 TABLESPOON OLIVE OIL, CHILLED

2 TEASPOONS FRESH LEMON JUICE

3/4 TEASPOONS APPLE CIDER VINEGAR

1/4 TEASPOON SEA SALT

1/8 TEASPOON AGAVE NECTAR

MAKES ABOUT 1 CUP

QUICK & EASY
GLUTEN FREE

Full-Fat Mayo: Combine the soymilk, mustard, milk powder, tapioca, guar gum, and xanthan gum in a 1-quart, wide-mouth Mason jar. Use an immersion blender to blend well, until thickened.

Lower-Fat Mayo: Combine the tofu, soymilk, mustard, and tapioca in a 1-quart, wide-mouth Mason jar. Use an immersion blender to blend well, until thickened.

Combine the grapeseed oil and olive oil in a measuring cup with a spout. While blending the ingredients in the Mason jar, slowly, in a thin, steady stream, add the oil mixture. Move the immersion blender around the jar to incorporate the oil, rotating it in a circle and moving it up and down so that the blender pulls the oil into the milk mixture, until it is incorporated.

Whisk in the lemon juice, vinegar, salt, and agave by hand. Cover and refrigerate for 30 minutes to chill. Whip the mayonnaise with a whisk before using. The mayo will keep in the refrigerator for up to two weeks.

CHEF'S TIP: Xanthan gum and guar gum are thickeners and stabilizers. They keep mixes emulsified by keeping the oil droplets suspended in a liquid. Guar gum comes from a seed and xanthan gum is made by a microorganism. They are quite popular in gluten-free baking and are readily available in the baking section or health food section of grocery stores, as well as online.

NOTE: Better Than Soymilk Original powder can be found in natural food stores, supermarkets, or online.

Vegan Protein Basics

Every vegan has heard the question: "Where do you get your protein?" The fact is, most plants contain protein, and this section has vegan power-packed proteins, from tofu and tempeh, to beans and seitan. Protein choices abound! Grains paired with beans contain all your essential amino acids, and they do not even need to be eaten in the same meal. One need only take care to eat a varied plant-based diet throughout the week to get the needed amino acids.

Protein-rich tofu is versatile because it can be transformed in many different ways with the proper preparation. Also referred to as bean curd, tofu is the pressed curds of coagulated soymilk. It comes in a variety of textures: silken, soft, firm, and extra-firm.

Tempeh is just as versatile. Made from fermented soybeans, it has an earthy flavor and chewy texture. It also needs to be prepared properly in order to achieve maximum flavor.

Soy Curls are relatively new to vegan fare, and although they are similar to textured vegetable protein, the preparation is slightly different.

Seitan, also known as wheat meat, is made by rinsing the bran and fiber from wheat gluten flour. What remains is rich in protein, and can be cooked in various ways to achieve different flavors and textures.

The proteins in this section can all be used to make the recipes in upcoming chapters.

Basic Beans

Canned beans are a great time-saver, but can become costly, especially when you purchase organic beans in BPA-free containers. Consider cooking up a pound of beans once a week and storing them in the freezer in portion containers. Simply thaw the beans before use. If you cook a different kind of bean each week, within a month you will have all the popular kinds of beans waiting for you in the freezer. It is important that you pick over your beans and make sure there are no small stones present.

2 CUPS DRY BEANS, EXCLUDING SPLIT PEAS AND LENTILS, PICKED OVER, RINSED, AND DRAINED

2-INCH PIECE OF KOMBU (KELP) (OPTIONAL)

WATER, AS NEEDED

MAKES ABOUT 4 CUPS

GLUTEN FREE
SOY FREE

Combine the beans and enough water to cover them by three inches in a large pot. Set the beans aside to soak overnight.

Drain and rinse the beans and transfer them back to the pot. Add the kombu and enough water to cover the beans by three inches again. Bring the water to a boil, reduce it to a simmer, and cook the beans until tender, from 1 1/2 to 2 1/2 hours, depending on the type and age of the beans. Older beans will need a longer cooking time. Remove the kombu and discard. Use the cooked beans in a recipe immediately or portion and freeze them in airtight containers for 6 months. Thaw before use.

CHEF'S TIP: To quick-soak the beans, place them in a pot in enough water to cover by three inches, bring to a boil, and lower the heat to a strong simmer. Simmer the beans for 5 minutes. Remove the pot from the heat and set aside to soak for 1 hour, then continue with the recipe.

Under Pressure

I recommend investing in a pressure cooker to cut down on the time spent cooking beans. A pressure cooker speeds up bean cooking considerably. For example, beans that can take 2 hours to cook on the stovetop can be ready in under 30 minutes using a pressure cooker. I use an electric pressure cooker that heats up the water and reduces the pressure automatically.

Marinated Tofu

We've all heard the jokes about tofu and how bland it is. Truth be told, it is bland—but that's a good thing, since we all know that a blank canvas can be the beginning of a masterpiece. You will need to press your tofu overnight (page 9), so plan accordingly.

14 OUNCES FIRM OR EXTRA FIRM TOFU, PRESSED OVERNIGHT

2 CUPS WATER

2 TABLESPOONS SAVORY BROTH MIX (PAGE 19)

1/4 TEASPOON SEA SALT

1 TABLESPOON GRAPESEED OR SUNFLOWER OIL

MAKES 2 1/2 TO 3 CUPS

QUICK & EASY
GLUTEN FREE

Cut the pressed tofu into 1/2-inch cubes.

Heat the water, broth mix, and salt in a medium saucepan. Bring to a boil, then reduce to a simmer.

Add the tofu and simmer for 10 minutes. Remove from the heat and allow the tofu to sit in the broth for an additional 10 minutes. You may also keep the tofu in the broth in an airtight container in the refrigerator for a week before continuing to the next step.

Drain the tofu. Heat the oil in a large skillet over medium heat. Add the tofu and cook, stirring, until golden brown, about 10 minutes. Season with salt and black pepper, as needed. The tofu is now ready to use in recipes. If not using right away, cool to room temperature, then store in an airtight container in the refrigerator for up to 3 days. This recipe easily doubles, but it does not freeze well since the texture of the tofu changes after being frozen.

CHEF'S TIP: Alternatively, the tofu can be cut into 1/2-inch slices, marinated in the broth as instructed above, and grilled in a grill pan, electric grill, or outdoor grill. Lightly oil the slices and grill them for 4 minutes per side.

VARIATION: Seafood Tofu. Slice the tofu into about 8 (1/2-inch) slices. Substitute 2 cups vegetable broth for the water. Omit the Savory Broth Mix. Add 4 teaspoons dulse seaweed flakes and 1 teaspoon Old Bay seasoning to the vegetable broth. Cook as directed above. Use in recipes without sautéing or, for an easy main dish, dredge the tofu in a little flour, sauté in a little oil, and serve with lemon wedge.

Tender Soy Curls

Butler Soy Curls are a delicious replacement for meat that is easy to prepare and use in recipes. They are made of non-GMO whole soybeans, and unlike textured vegetable protein, Soy Curls are not de-fatted and have no added chemicals or preservatives. Look for Butler Soy Curls online or visit www.butlerfoods.com for information about where to buy.

3 1/2 CUPS WATER

2 TABLESPOONS SAVORY BROTH MIX (PAGE 19)

1/4 TEASPOON SEA SALT

1 (8-OUNCE) PACKAGE SOY CURLS, ABOUT 4 1/2 CUPS

2 TABLESPOONS GRAPESEED OR SUNFLOWER OIL

MAKES ABOUT 4 CUPS

QUICK & EASY
GLUTEN FREE

Combine the water, broth mix, and salt in a medium saucepan. Bring to a boil, then reduce to simmer.

Stir in the Soy Curls and simmer until tender, 5 to 10 minutes, stirring occasionally.

Remove from the heat and allow the Soy Curls to sit in the broth for another 5 minutes. Drain, reserving any remaining cooking broth.

Heat the oil in a large skillet over medium heat. Stir in the Soy Curls and cook, stirring, until golden brown, about 10 minutes. If your pan isn't big enough to cook them in a single layer, it is best to cook them in batches or increase the cooking time in order to achieve a golden brown color. Scrape the bottom of the pan with a sturdy spatula as you cook and season to taste with salt and black pepper, as needed.

Stir in the reserved broth if they are beginning to burn. Discard any unused broth.

The Soy Curls are now ready to use in recipes. If not using right away, they can be stored in an airtight container in the refrigerator for 3 days. This recipe easily doubles and freezes well for 3 months. If frozen, thaw before use.

Bacon Tofu

Smoky, crispy, salty—all the reasons anyone would want bacon, right here, in all its vegan glory.

14 OUNCES FIRM OR EXTRA-FIRM TOFU,
   PRESSED OVERNIGHT, PATTED DRY

3 TABLESPOONS NUTRITIONAL YEAST FLAKES

1/4 CUP REDUCED SODIUM TAMARI

1 TO 2 TEASPOONS LIQUID SMOKE

MAKES ABOUT 20 SLICES

QUICK & EASY
GLUTEN FREE

Step 1: Slice the tofu into about 20 thin slices, each about 1/8-inch thick.

Step 2: Heat a large skillet over medium heat. Spray the skillet lightly with spray oil. Transfer the tofu slices to the skillet. Crowding the skillet is acceptable since the tofu slices will shrink. Cook the tofu slices, undisturbed, until golden on the bottom. Flip and cook them on the other side in the same way. Return all the slices to the pan and sprinkle with the nutritional yeast, tossing to coat the tofu on both sides.

Step 3: Mix the tamari and the liquid smoke (use 2 teaspoons if you like a very smoky bacon) in a small measuring cup. Pour the tamari mixture over the tofu slices and toss them with the liquid using tongs or a spatula. Do this quickly because the liquid will evaporate fast.

Step 4: Keep tossing the tofu until all of the liquid evaporates. It is ready to use as-is, or for extra crispy tofu, preoceed to Step 5.

Step 5: For crispy tofu: Oil a baking sheet with 2 tablespoons of oil and bake the prepared Bacon Tofu in a preheated 450°F oven until crisp, about 7 to 9 minutes. Alternatively, fry the tofu in 2 tablespoons oil over medium heat in a clean large skillet until crisp, 1 to 2 minutes.

Step 1

Step 2

Step 3

Step 4

Step 5

Savory TVP

Textured Vegetable Protein is considerably more readily available for purchase than other dry vegan proteins. When improperly prepared, TVP has a bland and off-putting flavor. Using the recipe here, you will learn the best method of preparing this vegan staple and making it taste superb.

For Ground TVP:

1 1/4 CUPS VEGETABLE BROTH

1 TABLESPOON HEARTY UMAMI FLAVORING (PAGE 20) OR SAVORY BROTH MIX (PAGE 19)

1 CUP GROUND TEXTURED VEGETABLE PROTEIN (TVP)

1 TABLESPOON GRAPESEED OR SUNFLOWER OIL

SEA SALT AND FRESH GROUND BLACK PEPPER

_____

MAKES ABOUT 1 CUP

GLUTEN FREE

Combine the vegetable broth and the umami flavoring in a medium bowl, mixing well. Add the TVP and set aside to rehydrate for 15 minutes.

Heat the oil in a large skillet over medium heat. Stir in the rehydrated TVP and cook until golden brown. Season to taste with salt and pepper. Store in an airtight container in the fridge for 1 week or in the freezer for 6 months.

For TVP Chunks or Strips:

2 CUPS VEGETABLE BROTH

2 TABLESPOONS HEARTY UMAMI FLAVORING (PAGE 20) OR SAVORY BROTH MIX (PAGE 19)

1 CUP TVP CHUNKS OR STRIPS

1 TABLESPOON GRAPESEED OR SUNFLOWER OIL

SEA SALT AND FRESH GROUND BLACK PEPPER

_____

MAKES ABOUT 2 CUPS

GLUTEN FREE

Combine the vegetable broth and umami flavoring in a medium saucepan, and mix well. Bring to a boil over medium heat. Stir in the TVP and simmer for 20 minutes.

Remove from the heat and cool the TVP in the broth mixture to room temperature, then refrigerate overnight to continue to rehydrate, placing an inverted bowl on top of the TVP to submerge it in the broth.

Heat the oil in a large skillet over medium heat. Stir in the rehydrated TVP and cook, stirring, until golden brown. Season to taste with salt and pepper. Store in an airtight container in the fridge for 1 week or in the freezer for 6 months.

Blackened Tempeh

This is a very quick way to cook tempeh, with no steaming necessary—and it tastes great. Blackening the tempeh has the potential to smoke up your kitchen, so have your stove fan on high and windows open, or move the cooking to the outdoors.

1 TEASPOON GARLIC POWDER

1 TEASPOON ONION POWDER

1 TEASPOON DRIED THYME

1 TEASPOON DRIED OREGANO

2 TEASPOONS PAPRIKA

1/2 TEASPOON SEA SALT

1/2 TEASPOON GROUND BLACK PEPPER

1/2 TEASPOON CAYENNE

1 (8-OUNCE) PACKAGE TEMPEH

1 TABLESPOON OLIVE OIL

_____

MAKES 4 PIECES

QUICK & EASY
GLUTEN FREE

Combine the garlic powder, onion powder, thyme, oregano, paprika, salt, black pepper, and cayenne in a small bowl. Transfer the spice mixture to a large plate and set aside.

Cut the tempeh block in half widthwise, and each half lengthwise. You should have four large, thin rectangles.

Coat both sides of each tempeh slab with oil. Dredge each side of the tempeh slabs in the spice mixture. For best flavor, use all of the spice mixture.

Heat a large skillet over medium-high heat. When the skillet is very hot, arrange the tempeh in the skillet in a single layer, working in batches, if needed. Cook until the spices are blackened, about 2 minutes per side. Use immediately or store in an airtight container in the refrigerator for up to 7 days.

Mock Meats

To people new to vegan cooking, faux meat products can supply a reassuring stepping stone. If you choose to use storebought mock meats, there are many options from companies such as Upton's Naturals, Lightlife, and Beyond Meat. Tofurky has a line of sandwich slices that are delicious. There is even vegan seafood by Sophie's Kitchen.

Such commercial products make suitable transitional options and are also great in a pinch when there's no time to cook. (Note: If a storebought protein such as vegan sausage links, for example, doesn't come pre-sautéed, it will more than likely taste much better if it is sautéed in a little water or oil before being used in the recipes.)

Simple Seitan Cutlets

This all-purpose seitan can be sautéed in a little olive oil or transformed into Country Fried Seitan. It is tender and flavorful, and is the simplest seitan to make, however, the ingredient amounts must be followed precisely to achieve the proper texture and flavor. This recipe easily doubles. Just double the amount of cooking broth and bake each batch in a separate baking pan.

1 CUP PLUS 2 TABLESPOONS STIRRED VITAL
    WHEAT GLUTEN FLOUR (SEE CHEF'S TIP)

3 TABLESPOONS SAVORY BROTH MIX (PAGE 19)

2 TABLESPOONS CHICKPEA FLOUR

1/2 TEASPOON GARLIC POWDER

1/2 TEASPOON SEA SALT

2 3/4 CUPS VEGETABLE BROTH, DIVIDED

2 TABLESPOONS GRAPESEED OR SUNFLOWER
    OIL

MAKES 8 CUTLETS OR 3 CUPS DICED

SOY FREE

CHEF'S TIP: All flour settles after a bit of sitting. Vital wheat gluten flour is no different. Stirring the flour before measuring will aerate it. Once the flour is stirred, it can be accurately measured. Sifting flour achieves the same goal, but gluten flour is not easily sifted. Grab a butter knife and stir your flour before measuring.

SLOW COOKER METHOD: Increase the cooking broth to 6 cups and cook the cutlets on low with the lid 1/4-inch ajar for 6 hours. Cool the seitan in the broth before using in recipes.

Step 1: In a large bowl, combine the vital wheat gluten, broth mix, chickpea flour, garlic powder, and salt. In a blender or small bowl, combine 3/4 cup vegetable broth, and oil and mix to combine. Pour the broth mixture into the flour mixture. Mix well.

Step 2: Knead for 5 minutes inside the mixing bowl.

Step 3: Shape into a thick log about 5-inches long. Set aside for 30 minutes to allow the gluten to relax.

Step 4: Cut the dough into 8 equal disk-shaped pieces; roll each piece into a 4- to 5-inch circle on a very dry surface using a rolling pin. Wipe the board with a clean, dry cloth if the gluten won't stick to the board. (As the gluten relaxes it will hold its shape better if it is stuck to the board.) You may have to wipe again after the first pass with the rolling pin to achieve a dry surface. Alternatively, lightly dust the work surface with vital wheat gluten. The dough will want to spring back into a small disk; that is okay.

Step 5: Pour 2 cups of the broth into a 9 x 13-inch baking pan amd add the cutlets (overlapping is okay). Cover tightly with aluminum foil. Bake in a 225°F oven (no need to preheat) for 2 hours, then turn off the heat and let the seitan rest in the oven for 1 hour. Transfer to the refrigerator to chill.

Step 6: Cool completely before using. Store submerged in the remaining cooking broth, tightly covered. It will keep refrigerated for 5 days or frozen for up to 3 months.

Step 1

Step 2

Step 3

Step 4

Step 5

Step 6

Creamy Tomato-Basil Soup (page 48)

CHAPTER 3

Soups

Soups are warming, comforting, easy to make meals, and they can be fantastic if you begin with a great recipe. There are thirteen delicious soup recipes in this chapter, including Mama's Hungarian Bean Soup, Comforting Noodle Soup, Manhattan Chowder, and Thai Thom Kha Coconut Soup. Some are one-pot wonders, while others are complete meals when served with an accompaniment. Each recipe is supplemented with suggestions to round out the soup and make it into a meal. These soups are among my family's favorites and are sure to satisfy and warm your heart and soul.

Comforting Noodle Soup

Chicken noodle soup, and its reputation for being a healing tonic, is almost as old as time. At our house, this is the soup we turn to when the weather turns sour and the cold season hits. Nutritional yeast, fresh vegetables, and the warming heat of the soup contribute to its healing comfort. Simple and satisfying, we enjoy this soup served with crackers and a green salad.

8 OUNCES SPAGHETTI, ANGEL HAIR, OR GLU-
  TEN-FREE PASTA

1 TABLESPOON OLIVE OIL

2 RIBS CELERY, FINELY CHOPPED

1 MEDIUM CARROT, CUT INTO 1/2-INCH DICE

1/2 CUP FINELY CHOPPED ONION

1 TEASPOON SEA SALT

1 BAY LEAF

FRESH GROUND BLACK PEPPER

8 CUPS WATER

6 TABLESPOONS SAVORY BROTH MIX (PAGE 19)

1 TEASPOON DRIED PARSLEY

SERVES 4

QUICK & EASY
GLUTEN FREE OPTION
SOY FREE

Break up the noodles and cook them in a large pot of boiling, salted water until al dente. Drain well and set aside.

Heat the oil in a large pot over medium heat. Stir in the celery, carrot, onion, salt, bay leaf, and black pepper. Cover the pot and cook until softened, about 3 minutes.

Stir in the water, broth mix, and parsley. Bring to a boil, then reduce to a simmer. Cook, uncovered, until the vegetables are tender, about 10 minutes. Adjust the seasoning by adding salt and black pepper, if needed. Remove and discard the bay leaf before serving.

When ready to serve, transfer a portion of the noodles into the bottom of each soup bowl and top with the hot soup.

CHEF'S TIP: Instead of cooking the noodles in a separate pot, you can cook them in the soup. If you decide not to enjoy it immediately, strain out the noodles so they do not absorb more liquid and become soggy. Store the soup and noodles separately.

Cream of Mushroom Soup

The cream of mushroom soup that comes condensed in a can was an American staple, used for soup or made into a variety of casseroles. This is a wink at that old favorite. It is neither canned nor condensed, but it's a snap to make and satisfying to enjoy. Serve with crusty bread and a simple spinach salad with Ranch Dressing (page 29). Dried porcini mushrooms are available in the produce section or bulk section of a supermarket. Porcinis tend to have sand in their folds, so rinse them well under running water.

3 TABLESPOONS VEGAN BUTTER, DIVIDED

2 GARLIC CLOVES, MINCED

1 MEDIUM RED ONION, FINELY CHOPPED

1 POUND BUTTON MUSHROOMS, WIPED CLEAN AND SLICED

3 CUPS PLAIN UNSWEETENED VEGAN MILK, DIVIDED

1 CUP COARSELY CHOPPED BLANCHED ALMONDS

1/2 TEASPOON SEA SALT

2 TABLESPOONS SAVORY BROTH MIX (PAGE 19)

2 OUNCES DRIED PORCINI MUSHROOMS, RINSED WELL

2 1/2 CUPS WATER OR PORCINI SOAKING LIQUID (SEE CHEF'S TIP)

1/4 TEASPOON FRESHLY GRATED NUTMEG

1 TEASPOON FRESH LEMON JUICE

FRESH GROUND BLACK PEPPER

SERVES 6

QUICK & EASY
SOY FREE
GLUTEN FREE

Melt 2 tablespoons of the butter in a large pot over medium-high heat. Add the garlic, onion, and button mushrooms and cook until the mushrooms release most of their liquid, stirring occasionally, 6 to 7 minutes.

Combine 1 cup of the milk and the almonds in a personal blender. Blend well until smooth. Set aside.

When the mushrooms begin to brown, stir in the salt, broth mix, and remaining 1 tablespoon of butter. Cook, stirring, until the mushrooms are golden brown, about 2 or 3 more minutes. Scoop out 1/4 cup of the mushrooms and set aside.

Stir in the porcini mushrooms and water. Cover the pot with a lid, reduce to a simmer, and cook until the mushrooms are tender, about 5 minutes.

Stir in the reserved almond cream and remaining 2 cups of milk. Use an immersion blender to blend until smooth.

Stir in the reserved mushrooms, nutmeg, and pepper, to taste. Bring to a simmer and cook until thickened. Stir in the lemon juice. Adjust seasoning as needed. Serve hot.

CHEFS TIP: To make porcini soaking liquid, soak the porcinis in 2 1/2 cups of boiling water in a deep container for 15 minutes. Remove them gently from the soaking water, so as not to stir up the grit on the bottom of the container. Strain the liquid through a coffee filter to remove any grit. The liquid is now ready to use in recipes.

Creamy Tomato-Basil Soup

Very classic and quite simple to make, this version of the traditional basil and tomato soup leaves nothing lacking. Using bread or rice is a traditional way of thickening soups. The surprise is that it isn't used more often. This soup makes an easy weeknight meal served with croutons (page 102) and an herb salad with Italian dressing. To make it gluten free, substitute 1 cup of cooked rice for the bread. (See photo page 42.)

2 (28-OUNCE) CANS WHOLE TOMATOES, UNDRAINED

2 TABLESPOONS PACKED BROWN SUGAR

2 TABLESPOONS OLIVE OIL

1 MEDIUM ONION, COARSELY CHOPPED

1 GARLIC CLOVE, COARSELY CHOPPED

1 TEASPOON DRIED BASIL

1 TEASPOON SEA SALT

FRESH GROUND BLACK PEPPER

2 CUPS VEGETABLE BROTH

3 SLICES OF GOOD-QUALITY WHITE BREAD, CRUSTS REMOVED AND CUT INTO 1-INCH CUBES

1/4 CUP FIRMLY PACKED FRESH BASIL, FINELY CHOPPED

6 TEASPOONS VEGAN SOUR CREAM, FOR GARNISH (OPTIONAL)

———

SERVES 6

QUICK & EASY
GLUTEN-FREE OPTION
SOY FREE

Preheat the oven to 475°F. Prepare a baking sheet with foil.

Gently squeeze excess liquid from the tomatoes and set aside all the tomato juice, including the juice from the cans. Place the tomatoes on the prepared baking sheet. Sprinkle the brown sugar over the tomatoes and bake for about 20 minutes, or until they begin to darken.

Strain the tomato juice to remove seeds. Set aside.

Heat the oil in a large pot over medium heat. Add the onion and cook, stirring, until softened, about 3 minutes. Stir in the garlic and dried basil and continue to cook for another minute.

Stir in the vegetable broth, bread, salt, and reserved tomato juice. Cook the soup for 10 minutes to blend the flavors and break down the bread.

Add the baked tomatoes to the soup. Continue to simmer for 5 more minutes.

Working in batches, transfer the soup to a blender and blend until smooth, then return to the pot. Alternatively, use an immersion blender to blend the soup in the pot.

Stir in the basil and another tablespoon of olive oil, for extra richness, if desired. Season to taste with salt and black pepper and reheat if needed. If the soup is too acidic, stir in another teaspoon of brown sugar. Serve the soup with the optional dollop of sour cream, if using.

Leek Potato Soup

This soup is another classic, one that is surprisingly easy to make and quite delicious. To be more economical, you can substitute up to half of the leeks with onions. This is my youngest daughter's favorite soup. Serve with crackers and a simple green salad.

1 TABLESPOON VEGAN BUTTER

3 SMALL LEEKS, WHITE PARTS ONLY, CUT INTO
1/4-INCH SLICES (ABOUT 3 CUPS)

6 CUPS WATER

5 MEDIUM WAXY POTATOES (ABOUT 1
1/2 POUNDS), PEELED AND COARSELY
CHOPPED

2 TEASPOONS SEA SALT

1 CUP PLAIN UNSWEETENED VEGAN MILK

FRESH GROUND BLACK PEPPER

VEGAN SOUR CREAM, FOR GARNISH

———————

SERVES 6

QUICK & EASY

GLUTEN FREE

SOY FREE OPTION

Melt the butter in a large pot over medium heat. Stir in the leeks, cover, and cook until they begin to soften and wilt, about 3 minutes. Do not brown.

Stir in the water, potatoes, and salt. Bring the soup to a boil and reduce it to a simmer. Cover the pot and cook until the potatoes are very tender and falling apart, about 15 minutes.

Stir in the milk. Use an immersion blender to blend the soup in the pot until smooth, or blend in batches in a blender. Add black pepper to taste and adjust the seasoning with salt.

Ladle the soup into bowls and garnish with a dollop of vegan sour cream, if desired.

Cleaning Leeks

To clean leeks, cut off the dark green parts and discard, or save them for making vegetable broth. Trim off the root end and cut the leek in half lengthwise. Slice each half into 1/4-inch slices. Fill a large bowl with water. Add the leeks to the water and swish them around. Allow the dirt to fall to the bottom of the bowl and scoop out the clean leeks with your hands.

Broccoli Cheese Soup

There are numerous ways to make cheesy vegan soups, but this one won't leave you feeling cheated. If you are hankering for an old favorite, you have found the perfect version. Serve the soup with breadsticks and/or a sandwich. To make this soup gluten free, omit the all-purpose flour. Set aside 1/4 cup of the milk and mix it with 3 tablespoons arrowroot starch. Stir the arrowroot mixture into the soup when the broccoli is tender. Bring the soup to a simmer and cook only until thickened.

4 CUPS PLAIN UNSWEETENED VEGAN MILK

1/4 CUP VEGAN CREAM CHEESE

2 TABLESPOONS SAVORY BROTH MIX (PAGE 19)

1/4 CUP DICED JARRED PIMIENTOS OR ROASTED RED PEPPERS

1 TABLESPOON NUTRITIONAL YEAST FLAKES

1/4 TEASPOON PAPRIKA

2 TABLESPOONS VEGAN BUTTER

1 SMALL ONION, FINELY CHOPPED

1/2 CUP UNBLEACHED ALL-PURPOSE FLOUR

12 OUNCES BROCCOLI, TOUGH STEMS REMOVED OR PEELED, FINELY CHOPPED

SEA SALT AND FRESH GROUND BLACK PEPPER

PINCH OF FRESHLY GRATED NUTMEG

1 TEASPOON APPLE CIDER VINEGAR

———

SERVES 4

QUICK & EASY
GLUTEN-FREE OPTION

In a blender, combine the milk, cream cheese, broth mix, pimientos, nutritional yeast, and paprika and blend until very smooth. Set aside.

Heat the butter in a large pot over medium heat. Add the onion and cook, stirring, until it begins to soften, about 3 minutes.

Add the flour and cook, stirring, until it begins to develop some color, about 2 minutes.

Slowly pour the milk mixture into the pot; mix the soup continuously using a whisk until there are no lumps. Bring the soup to a simmer and cook until thickened. (Do not boil.)

Stir in the broccoli. Add salt, black pepper, and nutmeg to taste. Simmer the soup on low until the broccoli is tender, about 15 minutes. Stir in the vinegar.

VARIATION: To make Cauliflower Cheese Soup, use finely chopped cauliflower instead of broccoli.

Hot and Sour Soup with Bok Choy

This is the soup traditionally found in Chinese restaurants, sans the eggs and other animal ingredients. It is spicy and sour at the same time, while being really quick to make. Serve the soup with fried wonton strips to complete the restaurant feel.

2 TEASPOONS GRAPESEED OR SUNFLOWER OIL

1 TEASPOON TOASTED SESAME OIL

4 OUNCES SHIITAKE MUSHROOMS, WIPED CLEAN, STEMMED, AND SLICED

1 SMALL ONION, CUT INTO 1/8-INCH SLICES

1 GARLIC CLOVE, MINCED

1 (1/2-INCH) PIECE FRESH GINGER, THINLY SLICED

5 CUPS VEGETABLE BROTH

3 TABLESPOONS REDUCED-SODIUM TAMARI

2 TABLESPOONS RICE VINEGAR

8 OUNCES BAKED TOFU, CUT INTO 1/4-INCH SLICES

1 TEASPOON RED PEPPER FLAKES

4 BABY BOK CHOY, QUARTERED THROUGH THE BOTTOM

SEA SALT AND FRESH GROUND BLACK PEPPER

GARNISH: 2 SCALLIONS, CUT INTO 1/4-INCH SLICES DIAGONALLY

SERVES 6

QUICK & EASY
GLUTEN FREE

Heat the oils in a large pot over medium heat. Add the mushrooms, onion, garlic, and ginger and cook, stirring, until the vegetables begin to brown, about 5 minutes.

Stir in the broth, tamari, vinegar, tofu, and red pepper flakes. Bring to a boil, reduce to a simmer, and cook for 5 minutes.

Stir the boy choy into the soup. Continue to simmer until tender, about 5 minutes. Season with salt, black pepper, and more vinegar if needed. Serve hot, garnished with the scallions.

Manhattan Chowder

There has always been a rivalry between the chowders: the red (Manhattan), and the white (New England). Manhattan is the tomato-based version of the coastal favorite. Make them both and pick a favorite between these two easy-to-make soups. Serve the soup with saltine crackers and a simple green salad. Pass the Tabasco at the table.

1 TABLESPOON VEGAN BUTTER

1 1/2 TEASPOONS TOASTED SESAME OIL

2 RIBS CELERY, CUT INTO 1/2-INCH DICE

4 GARLIC CLOVES, COARSELY CHOPPED

1 MEDIUM CARROT, CUT INTO 1/2-INCH DICE

1 MEDIUM ONION, CUT INTO 1/2-INCH DICE

1 MEDIUM GREEN BELL PEPPER, CORED,
    SEEDED, AND CUT INTO 1/2-INCH DICE

12 OUNCES OYSTER MUSHROOMS, WIPED
    CLEAN AND TORN INTO BITE-SIZED PIECES

1 TEASPOON DRIED OREGANO

1/2 TEASPOON FRESH OR DRIED THYME

1 BAY LEAF

3 CUPS MILD SEAWEED VEGETABLE STOCK
    (SEE VARIATION PAGE 21)

3 CUPS WATER

1 (14-OUNCE) CAN DICED TOMATOES, UND-
    RAINED

2 MEDIUM RUSSET POTATOES, PEELED AND
    CUT INTO 1/2-INCH CHUNKS

1 TEASPOON OLD BAY SEASONING

SERVES 6

QUICK & EASY

GLUTEN FREE

SOY FREE

Heat the butter and oil in a large pot over medium heat. Stir in the celery, garlic, carrot, onion, bell pepper, mushrooms, oregano, thyme, and bay leaf. Cook, stirring, until the vegetables begin to brown, about 10 minutes.

Stir in the stock, water, and tomatoes with their juice. Bring to a boil, then reduce the heat to a simmer. Cook, uncovered, for 5 minutes.

Stir in the potatoes and Old Bay seasoning, then season to taste with salt and pepper. Cook until the potatoes are tender, about 15 more minutes. Taste and adjust the seasonings, if needed. Remove and discard the bay leaf before serving.

New England Chowder

The great chowder rivalry continues even without the clams. You decide which you prefer, creamy vs. tomato-based. Even my family is divided between these two simple and savory classics. For a special treat, serve this soup in hollowed out, toasted bread bowls. Pass the Tabasco at the table.

2 TABLESPOONS OLIVE OIL

1 MEDIUM ONION, FINELY CHOPPED

4 GARLIC CLOVES, MINCED

12 OUNCES OYSTER MUSHROOMS, WIPED
    CLEAN, AND TORN INTO BITE-SIZED PIECES

1 CUP CORN KERNELS, THAWED, IF FROZEN

3 CUPS MILD SEAWEED VEGETABLE STOCK
    (SEE VARIATION PAGE 21)

2 MEDIUM RUSSET POTATOES, PEELED AND
    CUT INTO 1/2-INCH CHUNKS

2 TEASPOONS OLD BAY SEASONING

1 TEASPOON SEA SALT

FRESH GROUND BLACK PEPPER

1/2 TEASPOON LIQUID SMOKE

2 CUPS PLAIN UNSWEETENED VEGAN MILK

1/4 CUP ARROWROOT STARCH OR ORGANIC
    CORNSTARCH

SERVES 6

QUICK & EASY

GLUTEN FREE

SOY FREE

Heat the oil in a large pot over medium heat. Add the onion and garlic and cook, stirring, until they begin to soften, about 3 minutes.

Increase the heat to high and add the mushrooms and corn. Sear the mushrooms on both sides until golden, about 10 minutes. Cook and stir the corn until golden brown.

Stir in the stock, potatoes, Old Bay, salt, black pepper to taste, and liquid smoke. Bring the soup to a boil and reduce it to a simmer. Cook the soup, covered, until the potatoes are tender, about 15 minutes.

Whisk together the milk and arrowroot in a small bowl. Stir the arrowroot mixture into the soup. Bring the soup to a simmer and cook it only until it thickens; do not boil or it might break. Adjust the seasoning with salt and black pepper, if needed. Serve hot.

CHEF'S TIP: If using storebought broth to make the Mild Seaweed Vegetable Stock, add 1 teaspoon dried thyme, 1 teaspoon dried basil, and 1 teaspoon dried oregano to the chowder in the first step.

Minestrone Soup

This rendition of the classic Italian soup is quick and easy. Despite the lengthy ingredient list, it comes together in minutes. If that's not convincing enough, consider that my eldest, most discerning daughter, who also happens to be a minestrone connoisseur, compares all other minestrones to this one. Serve the soup with crusty bread for dipping.

2 TABLESPOONS OLIVE OIL

1/2 TEASPOON TOASTED SESAME OIL

1 SMALL ONION, FINELY CHOPPED

1 RIB CELERY, FINELY CHOPPED

1 SMALL CARROT, CUT INTO 1/2-INCH DICE

2 GARLIC CLOVES, MINCED

1/2 TEASPOON DRIED OREGANO

1/2 TEASPOON DRIED BASIL

1 BAY LEAF

1/4 TEASPOON RED PEPPER FLAKES

4 CUPS VEGETABLE BROTH

1 (15.5-OUNCE) CAN KIDNEY, PINTO, OR CAN-
   NELLINI BEANS, RINSED AND DRAINED

1 CUP CANNED DICED TOMATOES, UNDRAINED

1 SMALL POTATO, PEELED AND CUT INTO 1/2-
   INCH DICE

1/3 CUP ARBORIO RICE

1 TABLESPOON SAVORY BROTH MIX (PAGE 19)

1 SMALL ZUCCHINI, CUT INTO 1/2-INCH DICE

3 CUPS FRESH BABY SPINACH

SEA SALT AND FRESH GROUND BLACK PEPPER

———————

SERVES 6

QUICK & EASY
SOY FREE
GLUTEN FREE

Heat the oils in a large pot over medium heat. Add the onion and cook, stirring, until softened, about 3 minutes. Stir in the celery and carrot and cook until the celery softens, about 2 more minutes. Stir in the garlic, oregano, basil, bay leaf, and red pepper flakes. Cook, stirring, until the garlic is fragrant and the vegetables begin to brown, about 2 more minutes.

Add the vegetable broth, beans, tomatoes with their juice, potatoes, rice, and broth mix. Bring the soup to a boil and boil vigorously for 5 minutes.

Stir in the zucchini. Season to taste with salt and black pepper. Bring to a boil, then reduce to a simmer. Cook, uncovered, until the vegetables and rice are tender, about 15 minutes.

Taste and adjust seasoning with salt and black pepper. Stir in the spinach and cook until wilted, 1 to 2 minutes. Remove and discard the bay leaf before serving.

Split Pea Soup

The split pea is a delicious way to incorporate legumes into your diet. Traditionally, this soup is made with a ham hock to achieve a smoky flavor. This is easily accomplished without any animal ingredients, and again, nothing is lost in the translation. Serve this soup with plenty of croutons (page 102) and a crisp green salad. Legumes are notorious for needing more salt than you think they do, so be sure to season the soup well.

8 CUPS WATER

2 CUPS DRIED SPLIT PEAS, PICKED OVER, RINSED, AND DRAINED

1 BAY LEAF

1 TABLESPOON OLIVE OIL

1 TEASPOON TOASTED SESAME OIL

1 MEDIUM CARROT, FINELY CHOPPED

1 MEDIUM ONION, FINELY CHOPPED

1/2 RIB CELERY, FINELY CHOPPED

4 GARLIC CLOVES, MINCED

1 TEASPOON DRIED OR FRESH THYME

1 TEASPOON PAPRIKA

2 TEASPOONS LIQUID SMOKE

1 TEASPOON SEA SALT

FRESH GROUND BLACK PEPPER

SERVES 6

GLUTEN FREE
SOY FREE

Combine the water, split peas, and bay leaf in a large pot over high heat. Bring to a boil, then reduce the heat to a simmer and cook, partially covered, until the peas are tender, about 1 hour. The peas will be falling apart. If the soup is too thick, add another cup of water to thin. Remove and discard the bay leaf.

Heat the oils in a large skillet over medium heat. Add the carrot and cook, stirring, until it begins to brown, about 3 minutes. Stir in the onion and celery and continue to cook until the onion begins to brown, about 4 minutes. Stir in the garlic and thyme. Cook until the garlic is fragrant, about 30 seconds. Remove the skillet from the heat and stir in the paprika.

Stir the soup with a whisk until the peas are fairly smooth. Stir in the reserved vegetables, then stir in the liquid smoke, salt, and black pepper to taste. Serve hot.

Thai Thom Kha Coconut Soup

This delicious soup, with its coconut flavor and citrus tang, is a Thai restaurant favorite. Now you can enjoy this soup at home. Despite the long list of ingredients, it assembles quickly and is ready in 20 minutes, including prep time. For a protein boost, add 1 cup of cubed baked tofu to the simmering soup.

2 CUPS VEGETABLE BROTH

1 TABLESPOON SAVORY BROTH MIX (PAGE 19)

1 (1-INCH) PIECE FRESH GINGER, CUT INTO 1/4-INCH SLICES

2 TEASPOONS THAI RED CHILI PASTE, (OPTIONAL)

1 MEDIUM CARROT, CUT INTO 1/4-INCH SLICES

1 (15-OUNCE) CAN STRAW MUSHROOMS, RINSED AND DRAINED OR 1 CUP SLICED MUSHROOMS, ANY KIND, WIPED CLEAN, AND CUT INTO 1/4-INCH SLICES

1 CUP SMALL BROCCOLI FLORETS OR FRESH GREEN BEANS, TRIMMED AND CUT INTO 1-INCH PIECES

1 CUP SLICED GREEN CABBAGE

1 TABLESPOON NATURAL SUGAR

ZEST OF 2 LIMES, RESERVING THE LIME JUICE

ZEST OF 1 LEMON

1 (13-OUNCE) CAN FULL-FAT COCONUT MILK

2 TABLESPOONS REDUCED SODIUM TAMARI

3 CUPS FRESH BABY SPINACH

2 TABLESPOONS FRESH LIME JUICE

1/4 CUP BASIL OR CILANTRO LEAVES

SERVES 4

GLUTEN FREE
QUICK & EASY

Heat the vegetable broth, broth mix, ginger, and red chili paste, if using, in a large pot over medium heat. Bring to a boil, add the carrot, and cook for 3 minutes.

Stir in the mushrooms, broccoli or green beans, cabbage, sugar, lime zest, and lemon zest. Bring back to a boil and cook over medium heat for 5 minutes.

Stir in the coconut milk and tamari. Bring the soup just to a simmer. Do not boil again or the coconut milk might break. Simmer until the vegetables are tender, about 10 minutes.

Stir in the baby spinach to wilt. Stir in the lime juice. Taste and adjust the seasonings, adding more salt, sugar, and lime juice as needed. Serve hot, garnished with the basil or cilantro.

CHEF'S TIPS: Canned coconut milk is available as either reduced-fat or full-fat. This recipe works best using the full-fat kind.

If you can find them, add a stalk of smashed lemongrass and 5 kaffir lime leaves to the simmering soup. Omit the lime and lemon zest and reduce the lime juice to 1 tablespoon, or to taste.

Chipotle Chili

Everyone needs a fast, easy, and delicious chili recipe. This one is elevated by the addition of chipotle chiles, which are easily found in any grocery store. Use as much, or as little, as you'd like, since the chipotles can be quite hot. Serve the chili with Corn Muffins (page 236) and a simple green salad. Fixings for chili include vegan sour cream, vegan shredded cheese, finely chopped onion, and minced jalapeños.

1 TABLESPOON OLIVE OIL

4 RIBS CELERY, FINELY CHOPPED

3 GARLIC CLOVES, MINCED

2 MEDIUM ONIONS, FINELY CHOPPED

2 MEDIUM GREEN OR RED BELL PEPPERS, CORED, SEEDED, AND FINELY CHOPPED

1 TABLESPOON DRIED OREGANO

2 TEASPOONS SEA SALT

2 BAY LEAVES

1 TEASPOON GROUND CUMIN

FRESH GROUND BLACK PEPPER

2 (28-OUNCE) CANS WHOLE TOMATOES, UNDRAINED

3 (15.5-OUNCE) CANS KIDNEY OR PINTO BEANS, RINSED AND DRAINED

2 TABLESPOONS MILD CHILI POWDER

2 TABLESPOONS CHIPOTLE ADOBO PUREE (BELOW) OR 1 OR 2 FINELY CHOPPED CHIPOTLE CHILES IN ADOBO

SERVES 4 TO 6

QUICK & EASY
GLUTEN FREE
SOY FREE

Heat the oil in a large pot over medium heat. Stir in the celery, garlic, onions, bell pepper, oregano, salt, bay leaves, cumin, and black pepper to taste. Cover and cook until the vegetables begin to brown, about 7 minutes.

Stir in the tomatoes with their juice, breaking up the tomatoes with your hand as you add them. Stir in the beans, chili powder, and chipotle. Bring to a boil, then reduce to a simmer. Cook, partially covered, until the vegetables are tender and the flavors are blended, about 20 minutes. The chili may simmer for up to an hour. Taste and adjust the seasoning, if needed. Remove and discard the bay leaves before serving.

CHEF'S TIP: Leftover chili makes great Chili Mac (page 163) or can top a vegan burger, baked potato, or nachos.

Chipotle Adobo Puree

Makes about 3/4 cup

Blend the entire (7-ounce) can of chipotles with the adobo sauce and freeze in 1 tablespoon servings. Next time you need some chipotle, it'll be waiting for you in the freezer. 1 tablespoon of the puree equals about 1 chipotle chili.

Mama's Hungarian Bean Soup

After a long day's work in their restaurant, my mom would come home exhausted, but every night she still made us dinner. I still can't figure out where she got the energy from. This simple soup was one meal we always looked forward to. To make it even heartier, add slices of pan-sautéed vegan sausage during the final simmering step. Serve with crusty bread and Hungarian Tomato Salad (page 113). Garnish with a soy-free vegan sour cream to make this soy free.

6 CUPS WATER

1/2 CUP PEARL BARLEY, SOAKED OVERNIGHT WITH 1/2 TEASPOON SEA SALT AND DRAINED

2 (15.5-OUNCE) CANS RED KIDNEY BEANS, RINSED AND DRAINED

2 RIBS CELERY, MINCED

4 MEDIUM CARROTS, COARSELY CHOPPED

1 SMALL ONION, FINELY CHOPPED

3 BAY LEAVES

2 TEASPOONS LIQUID SMOKE

1 TABLESPOON HUNGARIAN PAPRIKA

1 TABLESPOON SAVORY BROTH MIX (PAGE 19)

1 TEASPOON SEA SALT

1/4 TEASPOON FRESH GROUND BLACK PEPPER

1/4 CUP GRAPESEED OR SUNFLOWER OIL

5 TABLESPOONS ALL-PURPOSE UNBLEACHED WHITE FLOUR

6 GARLIC CLOVES, MINCED

VEGAN SOUR CREAM, TO GARNISH

SERVES 6

QUICK & EASY
SOY FREE

Combine the water, barley, beans, celery, carrots, onion, bay leaves, liquid smoke, paprika, broth mix, salt and black pepper in a large pot over high heat. Bring to a boil, then reduce to simmer. Simmer, partially covered, until the vegetables and barley are tender, about 20 minutes.

Remove and discard the bay leaves. Strain out 2 cups of broth from the soup and set aside.

Heat the oil in a small saucepan over medium heat. Add the flour and mix well using a whisk. Cook the flour until it is dark golden brown, about 5 minutes, continually whisking to avoid burning it.

Stir the garlic into the flour mixture. Cook the garlic for 30 seconds. Add the 2 cups of reserved soup broth into the flour mixture, whisking continuously to avoid lumps. Whisk the mixture until smooth.

Pour the flour mixture into the pot of soup and mix with a wooden spoon. Bring the soup to a boil over high heat and reduce to a simmer. Simmer the soup until thickened, about 3 minutes.

Season with salt and black pepper to taste. Ladle the soup into bowls and garnish with a dollop of vegan sour cream.

BBQ Bean Burgers with Slaw (page 89)

CHAPTER 4

Sandwiches

Not much beats a delicious filling between two slices of fluffy bread, rolled in a soft tortilla or stuffed into crunchy lettuce leaves. Some are very fast to throw together and others are layers of flavors and textures. The recipes in this chapter elevate sandwiches from simple to spectacular. Among the mouthwatering offerings are Deli Reubens, Greek Gyros, and Portobello Fajitas with Roasted Poblano Cream Sauce. These hearty sandwiches are satisfying enough to serve anytime you're hungry for some everyday vegan eats. In this chapter you'll also find handy lists for cold and hot sandwich meals.

Egg-Free Salad Sandwiches

Tofu effortlessly replaces eggs in this vegan version of egg salad. This salad is quite delicious and very much a vegan "egg" salad if you add the black salt to complete the egg-like flavor. Serve between slices of toasted bread, in lettuce cups, on crackers, or on sliced cucumbers or celery. Use gluten-free bread to make this gluten-free.

14 OUNCES SOFT TOFU, PRESSED FOR 10 MIN-
  UTES (SEE PAGE 9), PATTED DRY

2 CELERY RIBS, FINELY CHOPPED

1/2 SMALL ONION, FINELY CHOPPED

1/4 CUP VEGAN MAYONNAISE, STOREBOUGHT
  OR HOMEMADE (PAGE 31)

2 TEASPOONS YELLOW MUSTARD

2 TABLESPOONS NUTRITIONAL YEAST FLAKES

1 TEASPOON BLACK SALT (PAGE 206)

1/2 TEASPOON GROUND TURMERIC

FRESH GROUND BLACK PEPPER

8 SLICES BREAD, TOASTED, OR BUTTER LET-
  TUCE LEAVES

SERVES 4

QUICK & EASY
GLUTEN-FREE OPTION

Mash the tofu in a medium bowl with a potato masher or fork. Stir in the celery, onion, mayonnaise, mustard, yeast, black salt, turmeric, and black pepper. Season to taste with sea salt, if needed. Stir in 2 more tablespoons mayo, if needed.

Assemble the sandwiches using either toasted bread or lettuce cups.

VARIATIONS:

Mediterranean: Stir in 1 tablespoon minced capers, 2 tablespoons minced moist sun-dried tomatoes, 3 tablespoons minced Kalamata olives, and 1/2 teaspoon dried oregano. Reduce the amount of black salt and sea salt; the olives add enough saltiness to the salad.

Indian: Stir in 1/4 cup minced cilantro, 2 teaspoons mild curry powder, 1/4 teaspoon ground coriander seed, and 1/8 teaspoon cayenne.

Mexican: Stir in 1/2 cup roasted corn (page 108), 3 tablespoons minced cilantro, 1 tablespoon chipotle puree (page 63), and 1/4 teaspoon mild or spicy chili powder.

Chicken-Free Salad Sandwiches

Your protein of choice – Soy Curls, tofu, or TVP – is right at home in this easy-to-make sandwich filling. You can take a step back in time to the eighties and stuff it into a tomato or just add it to a bed of crisp green salad. Of course, it's also fantastic between two slices of bread or served in lettuce cups.

4 CUPS COARSELY CHOPPED TENDER SOY
   CURLS (PAGE 35), MARINATED TOFU (PAGE
   34) OR SAVORY TVP (PAGE 38), COOLED
   THOROUGHLY
2 CELERY RIBS, FINELY CHOPPED
1/2 SMALL ONION, FINELY CHOPPED
1/2 SMALL RED BELL PEPPER, CORED, SEED-
   ED, AND FINELY CHOPPED
3/4 CUP VEGAN MAYONNAISE, STOREBOUGHT
   OR HOMEMADE (PAGE 31)
1 TABLESPOON SWEET RELISH
SEA SALT AND FRESH GROUND BLACK PEPPER
8 SLICES TOASTED BREAD, GLUTEN FREE
   BREAD, OR BUTTER LETTUCE

SERVES 4

QUICK & EASY
GLUTEN-FREE OPTION

In a large bowl, combine your protein of choice with the celery, onion, bell pepper, mayonnaise, relish, and salt, and pepper to taste. Set aside for 10 minutes to blend the flavors.

Make sandwiches with the mixture, using either toasted bread or lettuce cups.

VARIATION: Curry Chicken-Free Salad. Combine 3/4 cup mayonnaise, 1/2 cup mango chutney, and 2 tablespoons of vegan milk, if the dressing is too thick. Stir in 1/2 cup currants or raisins, 1/2 cup finely chopped scallions, 1/2 cup almond slices, 1 tablespoon mild curry powder, and 1/2 teaspoon sea salt. Mix well and fold in the 4 cups of your choice of vegan protein. Chill to combine flavors.

Easy Lunch Ideas

Having a dozen or so easy lunch meals to rotate through makes preparing lunch easy and quick. Most people have several go-to lunch items that include sandwiches, soups, salads, and pasta, as well as leftovers that pack and travel well for those who attend school or work out of the home.

Easy Cold Sandwiches:

Chicken-Free Salad Sandwich (page 70)
Egg-Free Salad Sandwich (page 68)
Tempeh No-Tuna Sandwich (page 84)
Hummus (page 188) sandwich with slices of veggies and sprouts or mashed avocados
Nut Butter and Jelly (or apple butter and sliced apple or Asian pear) sandwich
Bacon Tofu (page 36), lettuce, and tomato sandwich
Grilled Marinated Tofu (page 34) sandwiches with lettuce and vegan mayo
Olive Salad (page 102) and vegan cream cheese sandwich
Blackened Tempeh (page 39) sandwich with avocado and veggies
Sliced Glazed Holiday Roast (page 136) sandwich, with vegan mayo and mustard
Sliced Vegan Meatloaf (page 132) sandwich with vegan mayo and Quick Barbecue Sauce (page 22)
Blackened Tempeh (page 39) sandwich and Buttermilk-Style Cole Slaw (page 103)
Grilled Vegetables with Pesto Sauce (page 202) sandwich

Hot Sandwich Ideas:

(Note: For these sandwiches, if packing your lunch, it's best to pack the bread separately and assemble after reheating the filling.)

Tostadas topped with Refried Beans with Tomatoes (page 191) and Salsa Fresca (page 23)
Vegan burgers (check out the Bánh Mì Burgers on page 90)
Pan-sautéed artichoke hearts, vegan cheese, and pesto sauce (page 202) on ciabatta
Breakfast burritos with Morning Scramble (page 206) and Refried Beans with Tomatoes (page 191)

Don't forget to check out the hot sandwiches in this chapter, as well as the soups and salads which are automatic to-go meals. Pack the dressing or garnishes separately.

Mushroom Po' Boys

I fell in love with fried oyster po' boys in my pre-vegan days. I love to substitute oyster mushrooms for oysters, but you can use other mushrooms, such as shiitake or sliced Portobellos.

2/3 CUP VEGAN MAYONNAISE, STOREBOUGHT OR HOMEMADE (PAGE 31)

1 TABLESPOON MINCED PARSLEY

2 TEASPOONS DIJON MUSTARD

2 TEASPOONS MINCED CAPERS

2 TEASPOONS HOT SAUCE OR 1/4 TEASPOON CAYENNE

1 TEASPOON FRESH LEMON JUICE

1 GARLIC CLOVE, MINCED

SEA SALT AND FRESH GROUND BLACK PEPPER

3/4 CUP CORN FLOUR (PAGE 84)

1/4 CUP UNBLEACHED ALL-PURPOSE FLOUR OR RICE FLOUR

1 TEASPOON GARLIC POWDER

1/2 TEASPOON CAYENNE

1 CUP PLAIN UNSWEETENED VEGAN MILK

16 MEDIUM TO LARGE OYSTER MUSHROOMS, WIPED CLEAN

GRAPESEED OR SUNFLOWER OIL, FOR PAN-FRYING

4 (6-INCH) HOAGIE ROLLS OR (6-INCH) GLUTEN FREE WRAPS

2 CUPS BUTTERMILK-STYLE COLESLAW (PAGE 103) OR 4 ROMAINE LETTUCE LEAVES

TOMATO SLICES (OPTIONAL)

SERVES 4

QUICK & EASY
GLUTEN-FREE OPTION

In a small bowl, combine the mayonnaise, parsley, mustard, capers, hot sauce, lemon juice, garlic, and salt and pepper to taste. Mix well and set aside.

Line a baking sheet with paper towels and set aside. Combine the flours, 1 teaspoon of salt, garlic powder, cayenne, and 1/4 teaspoon black pepper in a medium bowl. Mix well and set aside.

Pour the milk into a separate medium bowl. Dip each mushroom first in the milk and then dredge in the flour mixture. Set them aside on a large plate.

Heat 1/2 inch of oil in a large skillet over medium heat. (Cast iron is best.) Fry the mushrooms in the hot oil until crispy, about 2 minutes per side. Drain on the prepared baking sheet. Season with salt, to taste. Fry the mushrooms in batches to avoid overcrowding the pan.

Split and toast the hoagie rolls, if using. Warm the wraps, if using, between two damp paper towels in the microwave or heat them in a toaster oven or skillet. Keep warm.

Assemble the sandwiches by loading each roll or wrap with four fried mushrooms, 1/2 cup of coleslaw or 1 lettuce leaf, tomato slices, if using, and the reserved sauce, to taste. Serve immediately.

No-Fish Filet Sandwiches

This is one of my family's favorite sandwiches. It's a simple combination of fried tofu, bun, lettuce, tomato, and tartar sauce. Most of the ingredients in the list are for the breading, which comes together fast. If you'd like an extra seafood kick, use the Seafood Tofu instead of just the plain tofu.

16-OUNCES FIRM OR EXTRA-FIRM TOFU, PAT-TED DRY, OR 8 SLICES SEAFOOD TOFU (VARIATION, PAGE 34)

1/4 CUP PLAIN UNSWEETENED VEGAN MILK

1/4 CUP ARROWROOT STARCH

1/2 CUP CORN FLOUR (PAGE 4)

1/4 CUP UNBLEACHED ALL-PURPOSE FLOUR OR BROWN RICE FLOUR

1 TEASPOON ONION POWDER

1 TEASPOON SEA SALT

1 TEASPOON DRIED PARSLEY

1 TEASPOON DRIED DILL

1/2 TEASPOON GARLIC POWDER

FRESH GROUND BLACK PEPPER

GRAPESEED OR SUNFLOWER OIL, FOR PAN-FRYING

4 BURGER BUNS OR GLUTEN-FREE BUNS, TOASTED

TARTAR SAUCE (PAGE 30)

LETTUCE LEAVES, TOMATO SLICES, TO SERVE

———

SERVES 4

QUICK & EASY
GLUTEN-FREE OPTION

Slice the tofu into eight (1/2-inch) slabs and set aside.

Combine the milk and arrowroot in a shallow bowl. Mix well and set aside.

In a separate shallow bowl, combine the corn flour, all-purpose flour, onion powder, salt, parsley, dill, garlic powder, and black pepper to taste. Set aside.

Preheat 1/2-inch oil in a large skillet (cast iron is best).

Gently dredge each tofu slab first in the milk mixture and then in the corn flour mixture, pressing the breading to the tofu.

Fry each dredged tofu slab in the hot oil until golden brown on both sides, about 2 minutes per side. Drain the fried tofu on paper towels.

To assemble, place two fried tofu slices on each bun. Top with tartar sauce, lettuce, and tomato. Serve immediately.

CHEF'S TIP: Corn flour is not the same as cornmeal. Corn flour is finely ground, unlike cornmeal, which is coarse.

Greek Gyros with Tzatziki Sauce

My love for this sandwich began when I attended college in Chicago and worked in numerous Greek restaurants where gyros are quite popular. Going vegan simply meant I had to make a kinder version of the original.

1/4 CUP OLIVE OIL

3 TABLESPOONS FRESH LEMON JUICE

8 GARLIC CLOVES, MINCED

4 TEASPOONS DRIED OREGANO

2 TEASPOONS DRIED ROSEMARY

SEA SALT AND FRESH GROUND BLACK PEPPER

8 SIMPLE SEITAN CUTLETS (PAGE 40), CUT DIAGONALLY INTO 1/4-INCH SLICES, OR GRILLED MARINATED TOFU SLICES (PAGE 34)

6 PITA BREADS (WARMED) OR GLUTEN-FREE WRAPS

TOMATO SLICES, SHREDDED LETTUCE, ONION SLIVERS

TZATZIKI SAUCE (RECIPE FOLLOWS)

———————

SERVES 6

GLUTEN-FREE OPTION

In a large shallow bowl, combine the olive oil, lemon juice, garlic, oregano, rosemary, 3/4 teaspoon salt, and 1/4 teaspoon black pepper and mix well. Add the sliced seitan to the bowl and toss with the marinade. Set aside for at least 1 hour.

Heat a large skillet over medium heat. Transfer the seitan slices with the marinade to the skillet in a single layer. Cook until golden brown, 2 to 3 minutes on each side. If needed, cook in batches to prevent overcrowding. Season to taste with salt and pepper.

To serve, in each pita bread, arrange a few slices of seitan, a tomato slice, some lettuce, a few onion slivers, and a few tablespoons of tzatziki sauce. Devour.

Tzatziki Sauce

1 MEDIUM CUCUMBER, PEELED, SEEDED, AND SHREDDED

SEA SALT

1 CUP PLAIN UNSWEETENED VEGAN YOGURT

2 GARLIC CLOVES, MINCED

1 TABLESPOON OLIVE OIL

1 TEASPOON FRESH LEMON JUICE

1 TEASPOON OREGANO

FRESH GROUND BLACK PEPPER

———————

MAKES ABOUT 1 1/2 CUPS

Place the shredded cucumber in a small bowl. Sprinkle with a few pinches of salt, mix to combine, then transfer the cucumber to a strainer set over a small bowl. Set aside for 10 minutes to allow it to drain. Using your hands, squeeze the drained cucumber of excess liquid. Discard the liquid. Transfer the drained cucumber back to the small bowl. Stir in the yogurt, garlic, olive oil, lemon juice, oregano, and salt and pepper to taste. Mix well and set aside until needed. If not using right away, cover and refrigerate until ready to use.

Easy Falafel Pitas

Traditional falafel are made with dried chickpeas (garbanzo beans) and are fried. I use canned beans for ease (or you can use your own home-cooked beans) and pan-sauté them. They have all the flavor of traditional falafel without all the work or fat.

1 (15.5-OUNCE) CAN CHICKPEAS, RINSED AND
   DRAINED

1 SMALL CARROT, SHREDDED

1/4 SMALL ONION, COARSELY CHOPPED

1/4 CUP FIRMLY PACKED PARSLEY LEAVES

1/4 CUP UNBLEACHED ALL-PURPOSE FLOUR
   OR 3 TABLESPOONS ARROWROOT STARCH

2 TEASPOONS GROUND CUMIN

3/4 TEASPOON SEA SALT

1/2 TEASPOON PAPRIKA

1/4 TEASPOON CAYENNE

FRESH GROUND BLACK PEPPER

2 TABLESPOONS FRESH LEMON JUICE

2 GARLIC CLOVES, MINCED

2 TABLESPOONS OLIVE OIL

2 PITA BREADS, HALVED OR 4 (6-INCH) GLUTEN
   FREE WRAPS, WARMED

ONION SLIVERS, FINELY SHREDDED RED OR
   GREEN CABBAGE, THINLY SLICED JALAPEÑO

YOGURT TAHINI SAUCE (OPPOSITE)

———

SERVES 4

QUICK & EASY
GLUTEN-FREE OPTION

Combine the chickpeas, carrot, onion, parsley, flour, cumin, salt, paprika, cayenne, black pepper to taste, lemon juice, and minced garlic cloves in a food processor. Pulse until the ingredients are finely ground but not pureed.

Divide the mixture into 8 parts and form them into 1/2-inch thick patties.

Heat the oil in a large skillet over medium heat. Cook each falafel until golden brown on both sides and cooked through, about 3 minutes per side.

To assemble the sandwiches, fill each pita pocket half with 2 falafel, onion slivers, some shredded cabbage, a few jalapeño slices, and 2 tablespoons of the sauce.

Yogurt-Tahini Sauce

1/4 CUP PLAIN UNSWEETENED VEGAN YOGURT

1 TABLESPOON TAHINI

1/2 TEASPOON FRESH LEMON JUICE

1 GARLIC CLOVE, MINCED

SEA SALT AND FRESH GROUND BLACK PEPPER

———

MAKES 1/2 CUP

Combine the yogurt, tahini, lemon juice, sugar, and garlic in a small bowl. Mix well with a fork. Stir in 1 tablespoon water to thin the sauce, if needed. Season to taste with salt and black pepper.

Asian Summer Rolls

Not exactly a sandwich, I included these summer rolls in this chapter because they make a refreshing handheld lunch—and a nice break from the usual bread sandwiches. Summer rolls, or fresh spring rolls, are crazy-easy to make once you know how to soak the rice paper. The package will likely direct you to soak the wrapper for up to a minute. Don't believe them! The wrappers only need to be soaked long enough to make them pliable. They will continue to soften after you wrap them, as they continue to absorb the moisture in the filling. Alternately, you may wrap the filling in large fresh lettuce leaves.

Dipping Sauce:

6 TABLESPOONS HOT WATER

6 TABLESPOONS PEANUT BUTTER

1 TABLESPOON REDUCED SODIUM TAMARI

1 1/2 TEASPOONS FRESH LIME JUICE

1 1/2 TEASPOONS PACKED BROWN SUGAR

2 GARLIC CLOVES, MINCED

Spring Rolls:

1 OUNCE RICE VERMICELLI NOODLES

4 SPRING ROLL WRAPPERS OR LARGE LET-
TUCE LEAVES

1/2 CUP CILANTRO LEAVES

1/2 RIPE HASS AVOCADO, PITTED, PEELED AND
CUT INTO 1/4-INCH SLICES

2 SLABS BLACKENED TEMPEH (PAGE 39), CUT
INTO MATCHSTICKS

1 SMALL CARROT, CUT INTO MATCHSTICKS

1/2 SMALL CUCUMBER, CUT INTO MATCH-
STICKS

———————

SERVES 4

QUICK & EASY
GLUTEN-FREE

Dipping Sauce: Combine the water, peanut butter, tamari, lime juice, sugar, and garlic in a small bowl. Mix well using a whisk and set aside.

Spring Rolls: Cook the rice noodles in a medium pot of water until al dente. Drain, reserving the cooking water for the spring roll wrappers, and set the noodles aside.

If using spring roll wrappers, transfer the reserved hot water to a shallow baking pan. Rehydrate a spring roll wrapper by soaking it in the hot water just until pliable, at the most 10 seconds. Transfer the pliable wrapper to a large plate. It should still be somewhat rigid, but soft enough to roll after a few seconds.

If using lettuce leaves, trim off any thick stems using a paring knife. Place a lettuce leaf on a large plate.

To make rolling the wrapper easier, you may optionally coarsely mash the avocado; this will prevent them from sliding while you assemble the rest of the ingredients.

Stack 1/4 of the cilantro, 1/4 of the avocado, 1/4 of the noodles, 1/4 of the tempeh, 1/4 of the carrots, and 1/4 of the cucumber in the middle of the wrapper or leaf.

Fold the right side of the rice paper or lettuce leaf over the ingredients, then the left side. Fold the bottom flap of the wrapper over the ingredients and, pulling gently to tighten, roll up the wrapper. Repeat until all the wrappers are rolled. Serve the rolls with the dipping sauce.

California Club Sandwiches

The Club is a tiered sandwich, held together with long hors d'oeuvres toothpicks and sliced diagonally into 4 sections, from corner to corner. While the sandwich may seem simple, it is a concoction that has stood the test of time.

12 SLICES BREAD OR GLUTEN-FREE BREAD, LIGHTLY TOASTED

1/2 CUP VEGAN MAYONNAISE, STOREBOUGHT OR HOMEMADE (PAGE 31)

16 LETTUCE LEAVES, JUST LARGE ENOUGH TO FIT THE BREAD SLICES

8 SLICES RIPE TOMATO

12 SLICES BACON TOFU (PAGE 36) OR 4 SLABS BLACKENED TEMPEH (PAGE 39)

1 RIPE HASS AVOCADO, PITTED, PEELED, AND CUT INTO 12 SLICES

1/2 CUP FIRMLY-PACKED ALFALFA SPROUTS

SEA SALT AND FRESH GROUND BLACK PEPPER

———————

SERVES 4

QUICK & EASY
GLUTEN-FREE OPTION

Place 4 slices of toast on a work surface and spread each with a thin layer of mayonnaise. Top each with a lettuce leaf, 2 tomato slices, and 3 slices Bacon Tofu.

Spread mayonnaise on 4 more slices of toast and place them, mayonnaise side down, on top of the bacon. Spread a thin layer of mayonnaise on top of the toast slices that are on the sandwich. The middle pieces of toast now have mayonnaise spread on both sides.

Arrange another lettuce leaf, three slices of avocado, and sprouts on each sandwich. Season the sprouts with salt and black pepper.

Spread a thin layer of mayonnaise on the remaining 4 slices of toast and place them on the sandwiches, mayonnaise side down.

Insert 4 toothpicks into each sandwich in a diamond pattern to allow you to cut through the sandwich diagonally. One toothpick at the top, one at the bottom, one on the right and one on the left, midway between the center and the sides. Cut the sandwich diagonally, making two cuts from corner to corner, before serving.

Tempeh No-Tuna Salad Sandwiches

As a young adult, Tuna Melt was my favorite sandwich. True, I'm a child of the eighties, but it was still pretty tasty, as odd as a mayo-based canned fish sandwich with melted cheese is. I'm supposing no one told the folks in the know that cheese and fish are not a match. This salad takes compassion to the next level and the tuna and dairy cheese are no longer part of the dish. Tempeh, which flakes quite beautifully, is the perfect replacement, and a hint of the sea completes the dish. Use gluten-free bread to make this gluten-free.

1 CUP VEGETABLE BROTH

1/2 TEASPOON OLD BAY SEASONING

2 TEASPOONS DULSE SEAWEED FLAKES OR 1/4 TEASPOON KELP GRANULES

SEA SALT

1 (8-OUNCE) PACKAGE TEMPEH, CUT INTO 1/2-INCH SLICES

1 SMALL CARROT, SHREDDED

1/2 CELERY RIB, FINELY CHOPPED

2 TABLESPOONS FINELY CHOPPED ONION

1/4 CUP VEGAN MAYONNAISE, STOREBOUGHT OR HOMEMADE (PAGE 31)

2 TEASPOONS DILL RELISH

1 TEASPOON FRESH LEMON JUICE

1/2 TEASPOON DRIED DILL

FRESH GROUND BLACK PEPPER

8 SLICES BREAD, TOASTED OR LETTUCE LEAVES

SERVES 4

QUICK & EASY
GLUTEN-FREE OPTION

Combine the vegetable broth, Old Bay seasoning, dulse, and 1/4 teaspoon of salt in a medium saucepan. Mix well. Add the tempeh slices. Bring the broth to a boil and reduce it to a simmer. Simmer the tempeh for 10 minutes. Remove the saucepan from the heat and set aside for 10 minutes to marinate. Drain and cool the tempeh completely. For a stronger seaweed flavor, cover and refrigerate the tempeh in the broth overnight.

Crumble the tempeh into a medium bowl. Stir in the carrot, celery, onion, mayonnaise, relish, lemon juice, and dill. Season with salt and black pepper to taste. Serve the salad on toast or lettuce.

VARIATION: Tempeh No-Tuna Melt. Butter a piece of bread. Heat a skillet over medium heat. Add the bread slice, buttered side down, to the skillet. Spread some Tempeh No-Tuna Sandwich filling on the slice of bread and top with a slice of vegan cheese. Cover the skillet with a lid and cook until the bread is golden and the cheese melts. Add a few tablespoons of water to the skillet to produce steam to help melt the cheese.

Portobello Fajitas with Roasted Poblano Cream Sauce

Originally I was going to include a seitan variation for fajitas, thinking fajitas just weren't that good without a really "meaty" protein. Boy, was I wrong! The grilled, marinated Portobellos are just right, and the creamy sauce makes any cheese or sour cream superfluous. If you don't have a grill pan, use your broiler, an electric grill pan, or even a skillet, but don't miss this sandwich!

1/2 CUP CILANTRO LEAVES

4 SCALLIONS, COARSELY CHOPPED

3 GARLIC CLOVES

4 TABLESPOONS GRAPESEED OR SUNFLOWER
    OIL, DIVIDED

3 TABLESPOONS FRESH LIME JUICE

2 TABLESPOONS WATER

1/2 TEASPOON GROUND CUMIN

4 LARGE PORTOBELLO MUSHROOM CAPS,
    WIPED CLEAN, AND CUT INTO 1/2-INCH
    SLICES

2 RED OR GREEN BELL PEPPERS, SEEDED,
    AND CUT INTO 1/2-INCH SLICES

1 MEDIUM ONION, CUT INTO 1/4-INCH SLICES

SEA SALT AND FRESH GROUND BLACK PEPPER

6 (7-INCH) FLOUR TORTILLAS OR 8 (5-INCH)
    CORN TORTILLAS

ROASTED POBLANO CREAM SAUCE (PAGE 88)

1 RIPE HASS AVOCADO, PITTED, PEELED, AND
    CUT INTO 1/8-INCH SLICES

SERVES 4 TO 6

QUICK & EASY
GLUTEN-FREE OPTION
SOY-FREE

Make the marinade by combining cilantro leaves, scallions, garlic, 2 tablespoons oil, lime juice, water, and cumin in a personal blender. Blend well to combine.

Combine the marinade and mushrooms in a medium bowl, rubbing the marinade into the mushrooms. Set aside for 10 minutes.

Heat 2 tablespoons oil in a large skillet over medium heat. Add the peppers and onion. Cook, stirring, until crisp-tender, 5 to 8 minutes. Season with salt and black pepper.

In the meantime, heat a grill pan, electric grill, or another skillet over medium-high heat. Grill the mushroom slices in batches until cooked through and grill marks appear, about 3 minutes per side. Season to taste with salt.

Heat the tortillas between 2 damp paper towels in the microwave for 1 minute or heat each tortilla in a large skillet over medium heat. Keep warm.

Assemble the fajitas with warm tortillas, mushrooms, peppers and onions, poblano sauce, and avocado.

Roasted Poblano Cream Sauce

We love poblano chiles at our house, especially roasted; the house smells so good when a pepper is being charred. We have noticed, however, that even though poblanos are supposed to be milder than jalapeños, we have had our fair share of pretty spicy ones. If you'd rather not risk getting a spicy poblano, replace it in this recipe with a medium green bell pepper.

1 POBLANO CHILE

1/3 CUP RAW CASHEWS

6 TABLESPOONS PLAIN, UNSWEETENED AL-
   MOND MILK

2 TABLESPOONS FRESH LIME JUICE

2 TABLESPOONS CILANTRO LEAVES

2 TABLESPOONS OLIVE OIL

1/2 TEASPOON GROUND CUMIN

1/2 TEASPOON ONION POWDER

1/4 TEASPOON GARLIC POWDER

SEA SALT AND FRESH GROUND BLACK PEPPER

MAKES ABOUT 1 CUP

QUICK & EASY

GLUTEN-FREE

SOY-FREE

Roast the poblano in a dry skillet, turning every few minutes. When well blistered and mostly charred, transfer the poblano to a bowl and cover the bowl with plastic wrap to steam for ten minutes. Peel the chile by rubbing the skin off. Remove the stem and seeds and coarsely chop. Set aside.

Blend the cashews in a personal blender until the nuts are finely ground. Add the milk, lime juice, cilantro, oil, cumin, onion powder, garlic powder, and the reserved poblano. Blend the sauce as smoothly as possible, in intervals, if necessary, to avoid overheating the blender. Season with salt and black pepper to taste.

CHEF'S TIP: Check out "Blending Nuts" (page 9) for a smoother sauce.

BBQ Bean Burgers with Slaw

If Sloppy Joe ever wanted a makeover, I'm pretty sure he would want to be transformed into this burger. A bit of spice, a bit of sweet, and a whole lot of flavor awaits you. You could substitute more barbecue sauce for the chipotle in the spread if you'd like more BBQ taste. The burger mixture will keep in an airtight container for up to 2 days in the refrigerator before being cooked. It makes for an even faster meal if the burger mixture is premade. (See photo page 66.)

1 CUP OLD-FASHIONED ROLLED OATS, DIVIDED

1 (15.5-OUNCE) CAN NAVY BEANS, RINSED AND DRAINED

1/2 CUP CHOPPED SCALLIONS (4 SCALLIONS)

1/2 TEASPOON SEA SALT, PLUS MORE AS NEEDED

1/4 CUP BARBECUE SAUCE (PAGE 22), OR STOREBOUGHT

1 TABLESPOON GRAPESEED OR SUNFLOWER OIL, PLUS MORE FOR SAUTÉING

2 TABLESPOONS CHIPOTLE ADOBO PUREE (PAGE 63) OR 2 CHIPOTLE CHILES, FINELY MINCED

1 TEASPOON DIJON MUSTARD

FRESH GROUND BLACK PEPPER

1/4 CUP VEGAN MAYONNAISE, STOREBOUGHT OR HOMEMADE (PAGE 31)

4 TOASTED BURGER BUNS OR GLUTEN-FREE BUNS

1 CUP BUTTERMILK-STYLE COLESLAW (PAGE 103)

———————
SERVES 4

QUICK & EASY
GLUTEN-FREE OPTION
SOY-FREE

Add 3/4 cup of the oats to a food processor and pulse about 5 times to break them up, then transfer to a large bowl.

Add the remaining 1/4 cup oats to the food processor and process into flour. Add 3/4 cup beans, scallions, and salt and process into a paste. Transfer the mixture to the large bowl with the broken oats. Add the remaining whole beans, barbecue sauce, 1 tablespoon oil, 1 tablespoon chipotle puree, mustard, and black pepper. Mix well, then set aside for 10 minutes to firm up.

In a small bowl, combine the mayonnaise and up to 1 tablespoon of chipotle adobo puree. Set aside.

Heat a large skillet over medium-low heat. Add enough oil to lightly coat the skillet (about 2 teaspoons). Form the burger mixture into 4 patties about 3/4-inch thick. Cook the burgers for 4 minutes per side. These burgers are best cooked low and slow to cook the inside and leave the outside with a nice crisp.

To assemble, spread the chipotle mayonnaise on each of the bottom buns, top each with a burger and 1/4 cup of the slaw. Serve immediately.

Bánh Mì Burgers

Bánh Mì is a unique sandwich which is a fusion of French and Vietnamese elements. Pickled vegetables are the requisite topping, and ginger and garlic are also a must. This is a Bánh Mì in vegan burger form. This recipe makes enough for eight burgers, so if not using them all right away, freeze any uncooked burgers in an airtight container for up to 3 months. Thaw slightly before cooking. To make this gluten-free, use gluten-free breadcrumbs and burger buns.

Sauce:

1/4 CUP VEGAN MAYONNAISE

1 TEASPOON REDUCED-SODIUM TAMARI

1/2 TEASPOON SRIRACHA SAUCE

Burgers:

4 TABLESPOONS GRAPESEED OR SUNFLOWER OIL

2 MEDIUM ONIONS, FINELY CHOPPED

1/2 CUP OLD-FASHIONED ROLLED OATS

1 CUP DRIED BREADCRUMBS

1 TABLESPOON TAPIOCA STARCH OR ARROW-ROOT STARCH

1 (15.5-OUNCE) CAN BLACK BEANS, RINSED AND DRAINED

1 CUP COOKED BROWN RICE

1 CUP FINELY CHOPPED SCALLIONS

1/2 CUP GRATED CARROT

1 TABLESPOON REDUCED-SODIUM TAMARI

1 TEASPOON GRATED FRESH GINGER

1 TEASPOON SRIRACHA SAUCE

1/2 TEASPOON SEA SALT

1/2 TEASPOON GARLIC POWDER

BURGER BUNS, TOASTED

1 JALAPEÑO CHILE, SEEDED, THINLY SLICED

QUICK PICKLED VEGETABLES (OPPOSITE)

MAKES 8 BURGERS

QUICK & EASY
GLUTEN-FREE OPTION

Sauce: Combine the mayonnaise, tamari, and sriracha in a small bowl. Set aside.

Burgers: Heat 1 tablespoon of oil in a large skillet over medium heat. Add the onions and cook, stirring, until golden brown, almost caramelized, about 10 minutes. Season to taste with salt. Set aside.

Add the oats to a food processor and process until coarsely ground. Add the crumbs, tapioca, beans, rice, scallions, carrot, tamari, ginger, sriracha, salt, garlic powder, 2 tablespoons oil, and the reserved onions. Using a spatula, carefully mix the ingredients to distribute them. Pulse the processor a few times just to break up the beans. Season to taste with salt.

Divide the mixture into 8 equal portions. Firmly pack each portion into a 1/2-cup measuring cup to help compress the mixture. Tap out the mixture and form it into a disk about 1/2-inch thick. Set aside to firm up, about 5 minutes.

Heat 1/2 tablespoon of oil in a large skillet over medium heat. Add the burgers, working in batches (do not crowd), and cook until well browned, about 2 minutes per side, adding more oil as needed.

To serve, arrange a burger on the bottom of each toasted bun. Spoon the sauce on each burger, and top with jalapeños and pickled vegetables, as desired.

Quick Pickled Vegetables

1/2 CUP DISTILLED WHITE VINEGAR

1/2 CUP WATER

2 TABLESPOONS NATURAL SUGAR

1 TEASPOON SEA SALT

1 CUP OF CRUNCHY VEGETABLES CUT INTO
    MATCHSTICKS (CELERY, CARROT, RADISH)

1 TEASPOON GRATED FRESH GINGER

MAKES 1 CUP

Heat the vinegar, water, sugar, and salt in a small saucepan. Bring to a boil, then reduce to a simmer and cook until the sugar dissolves, about 1 minute.

Place the sliced vegetables and ginger in a 2-cup mason jar or other heat-proof container. Pour the brine over the vegetables. Set the vegetables aside for at least 10 minutes. The pickles may be made days in advance and will keep for months when stored in a tightly covered container in the refrigerator.

Deli Reuben

I can never pass up a Reuben, that's for sure! I love the creaminess of the melted cheese and dressing, and I totally dig the sauerkraut. I also love the crunch of the grilled bread and the spice of the seitan or tempeh. This is a traditional version, from the dressing to the "corned" protein.

1 CUP VEGETABLE BROTH

1 TEASPOON PICKLING SPICE (PAGE 117), WRAPPED IN CHEESECLOTH

4 SIMPLE SEITAN CUTLETS (PAGE 40), CUT INTO 1/8-INCH SLICES OR BLACKENED TEMPEH (PAGE 39), CUT INTO QUARTERS

8 SLICES RYE BREAD OR GLUTEN-FREE BREAD

2 TABLESPOONS VEGAN BUTTER

1 CUP SHREDDED VEGAN CHEESE

1 CUP FIRMLY PACKED SAUERKRAUT, LIGHTLY RINSED AND DRAINED

1/2 CUP THOUSAND ISLAND DRESSING (PAGE 30)

———

SERVES 4

QUICK & EASY
GLUTEN-FREE OPTION

Heat the broth and the wrapped pickling spice in a medium saucepan. Bring to a low boil, reduce to a simmer, add the seitan or tempeh, and simmer for 5 minutes. Remove the saucepan from the heat and set aside for 10 minutes to marinate. Drain and set aside, discarding the spice packet.

Butter one side of each slice of bread.

Heat a large skillet over medium heat. Arrange 4 slices of buttered bread in the skillet, butter side down. Top each equally with cheese, seitan or tempeh, sauerkraut, and dressing. Top with the other 4 buttered bread slices, butter side up.

Cook the sandwiches until golden brown, about 4 minutes. Flip the sandwiches and continue to cook until the other side is golden brown. Serve.

CHEF'S TIP: To cut the seitan cutlets into thin slices, place the palm of one hand on the top of the cutlet, such as when cutting a bagel in half. Cut the seitan at a deep angle on the bias, not straight across horizontally, taking care to avoid cutting the hand that is securing the cutlet. Repeat slicing the seitan in this way every 1/8-inch until the cutlet is sliced into about 6 pieces.

Creamy Macaroni Salad variations (page 98)

CHAPTER 5

Salads

Salads can be as simple as a pile of dark leafy greens dressed with olive oil and vinegar or more substantial, such as my Seven-Layer Tex-Mex Salad or Autumn Harvest Salad. Salads, to me, are the perfect food. I love to dig into some robust greens, ripe fruits, and crisp veggies that are accompanied by the perfect dressing. I have taken inspiration from all kinds of dishes – from soups to stir-fries – in making these salads, just so I can enjoy my vegetables with as much variety as possible. You can serve any of these with a simple sandwich or enjoy many of them as a light meal.

German Potato Salad

Unlike the traditional American potato salad, this one is not mayo-based. It's quite tangy, but still creamy and, thanks to the Bacon Tofu, a bit smoky. Serve it warm, but if you find it too tangy, an overnight stay in the fridge mellows out the flavors nicely. Be sure that your whole-grain mustard lists mustard seeds as the first ingredient, otherwise your salad will not have the needed punch.

2 POUNDS MEDIUM YUKON POTATOES

1/2 CUP GROUND BACON TOFU (8 TO 12 SLICES) (PAGE 36), UNBAKED OR BAKED

4 TABLESPOONS GRAPESEED OR SUNFLOWER OIL, DIVIDED

1 MEDIUM ONION, MINCED

1/2 TEASPOON SEA SALT

1/2 TEASPOON CARAWAY SEEDS

1/4 TEASPOON NATURAL SUGAR

FRESH GROUND BLACK PEPPER

2 TABLESPOONS WHOLE-GRAIN MUSTARD

6 TABLESPOONS APPLE CIDER VINEGAR

1/4 CUP MINCED PARSLEY

1 TABLESPOON MINCED SUN-DRIED TOMATOES

4 SCALLIONS, MINCED

SERVES 4 TO 6

QUICK & EASY
GLUTEN-FREE

CHEF'S TIPS: Grind the Bacon Tofu by pulsing in a food processor or mince finely with a knife. You can substitute 1/3 cup storebought vegan bacon bits for the ground Bacon Tofu. Cook the storebought bits until they are crispy and refreshed, about 1 minute.

Cook the potatoes in their jackets in boiling water until just fork-tender, about 12 minutes. Do not overcook. Drain the potatoes, reserving 1/4 cup of cooking water. Set the potatoes aside to cool slightly.

Heat 3 tablespoons of oil in a large skillet over medium heat. Add the Bacon Tofu and cook, stirring, until crispy, about 4 minutes if the tofu is unbaked and 2 minutes if baked. Remove the tofu from the oil using a slotted spoon and set aside in a small bowl.

Add the onion to the same skillet and cook until golden brown, about 7 minutes.

Peel the cooled potatoes using a paring knife; the peels should easily slip off the potatoes. Cut the potatoes into 1/4-inch slices and set aside in a large bowl. Keep warm.

When the onion is golden brown, add the salt, caraway, sugar, and black pepper to taste. Cook, stirring, until the sugar melts, about 30 seconds. Stir in the mustard, vinegar, parsley, tomatoes, and reserved cooking water.

Transfer the vinegar mixture, scallions, half of the reserved Bacon Tofu and the remaining 1 tablespoon of oil to the potatoes and gently mix to combine. The hot liquid will quickly be absorbed by the warm potatoes. Taste and adjust seasoning using salt, fresh ground black pepper, and vinegar. Sprinkle the potatoes with the remaining Bacon Tofu before serving.

Creamy Macaroni Salad

Cooking pasta for a cold salad is radically different from cooking pasta for a hot dish. Going against the grain, you cook it not to al dente, but to tenderness. Overcooking it will leave you with a soggy mess instead of a salad, and undercooking it will produce hard-as-nails pasta once cool. Cooking the pasta just right will render this a perfect American staple. Make this dish soy free by choosing a soy-free vegan mayonnaise. Use gluten-free pasta to make it gluten-free.

8 OUNCES ELBOW MACARONI

3/4 CUP VEGAN MAYONNAISE, STOREBOUGHT OR HOMEMADE (PAGE 31)

1 TABLESPOON FRESH LEMON JUICE

1 TEASPOON DIJON MUSTARD

1 CELERY RIB, MINCED

1/4 MEDIUM RED BELL PEPPER, CUT INTO 1/4-INCH DICE

2 TABLESPOONS MINCED RED ONION

2 TABLESPOONS MINCED PARSLEY

2 TABLESPOONS SWEET PICKLE RELISH

SERVES 4

QUICK & EASY
GLUTEN-FREE OPTION
SOY-FREE OPTION

Cook the pasta in a large pot of boiling salted water until just tender. Drain well and transfer to a large baking dish to cool. Stir gently every few minutes to cool it faster. Once cool, transfer the pasta to a large bowl.

In a small bowl, combine the mayonnaise, lemon juice, and mustard and mix well. Add 1/2 cup to the pasta and set aside the remaining dressing.

Stir in the bell pepper, onion, parsley, and relish. Season to taste with salt and black pepper. Chill the pasta salad in the refrigerator for an hour to meld the flavors.

Stir the remaining dressing into the pasta salad before serving. Taste and adjust seasoning.

VARIATION: Tex-Mex Macaroni Salad. Replace the lemon juice with lime juice. Replace the mustard with 2 teaspoons of chipotle adobo puree (page 63). Reduce the celery to 1/2 celery rib. Replace the parsley with cilantro. Stir in 3/4 cup roasted corn kernels (page 108).

Muffuletta-Inspired Salad

You can use a commercial olive salad for this recipe or make the one on page 102. I highly recommend making the homemade version because the taste is superior and the cost is easier on your wallet. If you make your own, plan ahead; the olive salad needs 24 hours to marinate. Make this dish gluten free by doubling the tempeh and omitting the sausage if no gluten-free varieties of vegan sausage are available.

1 TABLESPOON OLIVE OIL

1/4 MEDIUM ONION, CUT INTO 1/4-INCH SLICES

1 LINK VEGAN SAUSAGE, CUT INTO 1/4-INCH
    SLICES

1 SLAB BLACKENED TEMPEH (PAGE 39), CUT
    INTO 1/2-INCH DICE

4 CUPS SHREDDED ROMAINE LETTUCE

8 RIPE CHERRY TOMATOES, CUT IN HALF

1 TABLESPOON TOASTED AND FINELY
    CHOPPED WALNUTS

1/2 CUP OLIVE SALAD (PAGE 102), BROUGHT
    TO ROOM TEMPERATURE

1/2 CUP SHREDDED VEGAN CHEESE (OPTIONAL)

SEA SALT AND FRESH GROUND BLACK PEPPER

1/2 CUP CROUTONS, STOREBOUGHT OR
    HOMEMADE (PAGE 102)

2 LEMON WEDGES

SERVES 2

QUICK & EASY
GLUTEN-FREE OPTION

Heat the oil in a large skillet over medium heat. Add the onion slices and vegan sausage. Cook, stirring frequently, until the onions and sausage are golden brown, about 4 minutes. Add a tablespoon of water to the skillet, cover, and continue to cook for 1 more minute. Remove from the heat. Combine the sausage mixture with the tempeh and set aside.

Combine the lettuce, tomato, nuts, Olive Salad, and optional cheese in a large bowl. Toss to combine. Season with salt and black pepper to taste. Divide the salad among two plates and top each with an equal portion of sausage and tempeh. Serve with croutons and lemon wedges.

Olive Salad

This zesty salad will keep well, and in fact, will get better with time. Remember to bring the salad to room temperature about 30 minutes before using.

3/4 CUP JARRED GIARDINIERA, DRAINED AND
    CHOPPED

1 (3-OUNCE) JAR DICED PIMIENTOS, DRAINED

1/2 CUP PITTED GREEN OLIVES, CHOPPED

1/2 CUP PITTED KALAMATA OLIVES, CHOPPED

1/4 CUP EXTRA-VIRGIN OLIVE OIL

1 TABLESPOON SOFT SUN-DRIED TOMATOES,
    MINCED

1 TEASPOON CAPERS, DRAINED AND CHOPPED

1 GARLIC CLOVE, MINCED

1/2 TEASPOON DRIED OREGANO

FRESH GROUND BLACK PEPPER

MAKES ABOUT 2 CUPS

GLUTEN-FREE
SOY-FREE

Combine the giardiniera, pimientos, green olives, Kalamata olives, olive oil, sun-dried tomatoes, capers, garlic, and oregano in a medium bowl. Season with black pepper.

Stir well and refrigerate for 24 hours in an airtight container before use. Bring to room temperature before using. This salad will keep in an airtight container in the refrigerator for up to 4 weeks.

Croutons

3 TABLESPOONS OLIVE OIL

1 TEASPOON PAPRIKA

1/2 TEASPOON GARLIC POWDER

1/2 TEASPOON SEA SALT

FRESH GROUND BLACK PEPPER

6 CUPS DAY-OLD RYE BREAD, CUT INTO 1/2-
    INCH CUBES

MAKES 5 CUPS

Preheat the oven to 335°F. In a large bowl, combine the olive oil, paprika, garlic powder, sea salt, and black pepper. Add the bread and toss to coat.

Transfer the coated bread cubes to a baking sheet. Bake until the bread is crunchy, about 15 minutes, stirring halfway through the baking and checking them again after 10 minutes.

Store the croutons in an airtight container for up to 5 days at room temperature or in the refrigerator.

Buttermilk-Style Coleslaw

This is a slightly sweet, slightly tangy, slightly creamy slaw that is quick and easy to prepare. This recipe can be easily doubled for potlucks or picnics. If you love celery seeds in your slaw, throw a teaspoon into the mixture. Make this dish soy free by choosing a soy-free vegan mayonnaise.

1 SMALL HEAD GREEN CABBAGE (ABOUT 1 POUND)

1/2 TEASPOON SEA SALT

1 MEDIUM CARROT, FINELY GRATED

1/2 SMALL ONION, MINCED

1/2 CUP VEGAN MAYONNAISE, STOREBOUGHT OR HOMEMADE (PAGE 31)

1 TABLESPOON FRESH LEMON JUICE

1 TABLESPOON APPLE CIDER VINEGAR

1 TABLESPOON NATURAL SUGAR

SERVES 4

QUICK & EASY
GLUTEN-FREE
SOY-FREE OPTION

Quarter the cabbage and cut out the core. Shred the cabbage using a food processor or a sharp knife. Transfer the shredded cabbage to a large bowl and toss with the salt.

Mix the cabbage with the carrots, onion, mayonnaise, lemon juice, vinegar, and sugar. Mix well. Taste and adjust seasoning. Set aside for 15 minutes for the flavors to unify.

If a creamier slaw is desired, stir in another 1/4 cup of vegan mayonnaise. Serve.

Grilled Summer Pasta Salad with Garlic Crostini

Summer is full of delicious fruits, vegetables, and grains. Grilling them in any season brings summer to mind and enhances the sweetness of the produce. Use a grill pan (or an outdoor grill) if you have one, but if not, a skillet will work just as well, although the grilled flavor will be missed. Use gluten-free pasta and bread to make this gluten free.

3 CUPS FUSILLI OR ROTINI

4 SMALL YELLOW SQUASH OR ZUCCHINI, CUT LENGTHWISE INTO 1/2-INCH SLICES

1/2 MEDIUM RED BELL PEPPER, CUT INTO 1-INCH SLICES

5 WHOLE SCALLIONS

2 TABLESPOONS OLIVE OIL, DIVIDED

SEA SALT AND FRESH GROUND BLACK PEPPER

1 (15.5-OUNCE) CAN CANNELLINI BEANS, RINSED AND DRAINED

1 1/2 CUPS RIPE CHERRY TOMATO HALVES

1 CUP ROASTED CORN KERNELS (PAGE 108)

1/4 CUP MINCED FRESH BASIL

1 TABLESPOON FRESH LIME JUICE

4 (1/2-INCH) SLICES FRENCH BREAD OR GLUTEN-FREE BREAD

1 SMALL GARLIC CLOVE

SERVES 4

QUICK & EASY
GLUTEN-FREE OPTION
SOY-FREE

Cook the pasta in a pot of boiling salted water until tender. Drain, cool, and return to the pot. Set aside.

In a large bowl, combine the squash, red bell pepper, and scallions with 1 teaspoon of oil. Season with salt and black pepper and toss to mix.

Grill the vegetable slices over medium heat on an outdoor grill, in a grill pan, or on an electric grill until tender, about 4 minutes per side. The scallions need only to be grilled for 2 minutes per side.

When the vegetables are tender, cut them into bite-sized pieces and add them back into the large bowl. Add the beans, tomatoes, corn, basil, lime juice, 1 1/2 tablespoons olive oil, and the reserved pasta. Toss well to mix. Taste and adjust seasoning using salt and black pepper.

Toast the French bread slices. Rub a garlic clove half on the warm toast. Serve the crostini with the pasta salad.

Autumn Harvest Salad

This whole-grain salad is full of the abundance that autumn brings. It is tossed with a horseradish dressing, in theme with the season. Delicious and easy to prepare, you can substitute 1 1/2 cups of another cooked whole grain for the cooked rice. Make this dish soy free by choosing a soy-free vegan mayonnaise.

1 TABLESPOON OLIVE OIL

1 POUND GOLDEN OR RED BEETS, PEELED AND CUT INTO 3/4-INCH DICE

SEA SALT AND FRESH GROUND BLACK PEPPER

1/2 HEAD MEDIUM RED CABBAGE, CORED AND SHREDDED

1/4 CUP VEGAN MAYONNAISE, STOREBOUGHT OR HOMEMADE (PAGE 31)

2 TABLESPOONS GRAPESEED OR SUNFLOWER OIL

2 TABLESPOONS DRAINED PREPARED HORSE-RADISH

1 TABLESPOON APPLE CIDER VINEGAR

1 TEASPOON MAPLE SYRUP

1 1/2 CUPS COOKED AND COOLED LONG-GRAIN BROWN RICE

10 DRIED FIGS, CUT INTO 1/4-INCH SLICES

2 CUPS BABY KALE OR ARUGULA

2 CUPS FRESH BABY SPINACH

SERVES 2 TO 4

GLUTEN-FREE
SOY-FREE OPTION

Heat the olive oil in a large skillet over medium heat. Stir in the beets, season with salt and black pepper. Cook the beets, stirring frequently, until they are golden brown, about 7 minutes. Add 1/4 cup water to the skillet, cover, reduce the heat to medium-low, and cook the beets until they are tender, about 7 more minutes. Transfer the beets to a medium bowl.

Stir half of the shredded cabbage into the same skillet. Season with salt and black pepper, cover, and cook over medium heat until tender and completely wilted, about 7 minutes. Stir occasionally. Transfer the cooked cabbage to the medium bowl with the beets.

In a small bowl, combine the mayonnaise, oil, horse-radish, vinegar, maple syrup, and salt and black pepper to taste. Mix well with a whisk and set aside.

Combine half of the dressing with the beets, cabbage, rice, and figs and toss to mix.

In a separate large bowl, combine the kale, spinach, and shredded raw cabbage with just enough dressing to coat. Season with salt and black pepper and toss to combine.

To serve, divide the kale mixture among either 2 or 4 plates and top with equal amounts of rice mixture.

Seven-Layer Tex-Mex Salad

Visually, this salad has a lot going for it; red, orange, green, and yellow make a beautiful presentation. But the taste is marvelous, too. Make my Salsa Fresca instead of buying it pre-packaged and you will have a feast of flavors. To make this soy free, use a soy-free vegan mayonnaise and/or vegan cheese.

1/2 CUP SALSA FRESCA (PAGE 23)

1/2 CUP VEGAN MAYONNAISE, STOREBOUGHT OR HOMEMADE (PAGE 31)

2 TEASPOONS FRESH LIME JUICE

1 MEDIUM HEAD ROMAINE LETTUCE, SHREDDED

1 (15.5-OUNCE) CAN BLACK BEANS, RINSED AND DRAINED

1 RIPE HASS AVOCADO, PITTED AND PEELED, CUT INTO 1/2-INCH DICE, AND TOSSED WITH 1 TEASPOON FRESH LIME JUICE

1 MEDIUM RIPE TOMATO, CORED AND CUT INTO 1/2-INCH DICE

1 SMALL CARROT, SHREDDED

1 RED BELL PEPPER, CORED, SEEDED, AND CUT INTO 1/2-INCH DICE

1 CUP ROASTED CORN KERNELS (BELOW)

1/2 TO 1 CUP SHREDDED VEGAN CHEESE (OPTIONAL)

1 CUP BROKEN TORTILLA CHIPS OR CORN CHIPS

SEA SALT AND FRESH GROUND BLACK PEPPER

———————————

SERVES 3 TO 4

QUICK & EASY

GLUTEN-FREE

SOY-FREE OPTION

To make the dressing, combine the Salsa Fresca, mayonnaise, and lime juice in a small bowl. Mix well, season to taste with salt and black pepper, and set aside.

In a large, clear bowl, layer the salad. Begin with the lettuce, then add the beans, avocado, tomato, carrot, bell pepper, corn, cheese (if using), and chips. Serve the salad with the dressing on the side.

Roasted Corn

To roast corn kernels, heat a medium skillet over medium heat. Cook fresh or thawed frozen corn in the dry skillet until the corn is golden, about 6 minutes, stirring only occasionally.

Gazpacho-Inspired Salad

Traditional gazpacho is thickened with bread, so the call for croutons in this recipe is not out of left field. A little spicy, a little tangy, and a little creamy: it's the best of the culinary world's soup bowl in a salad. To make this gluten free, use gluten-free croutons.

1 RIPE TOMATO, CORED, SEEDED, AND CUT INTO 1/2-INCH DICE

1 CUCUMBER, SEEDED AND CUT INTO 1/2-INCH DICE

1 MEDIUM RED BELL PEPPER, CORED, SEEDED, AND CUT INTO 1/2-INCH DICE

1/2 SMALL RED ONION, MINCED

1 GARLIC CLOVE, MINCED

2 TABLESPOONS OLIVE OIL

2 TEASPOONS SHERRY VINEGAR OR WHITE WINE VINEGAR

SEA SALT AND FRESH GROUND BLACK PEPPER

4 CUPS SHREDDED ROMAINE LETTUCE

1 RIPE HASS AVOCADO, PITTED, PEELED, AND CUT INTO 1/4-INCH SLICES

1 CUP CROUTONS, HOMEMADE (PAGE 102) OR STOREBOUGHT

SERVES 4

QUICK & EASY
GLUTEN-FREE OPTION
SOY-FREE

In a medium bowl, combine the tomato, cucumber, bell pepper, onion, garlic, oil, and vinegar. Season to taste with salt and pepper and toss to combine. Set aside for 10 minutes to allow the seasonings to mingle.

To serve, divide the lettuce among four bowls and top each equally with the vegetable mixture. Top with avocado slices and croutons. Serve immediately.

CHEF'S TIP: If you don't have sherry vinegar or white wine vinegar on hand, use apple cider vinegar instead.

Green Goddess Primavera Salad

Spring is a wonderful time for amazing produce. Asparagus, lemon, baby kale, and spring baby carrots are among the bounty. Tahini, quinoa, parsley, and garlic boost the nutrition in this healthful salad.

1 CUP QUINOA, WELL RINSED

1 1/2 CUPS VEGETABLE BROTH

SEA SALT AND FRESH GROUND BLACK PEPPER

2 SMASHED GARLIC CLOVES, DIVIDED

ZEST OF 1 LEMON

1 TEASPOON OLIVE OIL

1 POUND ASPARAGUS, TRIMMED AND CUT INTO 1-INCH PIECES

2 TABLESPOONS MINCED PARSLEY

2 TABLESPOONS GRAPESEED OR SUNFLOWER OIL

1 TABLESPOON TAHINI

1 TABLESPOON WATER

2 TEASPOONS APPLE CIDER VINEGAR

2 TEASPOONS MAPLE SYRUP

2 TEASPOONS REDUCED-SODIUM TAMARI

2 TEASPOONS FRESH LEMON JUICE

2 TEASPOONS DRIED CHIVES

4 SPRING BABY CARROTS, FINELY SHREDDED

5 CUPS BABY KALE

SERVES 4

QUICK & EASY
GLUTEN-FREE

Combine the rinsed quinoa, broth, 1/4 teaspoon salt, and 1 garlic clove in a medium saucepan. Bring to a boil, then reduce to a simmer, cover, and cook for 15 minutes. Remove the saucepan from the heat and set aside, still covered, for another 10 minutes to steam. Fluff the quinoa with a fork and transfer it to a baking sheet to cool and dry for 5 minutes. Stir a few times to dry the quinoa thoroughly.

Heat the olive oil in a large skillet over medium heat. Add the asparagus and stir-fry for 1 minute. Add 1 tablespoon of water to the skillet, cover, and cook the asparagus until crisp-tender, about 4 minutes. Set aside in a large bowl.

In a personal blender, combine the parsley, oil, tahini, water, vinegar, maple syrup, tamari, lemon juice, chives, and the remaining garlic clove. Blend well to combine.

Add the cooled quinoa to the asparagus in the large bowl. Add the carrots, kale, dressing, and lemon zest. Stir to combine. Season to taste with salt and pepper.

CHEF'S TIP: Spring baby carrots are not to be confused with the "baby carrots" that come packaged as a snack food. Spring baby carrots are about 4 to 5 inches long and they are fresh out of the ground at springtime. If making this salad out of season, substitute the sweetest carrots you can find and use 2 carrots instead of 4.

Asian Chopped Salad

I used to work at a famous pie restaurant in my early twenties and my favorite dish on the menu was a pita sandwich with teriyaki vegetables. I've brought the same teriyaki vegetables to this salad with the addition of tempeh. I highly recommend making your own teriyaki sauce—it is much simpler to make than it sounds, and so much better than anything you could buy.

1/4 CUP TERIYAKI SAUCE (PAGE 113)

1 TEASPOON TOASTED SESAME OIL

4 PIECES BLACKENED TEMPEH (PAGE 39) CUT INTO 1-INCH DICE

1 RED BELL PEPPER, CORED, SEEDED, AND CUT INTO 1/2-INCH DICE

1/2 SMALL ONION, CUT INTO 1/2-INCH DICE

1/4 CUP RAW CASHEW PIECES

2 TABLESPOONS REDUCED-SODIUM TAMARI

2 TEASPOONS BALSAMIC VINEGAR

1/4 CUP GRAPESEED OR SUNFLOWER OIL

1/4 CUP WATER

6 CUPS CHOPPED ROMAINE LETTUCE

3 CUPS CHOPPED NAPA CABBAGE, ABOUT 1/2 A SMALL HEAD

1 CUP SHREDDED RED CABBAGE

4 SCALLIONS, FINELY CHOPPED

2 MEDIUM CARROTS, SHREDDED

1 TEASPOON OLIVE OIL

SERVES 4

QUICK & EASY
GLUTEN-FREE

Combine the teriyaki sauce and sesame oil in a 9 x 9-inch baking dish. Gently toss the tempeh, bell pepper, and onion with the marinade. Set aside while you prepare the rest of the salad.

In a personal blender, combine the cashews, tamari, vinegar, oil, and water. Blend to make a creamy dressing with some small cashew pieces suspended in the dressing. Set aside.

In a large bowl, combine the romaine, cabbages, scallions, and carrots. Toss well to mix. Divide the salad among four bowls.

Heat the olive oil in a large skillet over medium heat. Add the tempeh and marinated vegetables, including the marinade, and cook, stirring until the vegetables are tender, about 5 minutes. Divide the tempeh and vegetables among the bowls. Serve with the dressing.

Ready Salad Mix

The salad mix in this recipe is a great go-to mix to have stashed in the fridge for when you need a lettuce fix. Mix another batch of romaine lettuce, Napa cabbage, red cabbage, scallions and carrots at the same time that you prepare the greens for this recipe. Store it in a zip-top bag or bowl and you are all set for a salad at any time.

Teriyaki Sauce

This teriyaki sauce is the real deal. It's hard to believe that such minimal ingredients yield such fantastic results. This recipe easily doubles.

1/2 CUP REDUCED-SODIUM TAMARI

1/2 CUP SWEET RICE WINE

2 SMALL GARLIC CLOVES

1 (1-INCH) PIECE GINGER

1 TEASPOON PACKED BROWN SUGAR

MAKES 1/2 CUP

QUICK & EASY
GLUTEN-FREE

Combine the tamari, rice wine, garlic, and ginger in a medium saucepan. Bring to boil, then reduce to a strong simmer; watch carefully so the sauce doesn't boil over. Simmer the sauce until it is reduced by half, about 15 minutes.

Remove the garlic and ginger and discard. Stir in the brown sugar. Set aside to completely cool. Store in an airtight container in the refrigerator where it will keep for 2 weeks.

Hungarian Tomato Salad

I love serving this salad alongside a rich-tasting dish. The cooling vegetables and vinegar-based dressing cut through spicy or heavy flavors.

1 CUP WATER

1/4 CUP DISTILLED WHITE VINEGAR

1 TABLESPOON NATURAL SUGAR

1 MINCED GARLIC CLOVE

1 TEASPOON SALT

1 TEASPOON FRESH GROUND BLACK PEPPER

1/4 CUP VEGAN SOUR CREAM (OPTIONAL)

1/2 SMALL ONION, THINLY SLICED

1/2 CUCUMBER, THINLY SLICED (THE THINNER THE BETTER)

1 LARGE RIPE TOMATO, THINLY SLICED

SERVES 4

GLUTEN-FREE
QUICK & EASY

Mix the water, vinegar, sugar, garlic, salt, and black pepper in a medium bowl until the sugar dissolves. Stir in the sour cream, if using. Add the onion, cucumber, and tomato and toss to combine. Set aside to marinate at room temperature for 10 minutes before serving.

Country-Fried Seitan (see variation, page 123)

CHAPTER 6

Everyday Mains

Comfort foods abound in this chapter, all of which are hearty enough for vegans and omnivores to enjoy. Our family indulges in satisfying bean dishes, tofu and seitan entrees, and vegetable-centered meals. Most of these recipes are complete meals in themselves, while others benefit from the addition of a starch or vegetable side dish. These are my family's most frequently-requested meals, with the Country Fried Portobello and Lima Bean Bake topping the list. Don't miss the Glazed Holiday Roast, fit to grace any festive table.

Irish Corned Cabbage

I started making this dish as Corned Seitan, the cabbage being a mere afterthought. By the second or third time, however, I noticed that the vegetables were more enjoyable than the seitan. Over the years, the seitan was left by the wayside and the vegetables took on the starring role. I added green beans to increase the nutrition, but you could omit it and add a side of kidney beans or black beans to the meal.

3 CUPS WATER

1/4 CUP REDUCED-SODIUM TAMARI

4 GARLIC CLOVES, CRUSHED

2 TABLESPOONS PACKED BROWN SUGAR

2 1/2 TEASPOONS SEA SALT

1 TABLESPOON PAPRIKA

3 TABLESPOONS PICKLING SPICE (BELOW)

1 TEASPOON RED PEPPER FLAKES

1 TEASPOON FRESH OR DRIED THYME

4 MEDIUM BEETS, PEELED AND QUARTERED

4 SMALL TO MEDIUM WAXY POTATOES,
    HALVED

3 CARROTS, CUT INTO THIRDS

8 SMALL ONIONS OR SHALLOTS, PEELED BUT
    LEFT WHOLE

1 MEDIUM HEAD SAVOY OR GREEN CABBAGE,
    CUT INTO 8 WEDGES THROUGH THE ROOT

1/2 POUND GREEN BEANS, TRIMMED

1/2 CUP VEGAN MAYONNAISE, STOREBOUGHT
    OR HOMEMADE (PAGE 31)

2 TABLESPOONS DRAINED PREPARED HORSE-
    RADISH

1 TEASPOON NATURAL SUGAR

SERVES 4

QUICK & EASY
GLUTEN-FREE

Combine the water, tamari, garlic, brown sugar, 2 teaspoons salt, and paprika in a large saucepan. Wrap the pickling spice, red pepper flakes, and thyme in a small muslin bag or in several layers of cheesecloth. This will make the removal of all the seeds and spices easy. Add the spice bag to the broth and bring to a boil.

Arrange the beets and potatoes on the bottom of the saucepan, making sure the spice bag is submerged in the broth. Arrange the carrots, onions, and cabbage on top of the potatoes and beets. Cover the pot and bring to a boil again, then reduce to a strong simmer and cook until the vegetables are tender, about 20 minutes.

Uncover, arrange the green beans on top of the cabbage, cover again, and cook until the beans are crisp-tender, about 5 minutes.

In a small bowl, combine the mayonnaise, horseradish, 1/2 teaspoon salt, and sugar.

To serve, place the vegetables on a plate and top with the horseradish sauce and a few tablespoons of the cooking broth.

PICKLING SPICE: The best pickling spice is one that includes coriander seeds, cloves, mustard seeds, bay leaves, dill seeds, and allspice. If you want to make a homemade version, combine 2 tablespoons mustard seeds, 1 tablespoon whole allspice berries, 1 tablespoon black peppercorns, 2 teaspoons dried dill seed, 6 whole cloves, 2 broken cinnamon sticks, and 2 crushed bay leaves in an airtight container.

Maple-Chipotle Crispers

Nothing beats tender seitan fried with a crisp coating and doused in a sweet, spicy, and garlicky sauce. These crispy delights are reminiscent of the wings you characteristically find at quality sports bars. Serve the Crispers with French fries or tater tots and a side of steamed broccoli. Make the sauce ahead of time so it's ready when you need it.

1 CUP PLAIN UNSWEETENED VEGAN MILK

3 TABLESPOONS FLAX SEED MEAL

1 TABLESPOON SAVORY BROTH MIX (PAGE 19)

2 1/2 TEASPOONS SEA SALT, DIVIDED

2 CUPS UNBLEACHED ALL-PURPOSE FLOUR, DIVIDED

8 SIMPLE SEITAN CUTLETS (PAGE 40)

GRAPESEED OR SUNFLOWER OIL, FOR PAN-FRYING

SWEET AND SPICY SAUCE (RECIPE FOLLOWS)

SERVES 4 TO 6

SOY-FREE

In a medium bowl, combine the milk, flax seed meal, broth mix, 1 1/2 teaspoons of the salt, and 3/4 cup of the flour. Whisk until smooth. Set the batter aside to thicken.

In a separate bowl, combine the remaining 1 1/4 cups of the flour and 1 teaspoon salt. Set aside.

Cut each cutlet into three pieces lengthwise. With your hands, gently squeeze out excess broth from each piece.

Preheat 1/2 inch of oil in a large skillet (cast iron is best). Line a baking sheet with a few layers of paper towels.

While the oil is heating, dip a prepared seitan piece in the wet batter, allow excess batter to drip off, and dredge it in the dry breading. Repeat with the remaining seitan pieces.

Add each battered seitan piece to the hot oil and cook until golden brown, about 2 to 3 minutes per side. Do not crowd the skillet or the seitan won't fry properly. Drain the fried seitan briefly on paper towels and then toss quickly with some of the prepared sauce. Repeat until all of the seitan is fried and sauced. Serve immediately.

Sweet and Spicy Sauce

1 TEASPOON GRAPESEED OR SUNFLOWER OIL

6 GARLIC CLOVES, MINCED

1/4 CUP KETCHUP

3 TABLESPOONS MAPLE SYRUP

3 TABLESPOONS WATER

2 TABLESPOONS AGAVE NECTAR

1 TABLESPOON CHIPOTLE ADOBO PUREE
 (PAGE 63)

1 TABLESPOON APPLE CIDER VINEGAR

1/2 TEASPOON SEA SALT

MAKES ABOUT 3/4 CUP

Heat the oil over medium heat in a small saucepan. Add the garlic and cook, stirring, until the garlic is beginning to brown, about 30 seconds. Stir in the ketchup, maple syrup, water, agave, chipotle, vinegar, and salt. Bring the sauce to a boil, then reduce it to a simmer and cook for 2 minutes. Remove from the heat, transfer to a medium bowl, and set aside until ready to use.

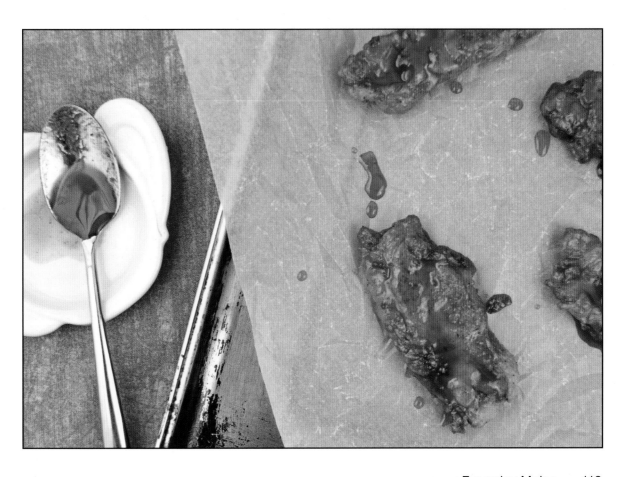

Meatless Pies in Buttermilk Herb Biscuits

Wrap flaky biscuits around a flavorful filling and you get a fun, portable meal. These don't last too long, but if you have any leftover, toast them in a toaster oven until heated through. This recipe may be a little more time-consuming than most of the others, but it's still quite easy to make and well worth the effort.

1/4 POUND BROCCOLI FLORETS (ABOUT 2 1/2 CUPS)

1 TABLESPOON OLIVE OIL

1/2 SMALL ONION, MINCED

2 GARLIC CLOVES, MINCED

3/4 CUP MINCED TENDER SOY CURLS (PAGE 35), MARINATED TOFU (PAGE 34), OR SIMPLE SEITAN (PAGE 40)

1 TABLESPOON SAVORY BROTH MIX (PAGE 19)

1 1/2 TEASPOONS UNBLEACHED ALL-PURPOSE FLOUR

1/2 CUP PLAIN UNSWEETENED VEGAN MILK

1/2 TEASPOON DIJON MUSTARD

SALT AND FRESH GROUND BLACK PEPPER

1 RECIPE FLAKY BUTTERMILK HERB BISCUITS (PAGE 239), ROLLED TO LESS THAN 1/4-INCH THICKNESS

———————

MAKES 9 PIES

SOY-FREE

Steam the broccoli until crisp-tender, about 4 minutes. Transfer to a large plate to cool. Once cool, finely mince and set aside.

Heat the oil in a large skillet over medium heat. Add the onion and garlic and cook, stirring, until soft, about 5 minutes. Add the protein, broth mix, and flour and stir well to combine. Cook the flour for 1 minute.

Add the milk, mustard, and reserved broccoli and cook until the sauce thickens, about 1 minute, stirring continuously. Season to taste with salt and black pepper. Remove the mixture from the heat and cool slightly. Preheat the oven to 450°F.

Cut the rolled-out dough into 18 (3-inch) circles. Place about 2 firmly-packed tablespoons of filling in the middle of a biscuit round, making sure to keep the edges of the dough clean. Place another round biscuit on top of the filling. Press the edges of the biscuits together using the tines of a fork, then pick up the pie and use your thumb and forefinger to seal it even better. Repeat until all the biscuits are used and filled. For quicker assembly, work in an assembly-line fashion; cut out all the rounds first, then fill them all, top them all, and lastly, seal them all.

Place the stuffed biscuits on a lightly greased baking sheet about 1 inch apart. Using a sharp knife, pierce the tops of the biscuits a few times to vent the steam. Bake until golden brown, about 15 minutes. Serve hot.

Peel the broccoli stems, slice them and steam them with sliced carrots for a nice side dish, while at the same time using all of the broccoli. You can also serve the pies with Herbed Gravy (page 134).

If you are short one biscuit round for a pie, piece together some of the bigger scraps to form another 3-inch round, instead of reforming and rerolling the dough. Bake any scraps alongside the pies and make Southern Biscuits and Gravy (page 216) the next morning.

Chickpeas and Dumplings

Who doesn't love classic chicken-style soup with billowy dumplings? This dish is thickened by the dumplings themselves, which you drop on the broth right before serving. You can substitute 4 finely chopped seitan cutlets for the chickpeas (garbanzo beans), if you wish; it's the dumplings that everyone will be after. A crisp green salad with a vinaigrette would nicely complement this dish. To make this soy free, use soy-free vegan milk and butter.

2 TABLESPOONS OLIVE OIL

2 RIBS CELERY, FINELY CHOPPED

2 MEDIUM CARROTS, FINELY CHOPPED

1 SMALL ONION, FINELY CHOPPED

3 GARLIC CLOVES, MINCED

1 (15.5-OUNCE) CAN CHICKPEAS, RINSED, DRAINED, AND PATTED DRY

5 CUPS WATER

1 TABLESPOON SAVORY BROTH MIX (PAGE 19)

1 TEASPOON DRIED PARSLEY

1 BAY LEAF

2 1/2 TEASPOONS SEA SALT, DIVIDED

FRESH GROUND BLACK PEPPER, TO TASTE

1 1/4 CUPS PLAIN UNSWEETENED VEGAN MILK

1 TEASPOON APPLE CIDER VINEGAR

2 CUPS UNBLEACHED ALL-PURPOSE FLOUR

1 TABLESPOON DOUBLE-ACTING BAKING POWDER

2 TEASPOONS NATURAL SUGAR

1 TABLESPOON DRIED CHIVES

1/4 CUP VEGAN BUTTER

SERVES 4 TO 6

QUICK & EASY
SOY-FREE OPTION

Heat the oil in a large saucepan over medium heat. Stir in the celery, carrots, onion, and garlic. Cook, stirring, until the onions begin to brown, about 7 minutes. Stir in the chickpeas and cook until they begin to brown, about 7 more minutes.

Stir in the water, broth mix, parsley, bay leaf, 1 1/2 teaspoons salt, and black pepper to taste. Bring the soup to a boil and reduce to simmer. Simmer the soup until the vegetables are tender, about 10 minutes. Taste and adjust seasoning as needed.

To make the biscuits, stir together the milk and vinegar in a small bowl; set aside for 3 to 5 minutes.

Stir together the flour, baking powder, sugar, chives, and 1 teaspoon salt in a medium bowl. Cut the butter into the flour using your fingers or a fork. Continue to work the butter into the flour until the butter pieces are about the size of peas.

Add the milk mixture to the flour and gently mix the batter with a large spoon.

When the soup is ready, drop the biscuit mix right on top of the soup in large spoonfuls. Cover and simmer the soup until the biscuits are cooked, about 10 minutes. Remove and discard the bay leaf before serving.

Country Fried Portobellos

For me, a perfect meal contains country-fried Portobellos, some mashed potatoes, and creamy White Pepper Gravy. For your enjoyment, this recipe makes enough gravy to smother your cutlets and potatoes. The seitan variation is just as good! Serve with Garlicky Greens (page 196) or the pesto veggies on page 202 and mashed potatoes, or a big salad with Ranch Dressing (page 29).

Portobellos:

4 LARGE PORTOBELLO MUSHROOMS, WIPED CLEAN

1 CUP PLAIN UNSWEETENED VEGAN MILK

1 1/2 TEASPOONS SEA SALT, DIVIDED

3/4 TEASPOON FRESH GROUND BLACK PEPPER, DIVIDED

2 CUPS UNBLEACHED ALL-PURPOSE FLOUR

2 TEASPOONS GARLIC POWDER

2 TEASPOONS PAPRIKA

GRAPESEED OR SUNFLOWER OIL, FOR PAN-FRYING

White Pepper Gravy:

5 TABLESPOONS GRAPESEED OR SUNFLOWER OIL

1/2 CUP UNBLEACHED ALL-PURPOSE FLOUR

3 CUPS PLAIN UNSWEETENED VEGAN MILK

SALT AND FRESH GROUND BLACK PEPPER

———————

SERVES 4

VARIATION: Country Fried Seitan. Use 8 Simple Seitan Cutlets (page 40) instead of the Portobello mushrooms. Dredge the seitan in the flour first, then into the milk, and once more into the flour. Fry as directed in the recipe above. (See photo on page 114.)

Portobellos: Preheat the oven to 250°F. Stem and scrape out the gills under each mushroom cap. Trim off any overhanging rim on the edge of each mushroom.

In a large, shallow baking dish, combine the milk, 1/2 teaspoon salt, and 1/4 teaspoon black pepper. In a separate large shallow dish, combine the flour, garlic powder, paprika, 1 teaspoon salt, and 1/2 teaspoon black pepper. Line a baking sheet with paper towels and set aside.

Preheat 1/2 inch of oil in a large skillet over medium heat (cast iron is best).

Dip a mushroom in the milk, then dredge it in the flour, then back into the milk, and once more in the flour. Repeat with the remaining mushrooms.

Fry the dredged mushrooms in the hot oil, cap-side down first, taking care not to crowd the skillet, about 3 minutes on each side, or until golden brown. Drain the mushrooms on the the paper towels, then transfer to another baking sheet and place in the oven to keep warm. Repeat until all of the mushrooms are fried.

White Pepper Gravy: Heat the oil in a medium saucepan over medium heat. Whisk in the flour, and cook until it gives off a nutty aroma, about 2 minutes. Slowly stir in the milk, whisking continuously until there are no lumps. Bring to a low boil and reduce to a simmer. Cook for 5 minutes, stirring occasionally. Season to taste with salt and pepper. Serve the fried mushrooms with the gravy.

Tandoori Tofu and Vegetables

Tandoori ovens get as hot as a whopping 900°F! In spite of that, this dish is very easily made at home. The Tandoori marinade is made of thick, spiced yogurt that cooks right onto the tofu and vegetables. Although not too spicy, the cooling effect of the raita is a welcome addition. Serve with Naan (page 126) or gluten-free wraps. Soak wooden skewers in water for 30 minutes before using.

Marinade:

2 CUPS PLAIN UNSWEETENED VEGAN YOGURT

1/4 CUP GRAPESEED OR SUNFLOWER OIL

3 TABLESPOONS MINCED GARLIC

3 TABLESPOONS MINCED FRESH GINGER

1 TABLESPOON PLUS 1/2 TEASPOON GARAM
    MASALA, DIVIDED

1 TABLESPOON GROUND CORIANDER

2 TEASPOONS GROUND CUMIN

2 1/4 TEASPOONS SEA SALT, DIVIDED

4 1/2 TEASPOONS PAPRIKA, DIVIDED

1 TEASPOON CAYENNE

Tofu and Vegetables:

14-OUNCES EXTRA-FIRM TOFU, PRESSED
    OVERNIGHT AND CUT INTO 1-INCH DICE

2 MEDIUM POTATOES, PEELED

4 CUPS MEDIUM-SIZED CAULIFLOWER FLO-
    RETS

4 RIPE TOMATOES, QUARTERED

1 SMALL RED ONION, CUT INTO 1-INCH DICE
    (OPTIONAL)

CORN FLOUR (PAGE 4), AS NEEDED

RAITA (PAGE 126)

NAAN (PAGE 126), OPTIONAL

SERVES 4

GLUTEN-FREE

Marinade: Combine the yogurt, oil, garlic, ginger, 1 tablespoon garam masala, coriander, cumin, 2 teaspoons salt, 4 teaspoons paprika, and cayenne in a large bowl.

Tofu and Vegetables: Gently mix the tofu with the marinade and set aside for 20 minutes or up to 3 days. (If marinating longer than 30 minutes, cover and refrigerate until ready to use.)

Cut the potatoes into quarters and cover with water in a medium saucepan. Add 1/2 teaspoon garam masala, 1/4 teaspoon salt, and 1/2 teaspoon paprika. Bring to a boil, then reduce to a simmer and cook until knife-tender, about 3 minutes. Drain and set aside.

Preheat the oven to 475°F. Prepare two baking sheets with oven-safe wire cooling racks to suspend the skewers off the bottom of the baking sheet so the ingredients don't sit in their juices while cooking. Transfer the tofu to skewers, leaving space between each piece. Add the par-boiled potatoes, cauliflower, tomato, and onion to the marinade. Toss gently to combine using your fingers to coat the veggies with the marinade.

Skewer each type of vegetable onto a different skewer; this will ensure even baking. Arrange the skewers on the racks. Lightly sprinkle the skewered tofu and vegetables with the corn flour using a small mesh strainer, covering all sides with a light coat of the corn flour. Bake for 15 minutes. Turn the skewers carefully and continue to bake until the coating is crispy, another 15 minutes. Serve with the raita and naan, if using.

Raita

Raita is an Indian yogurt condiment that is eaten with a spicy meal for its cooling effect. It is the perfect complement to the Tandoori.

1/2 CUP PLAIN UNSWEETENED VEGAN YOGURT

1/4 CUP PEELED AND FINELY CHOPPED CU-
CUMBER

2 TABLESPOONS MINCED CILANTRO

1 SCALLION, FINELY CHOPPED

1/2 TEASPOON FRESH LEMON JUICE

1/4 TEASPOON GROUND CORIANDER

PINCH CAYENNE

1/4 CUP MINCED TOMATO, (OPTIONAL)

SALT AND FRESH GROUND BLACK PEPPER

In a bowl, combine the yogurt, cucumber, cilantro, scallions, lemon juice, coriander, cayenne, tomato (if using), and salt and black pepper to taste. Set aside. If not using right away, cover and refrigerate until needed.

MAKES ABOUT 1 CUP

QUICK & EASY
GLUTEN-FREE

Naan

The well-known leavened Indian flatbread is sensational made with the whole-grain dough (page 128). Serve a basket of it with the Tandoori Vegetables and Tofu (page 124).

1/4 CUP OLIVE OIL

2 TEASPOONS GARLIC POWDER

1/2 TEASPOON SALT

VERSATILE WHOLE GRAIN DOUGH (PAGE 128),
AT ROOM TEMPERATURE

MAKES 8 NAAN

In a small bowl, combine the oil, garlic powder, and salt. Set aside and have a pastry brush handy. Prepare a bowl and towel to keep the cooked naan warm.

Heat a medium skillet over medium heat. Divide the dough into 8 equal pieces. Roll each piece about 1/8-inch thick.

Wet your hands and toss the dough back and forth to coat with water. Transfer the naan to the hot skillet, cover, and cook until it puffs up and the bottom blisters, about 20 seconds. Flip the naan, cover, and cook the other side until blistered, 20 seconds. Remove from the skillet, place in the reserved bowl, brush both sides with the garlic oil, cover with a towel, and repeat with the remaining dough. Serve warm.

Black Bean Feijoada

Feijoada is the national dish of Brazil. It is a black bean stew with different kinds of sausages, smoked meats, and bacon. It is served with quick-cooked collard greens and toasted cassava root meal. It also takes longer than a day to prepare, even with a pressure cooker. Here, I speed things up considerably. The ingredients list seems long because there are lots of spices and herbs—the same ones used in the making of sausages and smoked meats. This comes together in a flash, so have everything prepared when you begin. Serve over fresh cooked rice.

2 TABLESPOONS GRAPESEED OR SUNFLOWER OIL

2 BAY LEAVES

1/4 TEASPOON RED PEPPER FLAKES

1 TEASPOON FRESH OR DRIED THYME

1/2 TEASPOON GROUND CUMIN

1/2 TEASPOON GROUND CORIANDER

1/2 TEASPOON DRIED OREGANO

1/2 TEASPOON RUBBED SAGE

4 GARLIC CLOVES, MINCED, DIVIDED

3 (15.5-OUNCE) CANS BLACK BEANS, RINSED AND DRAINED

2 CUPS WATER, PLUS MORE AS NEEDED

2 1/2 TEASPOONS SMOKED PAPRIKA

FRESH GROUND BLACK PEPPER

1 TEASPOON PICKLING SPICE (PAGE 117), WRAPPED IN CHEESECLOTH AND TIED

1 LARGE ONION, FINELY CHOPPED

2 RED BELL PEPPERS, CHOPPED

1/2 CUP FINELY CHOPPED PARSLEY

SAUTÉED COLLARD RIBBONS (PAGE 198)

2 CUPS ROASTED CORN (PAGE 108) (OPTIONAL)

HOT COOKED RICE, TO SERVE

SERVES 4 TO 6

QUICK & EASY
GLUTEN-FREE
SOY-FREE

Heat 1 tablespoon of oil in a large saucepan over medium heat. Add the bay leaves and chili flakes and cook for 1 minute. Add the thyme, cumin, coriander, oregano, sage, and half of the garlic. Cook, stirring, for 30 seconds.

Stir in the beans, 2 cups water, paprika, black pepper to taste, and the cheesecloth with the pickling spice. Bring to a boil, then reduce to a simmer. With a potato masher, coarsely mash some of the beans. Simmer for 10 minutes, partially covered, stirring occasionally.

Heat 1 tablespoon of oil in a large skillet over medium heat. Stir in the onion and cook until softened, about 3 minutes. Add the bell pepper and cook, stirring, until tender, about 5 more minutes. Stir in the parsley and remaining garlic. Cook for 30 seconds, then transfer to the pot with the simmering beans. Stir well and season to taste with salt. Simmer for 4 more minutes, adding 1/2 cup more water, if needed. Remove the bay leaves and the pickling spice bag. Serve with collards, roasted corn, if using, and hot cooked rice.

CHEF'S TIP: If you have any Bacon Tofu (page 36) hanging around, chop it up, heat it in some oil until crispy, and sprinkle over each serving of the Feijoada. It adds another rich dimension.

A Versatile Whole Grain Dough

If you make your own pizza dough, chances are you won't have enough time to make the dough, rise it, and bake it just before dinner. This recipe allows you to make the dough ahead, refrigerate it overnight, and make something with it the next day. Take the dough out of the fridge early, and it'll warm even more and create a lighter result. All that is actually required is a good knead and a 30-minute warm-up before baking.

1/2 CUP WARM WATER

2 TABLESPOONS NATURAL SUGAR

2 TEASPOONS ACTIVE DRY YEAST

1 1/3 CUP PLUS 1 TABLESPOON WHOLE WHEAT FLOUR, DIVIDED

2/3 CUP SPELT FLOUR

3/4 TEASPOONS SEA SALT

1/4 CUP PLAIN UNSWEETENED VEGAN YOGURT

2 TABLESPOONS OLIVE OIL, DIVIDED

MAKES 1 POUND OF DOUGH

VARIATION: Versatile White Dough. Substitute 2 cups of bread flour for the whole wheat and spelt flour. Reduce the sugar to 1 tablespoon and the yeast to 1 teaspoon.

In a small bowl, combine the warm water, sugar, and yeast. Set aside for 5 minutes.

In a food processor, combine 1 1/3 cups whole wheat flour, spelt flour, and salt. Pulse to combine. Add the yeast mixture, yogurt, and 1 tablespoon olive oil. Process the dough until it starts forming a ball. Process for 20 more seconds. Add 1 tablespoon of whole wheat flour and process again for 10 more seconds. The dough should be soft and tacky, but not too wet.

Transfer the remaining 1 tablespoon of oil to a medium bowl or zip top bag. Form the dough into a ball and transfer it to the oiled bowl or bag. Roll the dough around in the oil and cover the bowl with a plastic wrap or seal the bag. Place the bowl in the refrigerator for at least 8 hours, or up to 3 days, to rise.

Thirty minutes before you are ready to bake the dough, remove it from the refrigerator and place the dough in a warm spot to rise for 30 minutes. Follow the directions for the specific bread variation.

Homemade Tomato Pizza

Whole grain pizza dough can lack flavor and good texture. This dough is both delicious and easy to work with. The pizza sauce is flavorful and quick to throw together. With the dough waiting in the fridge dinner can be ready in no time. This pizza works beautifully using a pizza stone, if you happen to have one. This pizza is soy free, depending on the toppings you choose.

Sauce:

1 TABLESPOON OLIVE OIL

1/4 TEASPOON DRIED BASIL

1/4 TEASPOON DRIED OREGANO

1/4 TEASPOON SEA SALT

2 GARLIC CLOVES, MINCED

1 (15-OUNCE) CAN DICED TOMATOES, LIGHTLY
   DRAINED

1 TABLESPOON TOMATO PASTE

1/4 TEASPOON NATURAL SUGAR

FRESH GROUND BLACK PEPPER

Pizza:

VERSATILE WHOLE GRAIN DOUGH (OPPOSITE)
   OR 1 POUND STOREBOUGHT PIZZA DOUGH

2/3 CUP PIZZA SAUCE (ABOVE) OR STORE-
   BOUGHT

2 TABLESPOONS OLIVE OIL, DIVIDED

TOPPINGS OF CHOICE: VEGAN CHEESE, VEG-
   AN PEPPERONI, VEGAN SAUSAGE, SAUTÉED
   MUSHROOMS AND PEPPERS, THINLY SLICED
   ONION, CRUSHED PINEAPPLE, SLICED
   OLIVES, THINLY SLICED TOMATO, MINCED
   GARLIC

MAKES 2 (9-INCH) PIZZAS

SOY FREE

Sauce: Combine the olive oil, basil, oregano, sea salt, garlic and tomato in a medium saucepan. Bring the sauce to a boil and reduce to a strong simmer. Cook until thickened, about 8 minutes.

Stir in the tomato paste and continue to cook for 2 more minutes. Season with salt, black pepper and the sugar. Transfer the sauce to a blender and blend until smooth, or use an immersion blender to blend the sauce right in the pot. The sauce will keep stored in an airtight container in the refrigerator for up to 3 days.

Pizza: Bring the dough to room temperature 30 minutes before using. Preheat the oven 450°F. Place the oven rack in the center of the oven.

Divide the dough into 2 equal pieces. On parchment paper or a clean dry surface (lightly floured if using storebought dough), roll out one of the dough pieces into a 9-inch circle. Spread 1 tablespoon of oil on a baking sheet. Transfer the pizza dough to the baking sheet. Spread half of the pizza sauce over the dough using an off-set spatula or the back of a spoon. Add toppings of choice, taking care not to overload the pizza, especially toward the center of the pizza. Do not add raw or very moist vegetables to the pizza as they will make the crust soggy. Instead, sauté the vegetables first and then add them as toppings.

Bake the pizza for 12 to 15 minutes, until the crust is golden brown and crisp. Slice and serve hot. Repeat with the other pizza dough.

Spinach and Artichoke Pizza

This dish is almost like having the Spinach-Artichoke Dip on page 190 spread over a pizza. With the added optional vegan cheese, it is ooey and gooey. The thinly sliced garlic cooks down to a mild and sweet flavor and the artichokes come out of the oven lightly browned. We love this pizza made using the dough in this book, but storebought pizza dough will serve you just as well. This pizza works wonderfully using a pizza stone, if you happen to have one.

1/2 (10-OUNCE) BAG FROZEN CHOPPED SPINACH, THAWED

1/4 CUP VEGAN CREAM CHEESE

2 SCALLIONS, COARSELY CHOPPED

1/2 TABLESPOON FRESH LEMON JUICE

SEA SALT AND FRESH GROUND BLACK PEPPER

1 (6-OUNCE) JAR ARTICHOKE HEARTS, RINSED AND DRAINED

3 TABLESPOONS OLIVE OIL, DIVIDED

4 GARLIC CLOVES, VERY THINLY SLICED

VERSATILE WHOLE GRAIN DOUGH (PAGE 128) OR 1 POUND STOREBOUGHT PIZZA DOUGH

1/2 CUP SHREDDED VEGAN CHEESE (OPTIONAL)

_____

MAKES 2 (9-INCH) PIZZAS

Bring the dough to room temperature 30 minutes before using. Preheat the oven 450°F. Place the oven rack in the middle of the oven.

Squeeze the excess moisture from the thawed spinach and transfer it to a food processor. Add the cream cheese, scallions, lemon juice, 1/4 teaspoon of salt, and black pepper, to taste. Process into a paste, scrapping down the sides of the bowl, as needed. Taste and adjust seasoning and set aside.

Squeeze the excess moisture from the artichokes, chop them and transfer to a medium bowl. Add 1 tablespoon olive oil, garlic, and salt and pepper, to taste. Mix well and set aside.

Divide the dough into 2 equal pieces. On parchment paper or a clean dry surface (lightly floured if using storebought dough), roll out one of the dough pieces into a 9-inch circle. Spread 1 tablespoon of oil on a baking sheet. Transfer the pizza dough to the baking sheet.

Spread half of the spinach mixture over the dough using an off-set spatula or the back of a spoon. If using, sprinkle half of the cheese over the spinach. Add half of the artichoke mixture.

Bake the pizza for 12 to 15 minutes, until the crust is golden brown and crisp. Slice and serve hot. Repeat with the other pizza dough.

Red Lentils and Cauliflower with Red Pepper Salsa

Despite the long ingredients list, this delicious meal goes together quickly. Cauliflower, chickpeas, and a zesty red pepper salsa combine to make this dish as pretty as it is healthful and flavorful.

2 1/2 CUPS VEGETABLE BROTH

1 CUP SPLIT RED LENTILS, PICKED OVER AND RINSED

1/2 CUP PARSLEY LEAVES

1/2 MEDIUM CUCUMBER, COARSELY CHOPPED

1/2 MEDIUM GREEN BELL PEPPER, COARSELY CHOPPED

10 RIPE GRAPE TOMATOES

2 SCALLIONS, COARSELY CHOPPED

1 MEDIUM JARRED ROASTED RED PEPPER, COARSELY CHOPPED

2 TABLESPOONS FRESH LEMON JUICE

1 GARLIC CLOVE, COARSELY CHOPPED

1/4 TEASPOON RED PEPPER FLAKES

1 1/2 TEASPOONS SEA SALT, DIVIDED

2 TABLESPOONS OLIVE OIL, DIVIDED

1 SMALL ONION, MINCED

1 SMALL HEAD CAULIFLOWER, CUT INTO BITE-SIZE FLORETS

FRESH GROUND BLACK PEPPER

2 TABLESPOONS TOMATO PASTE

1 (15.5-OUNCE) CAN CHICKPEAS, RINSED AND DRAINED

SERVES 4

QUICK & EASY
GLUTEN-FREE
SOY-FREE

Heat the broth in a medium saucepan over high heat, covered, to boiling. Add the lentils, reduce to a strong simmer and cook, uncovered, stirring occasionally, until tender, about 15 to 20 minutes. When the lentils are tender, puree them with an immersion blender. Set aside.

Mince the parsley in a food processor, then add the cucumber, bell pepper, grape tomatoes, and scallions and pulse to mince. Transfer the minced vegetables to a fine mesh strainer to drain excess liquid, about 10 minutes. After 10 minutes, use a large spoon to press on the vegetables to extract more liquid. Transfer the vegetables to a medium bowl.

In a personal blender, combine the red bell pepper, lemon juice, garlic, red pepper flakes, 1 teaspoon salt and 1 tablespoon olive oil. Blend until smooth. Combine the dressing with the reserved cucumber mixture. Taste and adjust seasoning. Set aside.

Heat 1 tablespoon of oil in a large saucepan over medium heat. Add the onion and cook, stirring, until softened, about 5 minutes. Add the cauliflower and 1/2 teaspoon salt. Cover and cook until the cauliflower is tender, stirring occasionally, about 8 to 10 minutes. Stir in the tomato paste and cook until the paste darkens, about 1 minute. Stir in the blended lentils, chickpeas, black pepper to taste, and more salt, if needed. Cook for 3 to 5 minutes to blend the flavors. To serve, spoon the cauliflower sauté into large bowls and top with the cucumber salad.

Vegan Meatloaf with Herbed Gravy

This moist, flavorful loaf is the ultimate "make ahead" dish. It's easy and quick to put together, but it needs to be made in advance for best results, so it has time to firm up in the refrigerator before slicing. I prepare it a day ahead of when I want to serve it so I can chill it and then slice it easily the next day when I simply reheat and serve.

5 TABLESPOONS OLIVE OIL, DIVIDED

1 MEDIUM ONION, FINELY CHOPPED

1/2 MEDIUM RED BELL PEPPER, FINELY
   CHOPPED (1/2 CUP)

1 MEDIUM CARROT, SHREDDED (1/2 CUP)

1 1/2 TEASPOONS DRIED THYME

1 TEASPOON DRIED OREGANO

1 TEASPOON RUBBED SAGE

FRESH GROUND BLACK PEPPER

5 GARLIC CLOVES, MINCED

1/2 TEASPOON PAPRIKA

1/2 CUP PLUS 2 TABLESPOONS HEARTY UMAMI
   FLAVORING (PAGE 20), DIVIDED

14-OUNCES FIRM TOFU, PRESSED FOR 10 MIN-
   UTES AND PATTED DRY

3 TABLESPOONS PLAIN UNSWEETENED VEGAN
   MILK

1 TABLESPOON REDUCED-SODIUM TAMARI

1/2 CUP DRY BREAD CRUMBS

2 TABLESPOONS MINCED PARSLEY

3/4 CUP PLUS 2 TABLESPOONS VITAL WHEAT
   GLUTEN FLOUR

3/4 CUP WATER

HERBED GRAVY (PAGE 134)

SERVES 4 TO 6

Preheat the oven to 230°F. Place a standard (9 x 5-inch) loaf pan on a baking sheet. Heat 2 tablespoons oil in a large skillet over medium heat. Add the onion, bell pepper, carrot, thyme, oregano, sage, and pepper to taste. Cook, stirring, until softened, about 7 minutes. Add the garlic and cook for 1 minute. Remove from heat and stir in the paprika and 1/2 cup of the umami flavoring. Set aside.

Cut the tofu in quarters and transfer 3/4 of the tofu to a food processor; reserve the rest for another use. Process for 10 seconds. Add the reserved vegetables and pulse just to combine. Do not break up too much. Transfer the mixture to a large bowl. Add the milk, tamari, breadcrumbs, parsley, and 1 tablespoon oil to the tofu. Mix in the vital wheat gluten. Knead the soft dough with your hands or a stand mixer with a dough hook for 5 minutes. Form into a loaf.

Add 2 tablespoons oil to the loaf pan. Transfer the dough to the loaf pan, gently pressing it into the pan. Mix the water with 2 tablespoons of the umami flavoring and pour it over the dough. Cover the pan with parchment paper and then tightly seal with foil. Bake for 3 hours or until most of the broth is absorbed. Remove from the oven and cool to room temperature. Refrigerate for 3 hours or overnight.

To serve, cut the chilled loaf into 8 slices. Heat a few teaspoons of oil in a skillet over medium heat. Sauté the slices in batches until heated through, about 3 minutes per side. Serve with the gravy.

Herbed Gravy

This gravy is well suited for an everyday meal of Vegan Meatloaf or on a holiday table alongside the Glazed Holiday Roast. Using fresh herbs elevates this humble gravy when something extra special is desired. The texture is rustic, but can become silky and smooth for that special occasion when strained.

3 TABLESPOONS VEGAN BUTTER

1/2 CUP MINCED ONION

3 GARLIC CLOVES, MINCED

1 TEASPOON DRIED THYME

1/2 TEASPOON DRIED ROSEMARY

1/4 TEASPOON DRIED RUBBED SAGE

1/2 TEASPOON DRIED OREGANO

1/4 CUP UNBLEACHED ALL-PURPOSE FLOUR

1 TABLESPOON SAVORY BROTH MIX (PAGE 19)

2 CUPS VEGETABLE BROTH

SEA SALT AND FRESH GROUND BLACK PEPPER

MAKES ABOUT 2 CUPS

QUICK & EASY
SOY-FREE OPTION

Melt the butter in a large skillet over medium heat. Stir in the onion, garlic, thyme, rosemary, sage, and oregano. Cook, stirring, until the onions are golden, about 5 minutes. Add the flour and cook, stirring, until the flour is golden and smells nutty, 3 to 4 minutes.

Stir in the broth mix and vegetable broth. Bring to a boil, reduce to a simmer, and cook for 5 to 10 minutes, until the gravy is thickened to your liking. For smooth and silky gravy, strain it through a fine mesh strainer. Season to taste with salt and black pepper.

CHEF'S TIP: During holidays, double the recipe, using a large saucepan. Omit the dried herbs and add 6 sprigs of fresh thyme, 2 sprigs of fresh oregano, 1 sprig of fresh rosemary, and 6 chopped fresh sage leaves to the gravy along with the vegetable broth.

Crustless Pot Pie Over Smashed Potatoes

To me, pot pie evokes thoughts of rolling pins and a flour-dusted kitchen. I decided that as delightful as the crust of a pot pie can be, it is not meant to be a quick and easy weeknight meal. This more accessible version keeps intact the creamy gravy, potatoes, and vegetables, and adds a vegan protein. If new potatoes are not available, use a thin-skinned potato such as red or gold. Cut them into chunks and proceed with the recipe as written.

2 POUNDS NEW POTATOES

3 TABLESPOONS VEGAN BUTTER, DIVIDED

SALT AND FRESH GROUND BLACK PEPPER

1 SMALL ONION, FINELY CHOPPED

2 GARLIC CLOVES, MINCED

2 TABLESPOONS UNBLEACHED ALL-PURPOSE FLOUR

2 TABLESPOONS SAVORY BROTH MIX (PAGE 19)

1/2 TEASPOON DRIED TARRAGON OR OREGANO

2 CUPS VEGETABLE BROTH

2 CUPS FROZEN MIXED VEGETABLES (CORN, PEAS, CARROTS, AND/OR BEANS), THAWED AND DRAINED

1/2 CUP PLAIN UNSWEETENED VEGAN MILK

4 CUPS COARSELY CHOPPED TENDER SOY CURLS (PAGE 35), SIMPLE SEITAN CUTLETS (PAGE 40), OR MARINATED TOFU (PAGE 34)

———————

SERVES 4

QUICK & EASY
GLUTEN-FREE OPTION
SOY-FREE

Cook the potatoes in just enough water to cover until tender, about 15 minutes. Drain the potatoes and coarsely smash them with 2 tablespoons of the vegan butter. Season to taste with salt and black pepper. Keep the potatoes warm.

Heat 1 tablespoon of vegan butter over medium heat in a skillet. Add the onions and garlic. Cook and stir until the onions are beginning to brown, about 5 minutes.

Stir the flour, broth mix, and tarragon into the onion mixture until the flour is well incorporated. Cook, stirring constantly, for 1 minute.

Slowly stir the vegetable broth into the onion mixture, whisking continuously. Bring the gravy to a simmer and cook for 5 minutes.

Stir in the protein, thawed vegetables, and milk. Mix well and cook the mixture until hot. Season with salt and black pepper to taste and serve over the smashed potatoes.

VARIATION: To make this gluten free, omit the all-purpose flour. Mix the milk with 1 1/2 tablespoons of arrowroot starch before adding it to the butter and onion mixture. Continue with the recipe as written, but cook the gravy only until thickened.

Glazed Holiday Roast

Not an "everyday" recipe, for sure, but perfect for those special occasions. Make the roast when you are able and reheat with the glaze when needed. This is a lovely dinner-party dish and the recipe easily doubles for a larger variation that makes a jaw-dropping, festive centerpiece when company's coming.

2 3/4 CUPS STIRRED VITAL WHEAT GLUTEN FLOUR

1/2 CUP CHICKPEA FLOUR

1 CUP WATER

14-OUNCES FIRM OR EXTRA-FIRM TOFU, RINSED AND PATTED DRY

1/4 CUP GRAPESEED OR SUNFLOWER OIL

1 TABLESPOON HEARTY UMAMI FLAVORING (PAGE 20)

1/4 CUP SAVORY BROTH MIX (PAGE 19)

1 TEASPOON ONION POWDER

1 TEASPOON GARLIC POWDER

1 1/2 TEASPOONS SEA SALT

4 CUPS VEGETABLE BROTH

5 GARLIC CLOVES

1 TEASPOON FRESH OR DRIED THYME

1 TEASPOON PAPRIKA

GLAZE (RECIPE FOLLOWS)

HERBED GRAVY (PAGE 134)

———————

SERVES 6 TO 8

Step 1: Combine the vital wheat gluten and the chickpea flour in the bowl of a stand mixer.

In a blender, combine the water, tofu, oil, umami flavoring, broth mix, onion powder, garlic powder, and salt and blend until very smooth.

Step 2: Stir the tofu mixture into the flour mixture to just combine. Knead the dough in a stand mixer fitted with a dough hook for 5 minutes, or until smooth and elastic. Alternatively, knead the dough by hand for 10 minutes, or until smooth and elastic.

Steps 3 and 4: With wet hands, form the dough into a thick 6- to 7-inch long cylinder. Place a damp cheesecloth, folded in half, on your work surface. Transfer the dough to the bottom section of the cheesecloth. Fold the left and right sides over the dough and firmly roll it up, burrito-style. Tie with twine, firmly but not tightly.

Step 5: Preheat the oven to 300°F. Transfer the vegetable broth, garlic cloves, thyme, and paprika to a medium (14 x 10-inch) roasting pan. Transfer the tied roast to the pan. Tightly cover the pan with a lid and foil. Bake the roast for 3 hours, removing the pan, turning the roast, recovering the pan, and returning the roast to the oven after 1 hour and again after 2 hours. Turn off the heat and allow the roast to remain in the cooling oven for 1 hour.

Cool the roast completely and reheat it at a later time or continue to the glazing step. If cooling the roast, store it covered in the cooking broth for up to 3 days in the refrigerator.

Step 1

Step 2

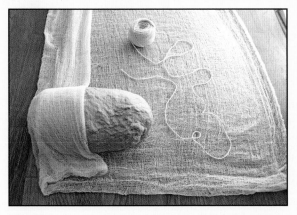

Step 3

Step 4

Step 5

To glaze the roast, preheat the oven to 350 degrees F. Remove the roast from the cheesecloth and discard the cooking broth. Return the roast to the roasting pan. If previously cooled, cover and bake for 30 minutes to reheat, then uncover and baste with the glaze. Continue to bake it for another 30 minutes, basting again after 15 minutes. If not previously cooled, baste the roast and bake for 30 minutes, basting after 15 minutes.

VARIATION: Large Holiday Roast. If company's coming, you can make a large holiday roast (enough to serve 12 to 16). To do so, double all of the ingredients for the roast (except the glaze). Bake as directed above as for the smaller roast, but increase the covered reheating time to 1 hour. Uncover, glaze, and continue to reheat the roast until an instant-read thermometer measures the internal temperature of the roast at 165-degrees.

Glaze

This scrumptious glaze glitzes up the roast beautifully. It is just sweet enough, and it gives the roast an amazing shine.

1 TABLESPOON OLIVE OIL

3 TABLESPOONS MINCED ONION

4 GARLIC CLOVES, MINCED

1 CUP APPLE JUICE

1/4 CUP TERIYAKI SAUCE (PAGE 113) OR STOREBOUGHT

1/2 CUP PACKED BROWN SUGAR

3 TABLESPOONS FRESH LEMON JUICE

1/8 TEASPOON CAYENNE

MAKES 1 CUP

Heat the oil in a medium saucepan over medium heat. Add the onion and cook, stirring, until softened, about 3 minutes. Stir in the garlic and cook for 30 seconds. Stir in the apple juice, teriyaki sauce, brown sugar, lemon juice, and cayenne. Bring the glaze to a boil, then reduce it to a strong simmer and cook until it reduces to 1 cup, about 10 to 13 minutes.

Remove from the heat, strain, and store in an airtight container in the refrigerator until needed, up to 7 days.

Mexican Red Rice and Beans (page 158)

CHAPTER 7

Pasta & Grains

This chapter is filled with flavorful grain and pasta recipes, ranging from Mushroom Stroganoff to Coco Loco Soba with Kale and Dulse (which, my family will tell you, is definitely a must-try). Most families, not just mine, automatically gravitate to pasta dishes since they are always a crowd favorite and a cook's best friend. Make sure to put on a large pot of boiling water before you do anything else to make pasta dishes as quick as possible. You can use gluten-free pasta, as I do, in many of these dishes with success. This is also the chapter where you will learn how to easily cook brown rice and properly prepare fluffy quinoa.

Pasta Primavera with Alfredo Sauce

This is one of my all-time favorite pasta dishes—creamy Alfredo sauce with tons of veggies makes a rich and delicious meal. Make the Alfredo sauce first and dinner will be ready in minutes.

8 OUNCES LINGUINE OR GLUTEN-FREE PASTA

1 TABLESPOON OLIVE OIL

1/2 SMALL ONION, FINELY CHOPPED

3 GARLIC CLOVES, MINCED

2 SMALL CARROTS, CUT INTO 1/4-INCH HALF-
    MOONS

1 CUP SMALL BROCCOLI FLORETS

1 CUP SMALL CAULIFLOWER FLORETS

1/2 MEDIUM RED BELL PEPPER, CUT INTO
    MATCHSTICKS

1/4 CUP WATER

2 CUPS ALFREDO SAUCE (RECIPE FOLLOWS),
    FRESHLY MADE

1/2 CUP FROZEN GREEN PEAS, THAWED

———————

SERVES 4

QUICK & EASY

GLUTEN-FREE OPTION

SOY-FREE

Cook the pasta in a large pot of boiling salted water until al dente. Drain well, return to the pot, and set aside.

Heat the oil in a large skillet over medium heat. Add the onion and garlic and cook, stirring, until softened, about 3 minutes. Stir in the carrot, broccoli, cauliflower, and bell pepper. Cook, stirring, until the bell pepper softens, about 3 minutes.

Add the water, cover the skillet, and steam the vegetables until tender, about 3 minutes.

Transfer the vegetables to the pot with the pasta and stir in the warm Alfredo Sauce. Cook over medium heat until the sauce thickens, about 3 minutes. Stir in the peas and cook for another minute. Serve hot.

Alfredo Sauce

This creamy, dairy-free Alfredo sauce is just as rich and enchanting as the original. For a quicker sauce, soak your cashews with the water overnight and skip the 15 minute waiting period after the first blend; just process the nuts until the milk is smooth.

2 CUPS WATER

1 1/4 CUPS CHOPPED RAW CASHEWS

1 TABLESPOON OLIVE OIL

3 TABLESPOONS NUTRITIONAL YEAST

1 GARLIC CLOVE, COARSELY CHOPPED

1/2 TEASPOON SEA SALT

FRESH GROUND BLACK PEPPER

MAKES 2 CUPS

QUICK & EASY

GLUTEN-FREE

SOY-FREE

Combine the water and cashews in a blender. Blend well and set aside for 15 minutes, then blend again until smooth.

Strain the cashew milk using a nut bag or several layers of fine cheesecloth. If you don't mind some fine cashew granules, there is no need to strain.

Rinse the blender jar, then transfer the strained cashew milk to the cleaned jar. Add the olive oil, nutritional yeast, garlic, salt and black pepper to taste. Blend until smooth.

Heat the sauce in a medium saucepan over medium-low heat until thickened, about 4 minutes, stirring continuously. Do not boil the sauce.

VARIATION: Chipotle Cream Sauce. Blend 1 tablespoon of chipotle adobo puree (page 63) into the sauce when adding the olive oil and other ingredients.

Rigatoni with Vodka Tomato Sauce

When vodka meets tomato sauce and cream, this sauce is the result. Using freshly-made almond cream makes it creamy and rich. While the vodka does add a bit of flavor, omitting it will not adversely affect the sauce. We used to love this sauce pre-vegan and are just as pleased with it vegan. Use only almonds for the cream base, as other nuts might not pair well with acid in the tomatoes. Use gluten-free pasta to make this gluten free.

12 OUNCES RIGATONI

3/4 CUP BLANCHED RAW ALMONDS

1 CUP WATER

2 TABLESPOONS OLIVE OIL

1 MEDIUM CARROT, FINELY SHREDDED

4 GARLIC CLOVES, FINELY CHOPPED

1 (28-OUNCE) CAN WHOLE OR DICED TOMA-
TOES, LIGHTLY DRAINED (SAN MARZANO OR
MUIR GLEN)

1/2 CUP VODKA

1 TABLESPOON FINELY CHOPPED BASIL
LEAVES

SEA SALT AND FRESH GROUND BLACK PEP-
PER

———

SERVES 4

QUICK & EASY
GLUTEN-FREE OPTION
SOY-FREE

Cook the pasta in a large pot of boiling salted water until al dente. Drain well and return to the pot. Set aside.

Combine the almonds and water in a personal blender and blend well. Strain the cream through a nut milk bag or through 8 layers of cheesecloth (rinse brand new cheesecloth very well under running water before use). Squeeze as much cream as possible from the nuts. Set aside.

Heat the oil in a large saucepan over medium heat. Add the carrot and cook, stirring, until softened, about 2 minutes. Add the garlic and cook, stirring, until golden, about 1 minute.

Stir in the tomatoes and vodka. If using whole tomatoes, break them up with your hand as you add them. Bring to a boil and lightly boil over medium heat until it thickens, about 10 to 12 minutes, stirring occasionally. Add salt and black pepper to taste. Stir the basil into the sauce 2 minutes before the sauce is ready.

Blend the sauce in a blender in batches to avoid over filling the blender, or blend with an immersion blender.

Toss the cooked pasta with the tomato sauce and stir in the reserved almond cream. Simmer the sauce until it is thickened and the pasta is reheated. Serve hot.

Coco Loco Soba with Dulse and Kale

When we lived in San Francisco, we ate at a charming little place called Feel Real. It was run by a couple of young guys who, although they could not manage to keep regular business hours and charged their customers for meals based on how much they felt like paying, made some amazing food! No surprise that they are no longer in business there, but my hubby and I fell in love with their kale and noodle dish, garnished with a hefty portion of nutritional yeast. I had to recreate it, and this is my version of their masterpiece. Thanks, guys—wherever you are!

2 BUNCHES KALE (ABOUT 1 POUND TOTAL), TOUGH STEMS REMOVED

1 (10-OUNCE) PACKAGE SOBA, UDON, OR LO MEIN NOODLES OR GLUTEN-FREE SPAGHETTI

2 TEASPOONS OLIVE OIL

6 GARLIC CLOVES, MINCED

1/2 CUP DULSE SEAWEED FLAKES

1/4 CUP REDUCED SODIUM TAMARI

1 (15-OUNCE) CAN UNSWEETENED FULL-FAT COCONUT MILK

1/2 CUP WATER

1 TABLESPOON FRESH LIME JUICE

1/2 CUP NUTRITIONAL YEAST FLAKES

SERVES 4

QUICK & EASY
GLUTEN-FREE OPTION

Steam the kale until tender, about 4 minutes. Remove from the heat and set aside.

Cook the soba in a large pot of boiling salted water until al dente. Drain well and set aside.

Heat the oil in a large skillet on medium heat. Stir in the garlic and cook until lightly golden, about 1 minute. Stir in the kale and dulse. Mix well and cook, stirring, for 3 minutes.

Stir in the tamari, coconut milk, water, and lime juice. Bring to a simmer and cook for 1 minute.

Divide the soba into four bowls and top equally with the kale, sauce, and nutritional yeast.

Have a fear of seaweed?

If so, the Coco Loco with Dulse and Kale is an ideal way to overcome it. So many assertive flavors are in this dish that the seaweed is just a lovely hint in the background. Seaweed is a wonderful, healthy addition to your diet, and this delicious noodle recipe is a gentle introduction to it.

Scampi Pasta with Asparagus and Walnuts

Scampi, in the seafood restaurant world, is a dish of shrimp sautéed in garlic butter and tossed with parsley and fresh lemon juice. In this version, dulse stands in for the flavor of seafood and the garlic-lemon sauce is tossed with thin pasta. This is a very fast meal, so get your pot of water boiling first.

8 OUNCES CAPELLINI OR ANGEL HAIR PASTA OR GLUTEN-FREE PASTA

1/4 CUP OLIVE OIL

2 TABLESPOONS MINCED GARLIC

1/2 CUP COARSELY CHOPPED RAW WALNUTS

1/4 CUP DULSE SEAWEED FLAKES

1/4 CUP PACKED FINELY CHOPPED PARSLEY

1 POUND ASPARAGUS, TRIMMED AND CUT INTO 1-INCH PIECES

3 TABLESPOONS FRESH LEMON JUICE, DIVIDED

SEA SALT AND FRESH GROUND BLACK PEPPER

SERVES 4

QUICK & EASY
GLUTEN-FREE OPTION
SOY-FREE

Cook the pasta in a large pot of boiling salted water until al dente. Drain the pasta, reserving 1 cup of the cooking water. Cool the pasta under running cold water, drain, and set aside.

Meanwhile, heat the olive oil in a large skillet over medium-low heat. Add the garlic and walnuts. Reduce the heat to low. Cook, stirring, until the garlic is golden, about 5 to 10 minutes.

Increase the heat to medium. Add the dulse, parsley, and asparagus. Cook, stirring, until the asparagus is partially cooked, about 3 minutes.

Stir in 1/2 cup of the reserved pasta cooking water and continue to cook until the asparagus is crisp-tender, another 2 minutes.

Stir in 2 tablespoons of lemon juice, the reserved pasta, and the other 1/2 cup of reserved pasta cooking water. Cook, stirring, until the pasta is heated through and the sauce has thickened.

Season to taste with salt, plenty of black pepper, and the rest of the lemon juice, if needed. Serve hot.

CHEF'S TIP: If you have a wok, this is a great place to use it. Garlic or walnut pieces can be pushed up the side of the wok, out of higher heat, if any of them brown faster than the others. When the sauce is ready to be tossed with the pasta, you'll have plenty of room to combine them.

Chilled Sesame Soba Noodles

Don't be tempted to reduce the sesame oil in this dish. It may seem like a large amount, but there are a lot of veggies in this pasta dish and the sesame oil completely balances out. If you are looking for a protein boost, toss the pasta with some sliced baked tofu.

1/4 CUP TOASTED SESAME OIL

2 TABLESPOONS RICE VINEGAR

2 TABLESPOONS REDUCED SODIUM TAMARI

1/2 TEASPOON NATURAL SUGAR

1/4 TEASPOON RED PEPPER FLAKES

1 (8-OUNCE) PACKAGE SOBA, UDON, OR LO
    MEIN NOODLES OR GLUTEN-FREE PASTA

1/2 SMALL HEAD CAULIFLOWER, CUT INTO
    BITE-SIZED PIECES

1 SMALL HEAD BROCCOLI, CUT INTO BITE-
    SIZED PIECES

1 SMALL RED BELL PEPPER, CORED, SEEDED,
    AND CUT INTO MATCHSTICKS

4 SCALLIONS, FINELY CHOPPED

2 TABLESPOONS TOASTED SESAME SEEDS

SERVES 4 TO 6

QUICK & EASY
GLUTEN-FREE OPTION

Combine the sesame oil, vinegar, tamari, sugar, and red pepper flakes in small bowl. Mix well and set aside.

Cook the noodles in a large pot of boiling salted water until al dente. Rinse under cold running water and drain. Toss with the sesame oil dressing and set aside.

Steam the cauliflower and broccoli until crisp-tender, about 4 minutes. Spread the vegetables on a baking sheet and set aside to cool.

When the vegetables are cool, add them to the bowl of noodles. Add the bell pepper, scallions, and sesame seeds. Mix well with your hands to avoid breaking up the noodles. Chill or serve at room temperature.

Hungarian March of the Grenadiers

When rations or supply lines were cut off during the Napoleonic Wars, cooks on the field devised this dish for the Austrian Grenadiers using nothing more than dry staples carried with them and any fresh vegetables they were able to procure along the way. Necessity was the mother of invention when this classic Hungarian dish was created made with coarsely mashed paprika potatoes tossed with cooked pasta. The whole shebang is then cooked until crispy pieces of pasta dot the landscape. It was a staple in my childhood household; now it is one my own kids love.

1 POUND BOWTIE PASTA OR GLUTEN-FREE
    PASTA
1 RECIPE HUNGARIAN PAPRIKA POTATOES
    (PAGE 192), COARSELY MASHED WITH THE
    COOKING LIQUID
SEA SALT AND FRESH GROUND BLACK PEPPER
GRAPESEED OR SUNFLOWER OIL, FOR FRYING

SERVES 6

GLUTEN-FREE OPTION
SOY-FREE

Cook the pasta in a large pot of salted water until al dente. Drain the noodles and set aside.

Gently mix the mashed potatoes and the cooked pasta in a large bowl. Season to taste with salt and black pepper.

Heat 1 tablespoon of oil in a large skillet over medium-high heat. Transfer about 2 cups of the potato-pasta mixture to the skillet. Spread the mixture flat. Cook until the bottom is golden brown and crisp. Flip the mixture, breaking it up and folding some of the crispy sections back into the mixture. Continue to cook and flip until about a third of the potato and pasta is crisp. Repeat the procedure to cook the rest of the potato-pasta mixture.

Alternatively, grease a baking sheet (or two) with 2 tablespoons of oil. Transfer the potato-pasta mixture to the baking sheet and spread it out with a spatula. Bake in a preheated 425 degree F oven until the bottom of the mixture is crispy, about 15 minutes. Flip and continue to bake for another 15 minutes, or until crispy. Taste and adjust seasoning as needed.

Penne with Pesto Sauce

My son would eat this at every meal, every day, given the chance – and given enough basil. Interestingly, his favorite of the two is the Lower-Fat Pesto version. Given that, he certainly should keep eating it as long as the basil holds out. When basil is in season, I make batches of this sauce and freeze it in large ice cube trays.

1 POUND PENNE OR GLUTEN-FREE PASTA

2 CUPS (ABOUT 2 OUNCES) TIGHTLY PACKED
   FRESH BASIL, LEAVES ONLY, BLANCHED
   (SEE CHEF'S TIP)

1/2 CUP EXTRA-VIRGIN OLIVE OIL

1/4 CUP CHOPPED BLANCHED ALMONDS OR
   PINE NUTS, TOASTED

4 GARLIC CLOVES, FINELY CHOPPED

SEA SALT AND FRESH GROUND BLACK PEPPER

SERVES 4

QUICK & EASY
GLUTEN-FREE OPTION
SOY-FREE

Cook the pasta in a large pot of boiling salted water until al dente. Drain well, reserving 1/2 cup of the cooking water, and return the pasta to the pot. Set aside.

While the pasta is cooking, make the pesto. In a food processor or personal blender, combine the basil, oil, nuts, garlic, and salt and pepper. Process until finely ground or smooth. Taste and adjust seasoning. Use immediately or store in an airtight container for up to 3 days or freeze for up to 3 months.

To serve, toss the pesto sauce with the hot cooked pasta. Add reserved cooking water, as needed, to thin out the sauce. Taste and adjust seasoning as needed. Serve hot.

VARIATION: Lower-Fat Pesto Sauce. Reduce the olive oil to 2 tablespoons and the nuts to 2 tablespoons; add 1/4 cup mashed soft tofu and 1/4 cup of water. Process the pesto in a personal blender until smooth. Season to taste.

CHEF'S TIP: Pesto traditionally oxidizes quickly and darkens to a drab green. To keep the pesto vibrantly green, blanch the basil leaves in a small pot of boiling water for 10 seconds and immediately cool them in a bowl of ice water. Gently squeeze excess moisture out of the basil before processing the pesto.

Mushroom Stroganoff

This is traditional stroganoff, minus the cow. The sauce is creamy and tangy enough and the mushrooms are meaty enough without the need for animal products. All that and, to boot, this meal can be on your table as soon as your pasta is cooked.

12 OUNCES LINGUINE

3 TABLESPOONS OLIVE OIL

1 1/2 POUNDS MUSHROOMS, WIPED CLEAN,
   CUT INTO 1/2-INCH SLICES

1 TEASPOON SEA SALT

1 SMALL ONION, FINELY CHOPPED

6 GARLIC CLOVES, MINCED

2 TEASPOONS TOMATO PASTE

2 TABLESPOONS UNBLEACHED ALL-PURPOSE
   FLOUR

2 CUPS VEGETABLE BROTH

2 TABLESPOONS SAVORY BROTH MIX (PAGE 19)

1 TABLESPOON DIJON MUSTARD

1/2 CUP VEGAN SOUR CREAM

FRESH GROUND BLACK PEPPER

FINELY CHOPPED FRESH PARSLEY

SERVES 4

QUICK & EASY
GLUTEN FREE OPTION

Cook the linguine in a large pot of boiling salted water until al dente. Drain and set aside.

Heat the oil in a large skillet over medium-high heat. Add the mushrooms and salt. Cook until the mushrooms begin to brown and release their liquid, stirring occasionally, about 5 minutes. Add the onion and garlic and cook, stirring, until the liquid has evaporated and the onion begins to brown, about 7 minutes. Stir in the tomato paste, then stir in the flour and cook for 30 seconds. Scrape up the brown bits on the bottom of the skillet as you stir.

Add the vegetable broth, broth mix, and mustard. Stir well to avoid lumps. Simmer the sauce until it thickens, about 3 minutes. Stir in the pasta. Continue to cook until the pasta is heated through.

Remove the skillet from the heat and stir in the sour cream. Season to taste with salt and black pepper. Garnish with parsley and serve.

NOTE: To make this dish gluten free, use gluten-free pasta. Also, omit the all-purpose flour and reserve 1/4 cup of the vegetable broth. Mix the reserved broth with 1 tablespoon of arrowroot starch and simmer the sauce for 3 minutes. Stir in the arrowroot mixture when you stir in the pasta and simmer only until the sauce is thickened and the pasta is heated through before proceeding with the recipe.

Pad Thai

You don't have to go to Thailand to enjoy some great pad thai. Tamarind is a sour, tangy fruit that is used frequently in Indian and Thai cuisine. Check international aisles, Indian grocery stores, and other Asian grocers for tamarind or look for it on the Internet.

1/4 CUP REDUCED SODIUM TAMARI

2 TABLESPOONS FRESH LIME JUICE

2 TABLESPOONS TAMARIND LIQUID OR 1 TEA-
SPOON TAMARIND PASTE MIXED WITH 2
TABLESPOONS WATER

1/4 CUP NATURAL SUGAR

8-OUNCES RICE NOODLES

4 TABLESPOONS GRAPESEED OR SUNFLOWER
OIL, DIVIDED

1 POUND SOFT OR FIRM TOFU, PATTED DRY
AND CRUMBLED

1 TABLESPOON NUTRITIONAL YEAST

1/4 TEASPOON GROUND TURMERIC

BLACK SALT (PAGE 206), OPTIONAL

4 OUNCES SHIITAKE MUSHROOMS, WIPED
CLEAN, AND CUT INTO 1/4-INCH SLICES

1 MEDIUM CARROT, SHREDDED

4 GARLIC CLOVES, MINCED

2 TEASPOONS THAI RED CHILI PASTE

1/2 MEDIUM RED BELL PEPPER, CUT INTO 1/4-
INCH SLICES

3 CUPS TIGHTLY PACKED FRESH SPINACH

2 CUPS FRESH BEAN SPROUTS

1/4 CUP CHOPPED ROASTED PEANUTS

CILANTRO LEAVES AND LIME WEDGES

———————

SERVES 4

QUICK & EASY
GLUTEN FREE

In a small bowl, combine the tamari, lime juice, tamarind, and sugar. Mix well and set aside.

Cook the noodles in a large pot of boiling water until just al dente, about 3 minutes. Drain the noodles, toss with 1/4 teaspoon of oil, and set aside.

Heat 1 tablespoon of oil in a large skillet over medium heat. Stir in the tofu, nutritional yeast, and turmeric. Stir and cook until the tofu is dry, 7 to 10 minutes. Transfer the tofu to a small bowl, season to taste with black salt, if using, and set aside.

Heat the remaining 2 tablespoons oil in the same skillet over medium heat. Stir in the mushrooms and carrots and cook, stirring, until the mushrooms begin to brown, about 5 minutes. Stir in the garlic, chili paste, and bell pepper and cook until the garlic is fragrant, about 30 seconds.

Stir in the noodles, spinach, bean sprouts, peanuts, reserved sauce, and reserved tofu. Cook, stirring, until the noodles are tender but not overcooked, the sauce has been absorbed, and everything is heated through. Serve hot with cilantro leaves and wedges of lime.

NOTE: Thai red chili paste, or red curry paste, contains red chiles, ginger, and lemongrass. Since the spice (heat) level of the different varieties depends on the particular chiles used, be sure to taste and adjust the amount that is called for in this recipe based on the heat of your chili paste. Any type of red chili paste should work equally well.

Mexican Red Rice and Beans

This is a hearty and economical dish that completes its cooking in the oven. Just add a salad and dinner's ready! (See photo on page 140.)

3 TABLESPOONS GRAPESEED OR SUNFLOWER OIL, DIVIDED

1 SMALL JALAPEÑO, SEEDED AND FINELY CHOPPED

3 MEDIUM RIPE TOMATOES, COARSELY CHOPPED

1/2 SMALL RED OR GREEN BELL PEPPER, FINELY CHOPPED

1 SMALL ONION, FINELY CHOPPED

5 GARLIC CLOVES, FINELY CHOPPED

2 TEASPOONS SEA SALT

2 CUPS LONG-GRAIN BROWN RICE

3 1/4 CUPS WATER

FRESH GROUND BLACK PEPPER

1 (15.5-OUNCE) CAN BLACK BEANS, RINSED AND DRAINED

SERVES 4 TO 6

GLUTEN FREE
SOY-FREE

Preheat the oven to 350°F. Heat 1 tablespoon oil in a large skillet over medium heat. Add the jalapeño, tomatoes, bell pepper, onion, and garlic. Cook, stirring, until the onion begins to brown, about 8 minutes. Remove from the heat and set aside.

Heat 2 tablespoons oil in a large oven-safe saucepan over medium heat. Stir in the salt and rice. Cook until the rice is beginning to brown, about 5 minutes, stirring continuously. Stir the reserved vegetables into the rice.

Add the water and bring the rice to a boil. Remove from the heat, cover tightly with foil, and bake until the rice is tender, about 60 minutes.

Check the rice for doneness at 60 minutes. Season with salt and black pepper to taste. If the rice is tender and there is no water remaining, remove from the oven and allow the rice to rest for 5 minutes before serving. Fluff the beans into the rice with a fork. The beans will warm up from the residual heat of the hot rice.

CHEF'S TIP: If the rice is tender but there is water remaining in the pot, return the pot, uncovered, to the oven and bake for another 10 minutes. If the rice is undercooked but there is water remaining in the pot, cover the pot and bake for another 15 minutes. If the rice is undercooked and there is no water remaining, add 1/4 cup of water to the rice, cover, and bake for another 15 minutes.

Creamy Cheesy Polenta

Medium grind cornmeal is the best for making a creamy polenta. Even if you think the cornmeal is cooked enough after 5 or 10 minutes, keep cooking it; the grains will absorb more water. Creamy polenta is great served with any southern-style meals, such as Country Fried Portobellos (page 123), Vegan Meatloaf (page 132), pan sautéed Seafood Tofu (page 34), or vegan sausage with sautéed onions and peppers.

2 TABLESPOONS OLIVE OIL

3 GARLIC CLOVES, MINCED

3 1/4 CUPS PLAIN UNSWEETENED VEGAN
MILK, DIVIDED

1 TEASPOON SEA SALT

1/4 CUP DICED JARRED PIMIENTOS OR ROAST-
ED RED PEPPERS

1/4 CUP NUTRITIONAL YEAST FLAKES

1 CUP MEDIUM GRIND CORNMEAL

1/4 CUP RAW CASHEW PIECES

4 TEASPOONS DRIED CHIVES

1/2 TEASPOON APPLE CIDER VINEGAR

FRESH GROUND BLACK PEPPER

_____

MAKES 3 CUPS

QUICK & EASY
GLUTEN FREE
SOY-FREE

Heat the oil in a medium saucepan over medium heat. Stir in the garlic and cook until golden, about 1 minute. Stir in 2 cups of milk and the salt.

While the milk is heating, combine 1/2 cup of the milk, pimientos, and yeast in a personal blender. Blend the mixture until smooth, then add it to the saucepan.

When the milk boils, reduce it to a simmer. Slowly whisk in the cornmeal in a steady steam. Whisk continuously for 2 more minutes to ensure that there are no lumps.

Bring the mixture to a low simmer, partially cover the pan, and simmer the polenta until it has thickened and there is no raw taste, about 20 minutes. Whisk the polenta every 5 minutes to prevent it from burning on the bottom.

While the polenta is cooking, make the nut cream by blending the cashews and 1/2 cup of milk in the small cup of a personal blender. Blend well and allow the nuts to sit for 15 minutes, then blend again to get the cream as smooth as possible.

When the polenta is cooked, stir in the nut cream, 1/4 cup of milk, chives, vinegar, and black pepper to taste. Taste and adjust seasoning, if needed. Serve hot.

Whole Grain Rice Pilaf

This is a foolproof way to make brown rice. Because each grain of rice is surrounded by water, it cooks faster. The steaming process makes sure the individual grains fluff up. Make this dish soy free by using soy-free vegan butter or substitute olive oil. This pilaf is delicious served with Garlicky Greens (page 196).

8 CUPS WATER

2 TEASPOONS SEA SALT, DIVIDED

2 TABLESPOONS VEGAN BUTTER, DIVIDED

1 CUP LONG-GRAIN BROWN RICE

1 SMALL ONION, FINELY CHOPPED

3 GARLIC CLOVES, FINELY CHOPPED

1/2 CUP WHOLE WHEAT ORZO OR SMALL GLU-
TEN-FREE PASTA

1 (15.5-OUNCE) CAN GARBANZO OR CANNEL-
LINI BEANS, RINSED AND DRAINED

1/4 CUP TOASTED SLIVERED TOASTED AL-
MONDS

1/4 CUP FINELY CHOPPED PARSLEY

———————

SERVES 4

GLUTEN FREE OPTION
SOY-FREE

In a large pot, combine the water and 1 teaspoon salt and bring to a boil. Heat 2 teaspoons of butter in a medium saucepan over medium heat. Add the rice and cook, stirring until golden brown and toasted, about 3 minutes. Transfer the rice to the boiling water. Return to a boil, reduce to a simmer, and cook until tender; check for doneness after 15 minutes.

Heat 2 teaspoons of butter in the same saucepan over medium heat. Add the onion and 1/2 teaspoon of salt and cook, stirring, until the onion softens and begins to brown, 5 minutes. Add 2 tablespoons water, cover, and cook until almost tender, 2 minutes. Uncover, stir in the garlic, and cook until fragrant, 30 seconds. Transfer to a small bowl and set aside.

Heat the remaining 2 teaspoons of butter in the same saucepan over medium heat. Stir in the orzo and 1/2 teaspoon of salt. Cook, stirring, until golden brown, 2 minutes. Carefully remove 3 cups of hot water from the pot of rice cooking and transfer it to the pasta. Alternately, use 3 cups of water heated in the microwave or in a separate saucepan. The orzo will sputter when you add the water, so be cautious. Add the beans to the orzo and simmer until the orzo is al dente. Drain and return to the saucepan. Cover and keep warm. When the rice is tender, drain with a strainer (not a colander) and return it to the large pot, off the heat. Add the reserved pasta and onions. Drape a kitchen towel over the pot, cover with a lid and steam the rice for 10 minutes. After the rice has steamed, fluff it with a fork. Gently stir in the toasted almonds and parsley. Season with salt and black pepper, as needed.

Mediterranean Quinoa
with Fresh Herbs

Most recipes call for cooking quinoa in a 1:2 ratio—1 cup quinoa to 2 cups liquid. This leads to soggy and over-cooked quinoa. This recipe produces fluffy, tender quinoa. If your package of quinoa doesn't specify that it is rinsed, make sure to rinse it well in a fine mesh strainer. To make this dish a meal, add cooked garbanzo beans and serve over lettuce greens with extra lemon juice and olive oil, if desired. Serve with pan-sautéed or grilled Marinated Tofu slices.

1 CUP QUINOA, WELL RINSED

1 1/2 CUPS VEGETABLE BROTH

1/4 TEASPOON SEA SALT

2 GARLIC CLOVES, MINCED, DIVIDED

1/4 CUP MINCED SCALLIONS OR 2 TABLE-
SPOONS MINCED FRESH CHIVES

2 TABLESPOONS FINELY CHOPPED PARSLEY

2 TABLESPOONS FINELY CHOPPED BASIL

2 TABLESPOONS FINELY CHOPPED MINT

2 TABLESPOONS FINELY CHOPPED SOFT SUN-
DRIED TOMATOES

1 TABLESPOON OLIVE OIL (OPTIONAL)

1/2 TEASPOON LEMON ZEST

1 TABLESPOON FRESH LEMON JUICE

2 TABLESPOONS MINCED PISTACHIOS OR
OTHER NUT

SALT AND FRESH GROUND BLACK PEPPER

SERVES 4

QUICK & EASY
GLUTEN FREE
SOY-FREE

Combine the rinsed quinoa, broth, 1/4 teaspoon sea salt and 1 clove minced garlic in a medium saucepan. Bring the broth to a boil, reduce to a simmer, cover, and cook for 15 minutes.

After 15 minutes, remove the saucepan from the heat and set the pan aside, still covered, for another 10 minutes to steam. Fluff the quinoa with a fork.

Add the scallions or chives, parsley, basil, mint, tomatoes, oil, zest, lemon juice, and nuts to the quinoa fluffing the mixture with a fork. Add additional lemon juice, salt, and black pepper to taste.

Chili Mac

Do you happen to have any Chipotle Chili leftover? Then you're in for an easy and quick lunch or dinner. Reheat the chili in another pan while the pasta is cooking to make this meal even quicker. Chili Mac is great with some warmed leftover Cheese Sauce (page 27).

1 POUND ROTINI, FUSILLI OR GLUTEN-FREE
   PASTA

5 CUPS CHIPOTLE CHILI (PAGE 63)

1 CUP SHREDDED VEGAN CHEESE (OPTIONAL)

1/2 CUP VEGAN SOUR CREAM

6 SMALL SCALLIONS, FINELY CHOPPED

––––––––––

SERVES 6

QUICK & EASY
GLUTEN FREE OPTION

Cook the pasta in a large pot of boiling salted water until al dente. Drain and return the pasta to the pot.

Stir in the chili and the cheese, if using. Cook the pasta and chili over medium heat until heated through and the cheese melts. Remove the pot from the heat.

Serve hot with a dollop of vegan sour cream and scallions.

Gotta Love Leftovers

Some dishes seem to taste even better when reheated the next day. Here are some recipes that are especially delicious the second time around and If you're cooking for just one or two, enjoying these recipes twice will give you a night off from cooking.

Chili Mac (page 163)

Chilled Sesame Soba Noodles (page 150)

Creamy Cheesy Polenta (page 159)

Meatless Pies in Buttermilk Herb Biscuits (page 120)

Black Bean Feijaoda (page 127)

Red Lentils and Cauliflower with Red Pepper Salsa (page 131)

Irish Corned Cabbage (page 117)

Lima Bean Bake (page 184)

Lasagna Americana (page 166)

Spinach and Bean Enchiladas (page 172)

Hearty Vegetable-Potato Au Gratin (page 176)

Arroz non Pollo (page 180)

Spinach and Bean Enchiladas (page 172)

CHAPTER 8

Casseroles

Casseroles have the distinct advantage of delivering complete, one-pot meals with ease. They bake up while the cook is engaged elsewhere, thereby freeing up much-needed time. I have included such classic comfort foods as Lasagna Americana and Arroz non Pollo, and new favorites such as Tater Tot Casserole and Hearty Vegetable-Potato Au Gratin. Leave those old hot dish ideas in the dust and get ready for a flavor explosion. Although these recipes take a little longer to cook, they are still easy to prepare, as much of the time is inactive, so you can do other things while your casserole bakes.

Lasagna Americana

A piping hot pan of lasagna makes regular appearances at our dinner table. Not only is it delicious, but it's easy to make, too, thanks to the use of uncooked regular lasagna noodles. With no need to first cook the noodles or look for hard to find no-boil vegan lasagna sheets, preparation is a snap.

14 OUNCES SOFT OR FIRM TOFU, MASHED

6 CUPS FRESH BABY SPINACH

1 CUP TIGHTLY PACKED BASIL LEAVES

2 GARLIC CLOVES, FINELY CHOPPED

1/4 CUP OLIVE OIL

1 TEASPOON SEA SALT

FRESH GROUND BLACK PEPPER

4 CUPS TIMELESS TOMATO SAUCE (PAGE 24)

4 TEASPOONS NATURAL SUGAR

15 DRY LASAGNA NOODLES (NOT THE NO-BOIL KIND)

2 CUPS GROUND TENDER SOY CURLS (PAGE 35), MARINATED TOFU (PAGE 34), OR SAVORY TVP (PAGE 38)

3 CUPS SHREDDED VEGAN CHEESE

———————

SERVES 8

Preheat the oven to 400°F. In a food processor, combine the tofu, spinach, basil, garlic, olive oil, salt, and black pepper to taste. Process until smooth. Taste and adjust seasoning. Set aside.

Combine the tomato sauce and sugar. Ladle 1/4 cup of the tomato sauce and 3/4 cup water on the bottom of a 9 x 13-inch baking dish. Stir to combine. Arrange 3 noodles on the bottom of the baking dish. Spread 2/3 cup of the tofu filling on the noodles. Arrange 1/2 cup of the protein over the tofu filling. Spread 3/4 cup tomato sauce over the protein. Sprinkle 1/2 cup cheese over the tomato sauce. Arrange 3 more noodles over the cheese. Press lightly to spread the fillings equally. Take care not to break the noodles.

Repeat the above layering 3 more times, ending with the noodles. Ladle the rest of the tomato sauce over the noodles and sprinkle the remaining cheese on top.

Cover tightly with parchment paper and then with foil. Bake until the noodles are tender, about 1 hour. Remove from the oven and set aside for 15 minutes before serving.

Baked Macaroni and Cheese

This is the vegan version of baked mac and cheese you've been craving. For a variation, stir in 1 cup of broccoli florets into the pasta cooking water 2 to 3 minutes before draining it or 3 cups of fresh baby spinach into the pasta before baking the casserole.

8 OUNCES ELBOW MACARONI (DO NOT USE GLUTEN-FREE PASTA)

2 1/2 CUPS PLAIN UNSWEETENED VEGAN MILK, DIVIDED

1/4 CUP VEGAN CREAM CHEESE

3 TABLESPOONS DICED JARRED PIMIENTOS OR ROASTED RED PEPPERS

3 TABLESPOONS NUTRITIONAL YEAST FLAKES

1 TEASPOON SEA SALT

1/2 TEASPOON ONION POWDER

1/2 TEASPOON PAPRIKA

2 TABLESPOONS VEGAN BUTTER

5 TABLESPOONS UNBLEACHED ALL-PURPOSE FLOUR

1 TEASPOON APPLE CIDER VINEGAR

FRESH GROUND BLACK PEPPER

———————

SERVES 4

CHEF'S TIP: To easily tell if the pasta is just shy of al dente, cut a piece in half. If there is a very thin line of white (uncooked dough) in the middle, it is ready to be drained and sauced.

Preheat the oven to 450°F. Cook the pasta in a large pot of boiling salted water until 1 minute shy of al dente. Drain and transfer to a 2-quart, wide baking dish and set aside.

Blend 1 cup of milk, cream cheese, pimientos, yeast, salt, onion, and paprika in a blender until smooth. Set aside.

Melt the butter in a medium saucepan over medium heat. Stir in the flour and cook, stirring, until the flour smells nutty, about 3 minutes. This is a very thick roux; use a wooden spoon to stir it well.

Transfer the roux to the blender with the milk mixture; make sure there is enough room in the blender jar for the added roux. Blend until smooth and return to the pan. Stir in the rest of the milk and whisk to combine.

Bring the sauce to a boil and reduce to a simmer. Stir in the vinegar. Simmer for 2 minutes to thicken and cook out the flour taste.

Add about 2 cups of the sauce to the pasta. Mix well. Spread the pasta evenly in the baking dish. Pour the remaining sauce over the pasta and smooth the surface. There will seem to be too much sauce for the amount of pasta, but it will all come out fine in the end.

Bake until the sauce is bubbling and a crust has developed, about 15 minutes. Remove from the oven, set aside to rest for 5 minutes before serving.

Baked Eggplant Parmesan

I love baked eggplant parmesan and this is my favorite recipe, as it always comes out perfect. When you make it, be sure to leave some of the crunchy eggplant un-sauced to keep them crispy. This is especially delicious served with a side of pasta.

2 MEDIUM EGGPLANTS, EACH 1 POUND, CUT INTO 1/4-INCH THICK SLICES

1/2 TABLESPOON KOSHER SALT

8 SLICES SANDWICH BREAD, CUT INTO QUARTERS

1/4 CUP NUTRITIONAL YEAST FLAKES

1 TEASPOON DRIED OREGANO OR DRIED BASIL

1 CUP WATER

6 TABLESPOONS FLAX SEED MEAL

1/2 CUP UNBLEACHED ALL-PURPOSE FLOUR OR ARROWROOT STARCH OR CORNSTARCH

FRESH GROUND BLACK PEPPER

6 TABLESPOONS GRAPESEED OR SUNFLOWER OIL

2 CUPS SHREDDED VEGAN CHEESE

4 CUPS TIMELESS TOMATO SAUCE (PAGE 24)

_____

SERVES 4 TO 6

Toss the eggplant slices with the salt in a large bowl. Transfer the slices to a colander set over a bowl and set aside for 30 minutes to drain. Place two baking sheets in the oven and preheat to 400°F.

Add the bread to a food processor and process into crumbs, then transfer to a large bowl and toss with the nutritional yeast, oregano, and pepper. Set aside.

Whisk the water and flax meal in a medium bowl. Set aside, but whisk again before dredging the eggplant.

Mix the flour and pepper to taste in a separate medium bowl. Set aside.

Prepare the work surface with three layers of paper towels. Arrange the eggplant in a single layer on top of the paper towels, place three more layers of paper towels over the eggplant, and press down firmly to remove more liquid. Do this in batches, if needed.

Dredge each slice of eggplant first in the flour, shaking off any excess flour, then in the flax mixture. Finally, gently toss in the bread crumbs; do not press the bread crumbs onto the eggplant.

Carefully remove the hot baking sheets from the oven, add 3 tablespoons of oil to each baking sheet and arrange the eggplant slices, in a single layer, on the two sheets. Bake for 7 minutes. Rotate the baking sheets. Bake 7 more minutes. Flip the eggplant on both sheets. Bake for 7 more minutes. Again, rotate the baking sheets and bake another 7 minutes, or until golden brown.

Spread 1 cup of the tomato sauce in the bottom of a 9 x 13-inch baking dish. Transfer half of the eggplant slices, overlapping slightly, to the baking dish. Spread 1 cup of tomato sauce over the eggplant and sprinkle with 1 cup of cheese. Layer the remaining eggplant over the cheese, spread another cup of tomato sauce over the eggplant and sprinkle with the remaining cheese. Leave some eggplant unsauced. Bake until the cheese melts and the sauce bubbles, about 15 minutes. Serve with the remaining sauce.

Spinach and Bean Enchiladas

Spinach, beans and a little vegan cheese are rolled in corn tortillas. Enchilada sauce smothers the casserole and a drizzle of cilantro-lime cream sauce complete it. It's great served with Mexican Red Rice and Beans (page 158) or Refried Beans with Tomatoes (page 200). Or keep things simple and serve with a crisp green salad with Mexican Ranch Dressing (page 29). (See photo on page 164.)

2 TABLESPOONS GRAPESEED OR SAFFLOWER OIL

1 LARGE ONION, FINELY CHOPPED

3 GARLIC CLOVES, MINCED

2 TEASPOONS GROUND CUMIN

1 TEASPOON GROUND CORIANDER

1 TEASPOON SEA SALT

3 TABLESPOONS MILD CHILI POWDER

1 CUP DICED FRESH OR CANNED TOMATOES, UNDRAINED

3 TABLESPOONS UNBLEACHED ALL-PURPOSE FLOUR

2 1/2 CUPS WATER, PLUS MORE FOR STEAMING

1 CUP SHREDDED VEGAN CHEESE

1 (15.5-OUNCE) CAN PINTO BEANS, RINSED AND DRAINED

6 CUPS FRESH BABY SPINACH

10 (5-INCH) CORN TORTILLAS

CILANTRO-LIME CREAM SAUCE (RECIPE FOLLOWS)

SERVES 4 TO 6

Preheat the oven to 350°F. Heat the oil in a medium saucepan over medium heat. Add the onion, garlic, cumin, coriander, and salt. Cook, stirring, until the onions are golden, 7 minutes. Remove from the heat and stir in the chili powder. Transfer half of the onion mixture to a large skillet and set aside.

Return the saucepan to medium heat. Add the tomatoes with their juice and cook, stirring, for 4 minutes. Stir in the flour and cook for 1 minute. Stir in 1/2 cup water and whisk until smooth. Stir in the remainiing water and bring to a boil, then reduce to a simmer and cook until it thickens, about 15 minutes. Blend with an immersion blender until smooth. Adjust seasoning and set aside.

Heat the reserved onions in the skillet over medium heat. Stir in the beans, spinach, and 2 tablespoons of water. Cover and cook until the spinach wilts, about 3 minutes. Stir in the cheese and 3 tablespoons of the reserved red sauce. Mix well, remove from the heat, and season with salt and black pepper. Set aside.

Transfer 1 cup of the red sauce to a 9 x 13-inch baking dish. Heat the tortillas between 2 damp paper towels in the microwave for 1 minute or heat each tortilla in a large skillet over medium heat. Fill a tortilla with 2 heaping tablespoons of bean mixture, roll it up and place it seam-side down in the baking dish. Repeat with all the tortillas. Ladle the remaining red sauce over the filled tortillas. Bake until heated through, about 20 minutes. Serve with the cream sauce.

Cilantro-Lime Cream Sauce

1/2 CUP RAW CASHEWS

1/2 CUP PLAIN UNSWEETENED VEGAN MILK

1/2 CUP CILANTRO LEAVES

2 TABLESPOONS FRESH LIME JUICE

SALT AND FRESH GROUND BLACK PEPPER

———————

MAKES 1 CUP

Blend the cashews in a dry personal blender until the nuts are finely ground. Add the milk, cilantro, lime juice, and salt and pepper to taste. Blend until smooth. If the sauce is too thick, add a tablespoon more milk. Set aside.

Ovens and Stoves Are All Alike, Right?

It is important to know how hot your stove and oven get. Medium heat is the most-used setting on the stovetop. Each stove heats differently, and even if you are using an electric stove with markings, the numbers on your stove might not heat at the same temperature as mine. For this reason, you should become completely familiar with your stove's medium setting.

To check your stove's medium setting, heat 1 tablespoon of oil in a pan over medium heat. When the oil is hot, add 1/2 cup of chopped onions and cook until golden brown over medium heat. It should take 5 to 6 minutes. Adjust the heat each time you cook onions until this is consistently true. Remember the marking on the stove's knob that indicated where your "medium" setting is. You can save this "onion test" until you need to cook some onions; no need to waste time and ingredients.

Although there are "hot spots" and "cool spots" within your oven, you should have a general idea of how high or low your oven runs. When I checked my oven it was a whopping 25°F off, running too cold. If I had not used an oven thermometer (around $5) to check, I would have wasted loads of food. The thermometer paid for itself with the first batch of cookies.

Tater Tot Casserole

Made famous by a television family, this casserole, completely veganized, is addictive! If it isn't one already, this is a future comfort food for sure. It certainly has been elevated to that status in our family. This casserole is great with Braised Brussels Sprouts (page 195), Garlicky Greens (page 196), Asparagus with Sesame Seeds (page 198), Sautéed Pesto Vegetables (page 202) , or a crisp salad of greens with Ranch Dressing (page 29).

1 TABLESPOON OLIVE OIL

1 MEDIUM ONION, FINELY CHOPPED

3 CUPS PLAIN UNSWEETENED VEGAN MILK, DIVIDED

1 TABLESPOON SAVORY BROTH MIX (PAGE 19)

1/2 TEASPOON SEA SALT

3 TABLESPOONS ARROWROOT STARCH

4 CUPS COARSELY CHOPPED TENDER SOY CURLS (PAGE 35)

1 CUP FROZEN PEAS, THAWED AND DRAINED

SALT AND FRESH GROUND BLACK PEPPER

2 POUNDS FROZEN TATER TOTS

SERVES 4 TO 6

GLUTEN-FREE

Preheat oven to 425°F. Heat the oil in a large saucepan over medium heat. Add the onion and cook until golden, about 4 minutes. Stir in 2 1/2 cups of the vegan milk, the broth mix, and 1/2 teaspoon salt, and bring to a simmer.

In a small bowl, whisk together the arrowroot starch, and the remaining 1/2 cup of vegan milk.

Pour the arrowroot mixture into the saucepan and whisk thoroughly. Simmer only until it thickens, about 30 seconds, whisking continuously. The gravy will be quite thick. Remove from the heat.

Add the Soy Curls and the thawed peas to the gravy and mix well. Season to taste with salt and pepper.

Lightly oil a 9 x 13-inch baking dish. Pour the gravy mixture into the dish and smooth it out. Arrange the tater tots on the filling, standing them upright in order to fit them all and season the tots with a little salt. Place the casserole dish on a baking sheet in case the filling bubbles over. Bake for 45 minutes or until the tots are golden brown.

VARIATION: This dish is best using the soy curls, but you may instead use Marinated Tofu (page 34) or coarsely chopped Simple Seitan Cutlets (page 40) instead. If using chopped Simple Seitan, heat 2 tablespoons of oil in a large skillet over medium-high heat. Add the seitan and cook, stirring, until the seitan is golden brown, about 10 minutes. Season with salt and pepper. Remove from the heat and set aside.

Hearty Vegetable-Potato Au Gratin

This homage to Hungarian layered potatoes makes a satisfying one-dish meal with the addition of kale, squash, and your choice of vegan protein. While the original is full of rich sour cream and butter (and therefore fat), this version uses hearty cool-weather vegetables and only hints at decadence.

6 CUPS WATER

1 (8-OUNCE) BUNCH KALE, TOUGH STEMS RE-MOVED

1 TABLESPOON OLIVE OIL

2 CUPS COARSELY CHOPPED TENDER SOY CURLS (PAGE 35), SIMPLE SEITAN CUTLETS (PAGE 40), OR OTHER VEGAN PROTEIN, SAU-TÉED (OPTIONAL)

1/2 SMALL ONION, COARSELY CHOPPED

2 1/2 CUPS PLAIN UNSWEETENED VEGAN MILK

1 BAY LEAF

1 TEASPOON TOASTED SESAME OIL

1 TEASPOON SEA SALT

2 POUNDS RUSSET POTATOES (4 TO 5 POTA-TOES), PEELED AND CUT INTO 1/8-INCH SLICES

10 OUNCES BUTTERNUT SQUASH OR SWEET POTATO, PEELED AND CUT INTO 1/4-INCH SLICES

1 CUP VEGAN SOUR CREAM

HUNGARIAN PAPRIKA

FRESH GROUND BLACK PEPPER

SERVES 4 TO 6

GLUTEN-FREE

Bring 6 cups of water to a boil in a large pot over medium-high heat. Add the kale and cook until almost tender, about 4 minutes. Drain and set aside. When cool enough to handle, squeeze the excess water out of the kale and coarsely chop it.

Heat the oil in a large skillet over medium heat. Add the onion and cook, stirring, until golden, about 7 minutes. Stir in the protein, if using, then remove from the heat and stir in the cooked kale. Preheat the oven to 375°F.

Heat the milk in a large pot over medium heat. Add the bay leaf, sesame oil, and salt, and bring to a light boil. Add the potatoes, cover the pot and cook over medium heat for 5 minutes. Remove from the heat.

Lightly oil a deep 3-quart baking dish. Use a slotted spoon to gently remove the potatoes from the milk. Layer one-third of the potato slices in the bottom of the baking dish, top with half of the squash slices followed by half of the kale mixture. Layer another one-third of the potatoes, the remaining squash, remaining kale mixture, and remaining potatoes.

Stir the sour cream into any milk remaining in the pot. If none remains, stir in an additional 1/4 cup milk. Remove the bay leaf and discard. Spread the sour cream mixture over the potatoes and sprinkle with paprika and black pepper. Tightly cover with foil and bake for 50 minutes. Remove the foil and bake for 10 minutes longer. Remove from the oven and let rest for 10 minutes before serving.

Butternut Squash and Sweet Potato Casserole

The holiday table would not be complete without a sweet potato dish to share. This is a rendition of the traditional casserole, but without all the added sugar that usually gets crammed into the dish. Baked sweet potatoes are sweet unto themselves, and the topping adds that just-right sweetness for the holiday season. Since the casserole feeds a crowd, you can halve the recipe but bake for the same amount of time. The topping can be skipped for everyday fare if it might be too much of a sweet thing.

4 LARGE SWEET POTATOES, ABOUT 1 POUND EACH

2 SMALL BUTTERNUT SQUASH, ABOUT 1 POUND EACH

2 TABLESPOONS GRAPESEED OR SUNFLOWER OIL

1/2 CUP PACKED BROWN SUGAR

1/4 CUP OLD-FASHIONED ROLLED OATS

1 CUP RAW WALNUTS OR PECANS, FINELY CHOPPED

6 TABLESPOONS VEGAN BUTTER

2 TEASPOONS FRESH LEMON JUICE

2 TEASPOONS SEA SALT

1/2 TEASPOON FRESHLY GRATED NUTMEG

1/8 TEASPOON FRESH GROUND BLACK PEPPER

―――――――――

SERVES 6 TO 8

Preheat the oven to 350°F. Pierce the potatoes and squash with a knife in a few places and place them on a baking sheet. Bake until soft, about 1 hour and 15 minutes to 1 hour and 30 minutes. When the vegetables are soft, remove them from the oven and immediately (but carefully) cut them in half lengthwise to allow the steam to escape. Cool them enough to handle.

While the vegetables are baking, make the topping by combining the oil, sugar, oats, and walnuts in a medium bowl. Stir well to combine.

When the potatoes and squash are cool enough to handle, remove the seeds from the squash and scoop the flesh from the vegetables into a large bowl. Add the butter, lemon juice, salt, nutmeg, and black pepper. Use a potato masher to mash all the ingredients together. Stir and mash until well combined.

Transfer the vegetable mixture to a 9 x 13-inch baking dish. Smooth the surface of the casserole and sprinkle evenly with the topping. Bake until the topping is crisp and the casserole is heated through, about 25 to 30 minutes.

Green Bean Casserole

This American holiday staple was actually invented by Campbell's. While my version keeps the intent of the iconic casserole intact, it brings it to the natural culinary forefront. For the holidays, do the full-fat version, but for everyday cooking, cut the fat in half by sautéing the mushrooms in 2 teaspoons of butter, the green beans in 1 teaspoon of butter, and make the gravy using 2 tablespoons of butter.

6 TABLESPOONS VEGAN BUTTER, DIVIDED

10 OUNCES MUSHROOMS, ANY KIND, WIPED
   CLEAN, AND SLICED

2 GARLIC CLOVES, MINCED

1 POUND FRESH GREEN BEANS, TRIMMED AND
   CUT IN HALF

1/4 CUP UNBLEACHED ALL-PURPOSE FLOUR

2 TABLESPOONS SAVORY BROTH MIX (PAGE 19)

2 CUPS PLAIN UNSWEETENED VEGAN MILK

2 CUPS FRIED ONIONS, STOREBOUGHT OR
   HOMEMADE (OPPOSITE)

SEA SALT AND FRESH GROUND BLACK PEPPER

SERVES 4 TO 6

Heat 2 tablespoons of vegan butter in a large skillet over medium-high heat. Stir in the mushrooms and cook until golden brown, 8 minutes. Stir occasionally to allow them to release their moisture and sear instead of steam. Season with salt and pepper to taste. Add the garlic and cook for 30 seconds. Transfer to a greased 9 x 9-inch baking dish and set aside.

Heat 1 tablespoon of vegan butter in the same skillet over medium heat. Add the green beans and cook for 2 minutes. Stir in 1/4 cup water, cover, and steam the beans until crisp-tender, about 2 minutes. Transfer the beans to the dish with the mushrooms and set aside.

Heat the remaining 3 tablespoons of vegan butter in the same skillet over medium heat. Whisk in the flour. Continue whisking until the flour smells nutty, 3 to 5 minutes. Stir in the broth mix.

Slowly add 1/2 cup of the milk, continuously whisking until smooth. Add another 1/2 cup of milk, continuously whisking until smooth. Repeat adding the milk and whisking until all the milk is used. Simmer the gravy for 2 minutes. Season to taste with salt and pepper.

Stir in the reserved green beans, mushrooms, and 1 cup of fried onions. Gently mix to combine. Transfer the mixture to the baking dish. Smooth out the casserole. Sprinkle the remaining cup of fried onions over the top. Serve immediately. If not serving right away, reheat in preheated 350°F oven for 15 to 20 minutes or until hot and bubbling.

Fried Onions

You can purchase fried onions at the store, or you can go all-out and make a homemade batch. It's surprisingly easy; just keep them away from wandering hands, otherwise you'll discover that not much remains of your onions when they are needed for the casserole.

2 MEDIUM ONIONS

3 TABLESPOONS UNBLEACHED ALL-PURPOSE FLOUR

1 TEASPOON SEA SALT

GRAPESEED OR SUNFLOWER OIL, FOR PAN-FRYING

———————————————

MAKES ABOUT 2 CUPS

Very thinly slice the onions using a mandoline or a very sharp knife. If using a knife, cut the onions in half through the root-end to make slicing easier.

Toss the sliced onions with the flour and salt. Prepare a baking sheet with paper towels.

Heat 1/2-inch of oil in a medium saucepan until hot. Cook the onions in the hot oil in batches until golden brown and crisp, about 5 minutes, stirring the onions after a few minutes. Remove to paper towels to drain. Repeat until all the onions are fried.

Baked Potato Bar

Try this fun idea the next time you want an easy dinner. All you need is enough time for the potatoes to bake and a selection of toppings (hint: this is a great way to use up small amounts of leftover chili or cooked vegetables) and dinner will be ready in 1- 2- 3.

Bake the potatoes: Preheat the oven to 375°F. If you do not regularly keep foil on the bottom rack of your oven, place a large sheet there now to catch any oil that might drip from the potatoes during baking. Poke holes all over your clean and dry Russet potatoes with a fork to vent the steam during baking. Rub the potatoes with some vegetable or olive oil, sprinkle with salt and bake them for 50 to 60 minutes directly on the middle oven rack.

When the potatoes are tender, remove them from the oven and split them in half.

Serve the potatoes with your choice of toppings: chopped Bacon Tofu (page 36), vegan sour cream, vegan butter, Cheese Sauce (page 27), chives, steamed broccoli or cauliflower, Chipotle Chili (page 63), vegan cheese, Roasted Corn (page 108), warm black beans, Salsa Fresca (page 23), or Ranch Dressing (page 29).

Arroz non Pollo

This classic Latin American dish is made with browned chicken, rice, sofrito, and spices. To achieve a deep flavor, cook the vegan protein very well before using it in the recipe. I cook the protein until it is beginning to char; that gives it a satisfying smoky flavor.

1 RED BELL PEPPER, SEEDED, AND CHOPPED INTO LARGE PIECES

1 GREEN BELL PEPPER, SEEDED, AND CHOPPED INTO LARGE PIECES

1 LARGE ONION, CHOPPED INTO LARGE PIECES

1 MEDIUM RIPE TOMATO, CORED AND CUT INTO LARGE PIECES

8 GARLIC CLOVES

1/4 CUP PARSLEY LEAVES

1/4 CUP OLIVE OIL

1/2 CUP CILANTRO LEAVES, COARSELY CHOPPED

2 TEASPOONS GROUND CUMIN

1 TEASPOON DRIED OREGANO

1 TEASPOON SEA SALT

1/4 TEASPOON FRESH GROUND BLACK PEPPER

2 BAY LEAVES

2 CUPS LONG-GRAIN BROWN RICE

1 1/2 TABLESPOONS SAVORY BROTH MIX (PAGE 19)

1 TEASPOON PAPRIKA

1 TEASPOON GROUND TURMERIC

3 1/2 CUPS WATER

4 CUPS TENDER SOY CURLS (PAGE 35), OR MARINATED TOFU (PAGE 34), OR SIMPLE SEITAN CUTLETS (PAGE 40), SAUTÉED WELL FOR ADDED FLAVOR

SERVES 4 TO 6

GLUTEN-FREE

Preheat the oven to 350°F. Make the sofrito by combining the bell peppers, onion, tomato, garlic, and parsley in a food processor. Process until the mixture is finely minced but is not a paste. Set aside.

Heat the oil in a large oven-safe saucepan over medium heat. Stir in the cilantro and cook until it begins to fry, about 1 minute.

Stir in the sofrito mixture, cumin, oregano, salt, black pepper, and bay leaves. Cook, stirring, until the liquid has almost completely evaporated, about 10 minutes.

Stir in the rice, broth mix, paprika, turmeric, and water. Bring to a boil, then remove from the heat. Stir in the protein and cover the pot tightly with aluminum foil. Transfer to the preheated oven and bake for 1 hour.

If the rice is tender and there is no water remaining, remove the pot from the oven and let rest for 10 minutes, covered, before serving. Remove the bay leaves and discard. Fluff the casserole using a fork and serve hot.

CHEF'S TIP: If the rice is tender but there is water remaining in the pot, return the pot, uncovered, to the oven and continue to bake for another 10 minutes. If the rice is undercooked but there is water remaining in the pot, recover the pot and bake for another 15 minutes. If the rice is undercooked and there is no water remaining, add 1/4 cup of water to the rice, cover, and bake for another 15 minutes.

Mike and Judy's Stuffed Cabbage

My parents operated many restaurants in South Florida. One of the most popular offerings on the menu was stuffed cabbage. After many years of trial and error, I've finally created a vegan version that tastes just like their famous rolls. Serve the cabbage rolls with cooked rice or baked potatoes and Hungarian Tomato Salad (page 113); omit the tomatoes from the salad and substitute with 1/2 green pepper, thinly sliced. **Note:** whichever protein you use should be ground first in a food processor.

1 LARGE HEAD GREEN CABBAGE, FROZEN
    OVERNIGHT AND THAWED

2 TABLESPOONS OLIVE OIL

1 LARGE ONION, FINELY CHOPPED

4 GARLIC CLOVES, MINCED

3/4 CUP ARBORIO RICE

3 1/2 CUPS VEGETABLE BROTH

5 CUPS GROUND SAVORY TVP (PAGE 38), TEN-
    DER SOY CURLS (PAGE 35), MARINATED
    TOFU (PAGE 34), OR SIMPLE SEITAN CUT-
    LETS (PAGE 40)

1 TABLESPOON HUNGARIAN SWEET PAPRIKA

2 (28-OUNCE) CANS TOMATO PUREE

1/4 CUP PACKED BROWN SUGAR

3 TABLESPOONS FRESH LEMON JUICE (OP-
    TIONAL)

1 TEASPOON SEA SALT

FRESH GROUND BLACK PEPPER

MAKES 14 ROLLS

GLUTEN-FREE

Core the thawed cabbage. Remove 16 of the largest leaves. Trim the thicker parts of the stems with a paring knife. Set the leaves aside for stuffing. Cut the rest of the cabbage into thin slices and arrange on the bottom of a large saucepan or slow cooker.

Heat the oil in a separate large saucepan over medium heat. Add the onion and cook, stirring, until softened, about 5 minutes. Stir in the garlic and rice and cook until the rice is translucent, about 1 minute. Stir in 1/2 cup of the broth and cook, stirring, until the rice has absorbed the broth, about 4 minutes.

Add another 1/2 cup of the broth and cook until the rice has absorbed the broth, about 4 minutes. Repeat this procedure until the rice is tender and creamy and most of the broth has been used, about 20 to 25 minutes.

Stir in the protein and paprika and mix well. Taste and adjust the seasoning, as needed, with salt and pepper.

Place a cabbage leaf on a work surface in front of you, with the core end of the leaf toward you and the cabbage leaf up in the form of a cup. Place about 1/3 cup of filling near the bottom of each leaf. Roll the leaf all the way up around the filling. Pick up the rolled cabbage and tuck each end of the leaf in with your finger, so that it doesn't unroll. Place the filled and sealed cabbage leaf, seam side down, on top of the shredded cabbage in the other large pot. Repeat until the leaves and filling are used.

Pour the tomato puree over the stuffed cabbages. Evenly sprinkle the tomato puree with brown sugar, salt, and the lemon juice, if using (for a sweet and sour version). Add black pepper to taste. Cover and cook on medium-low until the cabbage leaves are very tender, 6 hours in a slow cooker or 2 hours on the stove-top. Serve hot.

Lima Bean Bake

This recipe takes two hours to bake, so plan accordingly. The good news is that the preparation is easy, especially with canned lima beans, and the result is delicious! This is an ancient dish dating back to the middle ages in France. It is imperative that you use large beans for this dish. They are buttery and creamy and irreplaceable; smaller beans just don't do justice here. Search high and low and find large Lima or butter beans. This dish is decidedly great on its own, but it is even better served with crusty bread to soak up the flavorful broth and Garlicky Greens (page 196), which add a wonderful bitterness to the sweet beans.

1 SMALL ONION

3 TABLESPOONS OLIVE OIL

3 GARLIC CLOVES, MINCED

1 LARGE CARROT, CUT INTO 1/2-INCH HALF
   MOONS

1 RIPE TOMATO, CORED AND COARSELY
   CHOPPED

8 OUNCES LARGE LIMA BEANS, COOKED OR
   2 (15.5-OUNCE) CANS LARGE LIMA BEANS,
   RINSED AND DRAINED

3 CUPS BEAN COOKING LIQUID, WATER, OR A
   COMBINATION

1 TEASPOON DRIED OREGANO

1 TEASPOON SEA SALT

1/2 TEASPOON FRESH GROUND BLACK PEP-
   PER

SERVES 4

GLUTEN-FREE
SOY-FREE

Preheat the oven to 350°F. Peel the onion, slice it in half through the root, cut off the root, and cut the onion into thin half-moon slices.

Heat the oil in an oven-safe saucepan over medium heat. Cook the onion, garlic, and carrot until softened, about 5 minutes. Stir in the tomatoes. Cover and cook the vegetables until the tomatoes soften, stirring occasionally, about 5 minutes.

Stir in the cooked beans, water, oregano, salt, and pepper. Bake in the preheated oven, uncovered, for 1 1/2 hours.

Taste and adjust seasoning with salt and black pepper. Serve.

Everyday Nachos (page 200)

CHAPTER 9

Sides & Snacks

Side dishes round out any meal and complement a main dish. In this chapter I have included some of my family's favorites side dish recipes such as Braised Brussels Sprouts and Sautéed Pesto Vegetables. In addition, there are some delectable appetizers that not only whet the appetite, but can be complete meals in themselves. In my house, we will frequently choose two appetizers and a vegetable side and call it a meal. But don't assign appetizers to just meals; they make great snacks any time of day.

Classic Hummus

Hummus can be a vegan's best friend. It's quick and easy to make, loaded with flavor and protein, and can be enjoyed as a dip or a sandwich spread and more. The secret to a super smooth and silky hummus is in removing the skin of the chickpeas. I recall my mother cooking beans with baking soda to loosen and soften their skins. This same process works equally well for canned beans, making restaurant-quality hummus an everyday possibility.

1 (15.5-OUNCE) CAN CHICKPEAS, RINSED AND DRAINED

1/2 TEASPOON BAKING SODA

2 SMALL GARLIC CLOVES, CHOPPED

2 TO 3 TABLESPOONS TAHINI

2 TABLESPOONS FRESH LEMON JUICE

1 TO 2 TABLESPOONS WATER

3/4 TEASPOON SEA SALT AND FRESH GROUND BLACK PEPPER

1 TEASPOON PAPRIKA, FOR SERVING (OPTIONAL)

OLIVE OIL, FOR SERVING (OPTIONAL)

MAKES 1 CUP

QUICK & EASY
GLUTEN FREE
SOY-FREE

Combine the chickpeas, baking soda, and enough water to cover in a medium saucepan. Bring to a boil and simmer for 5 minutes, stirring occasionally. Drain the beans and transfer them to a large bowl of water. Use your fingers to agitate the beans to remove as much skin as possible. The skins will float to the top of the water. Carefully drain the chickpeas, pouring off the skins along with the water, while holding back the beans with your hand. Fill the bowl again with water and repeat the procedure until most of the chickpea skins are removed and drained off.

Transfer the chickpeas and garlic to a food processor. Process to a fine paste. Add the tahini, lemon juice, 1 tablespoon of water, salt, and black pepper to taste. Process the hummus until smooth, at least 1 full minute. Add another tablespoon of water if the hummus is too thick. Adjust seasoning with salt and pepper as needed.

Serve the hummus spread on a plate, sprinkled with the paprika and drizzled with the olive oil, or store in an airtight container in the refrigerator for up to 3 days.

VARIATION: Roasted Red Pepper Hummus. Add 1 medium roasted red bell pepper, storebought or homemade (page 8), to the bowl of the food processor with the tahini, omitting the water, and process as indicated.

Hummus Among Us

No surprise, hummus is great in sandwiches as a spread, but it also makes a great Mediterranean-type pizza. Spread hummus on pizza dough (page 128) or a pita bread, top with grilled veggies and vegan cheese, and bake or broil until the cheese melts.

Spinach-Artichoke Dip

I used to make this dip and take it to my kids' group get-togethers. It was the first thing to disappear and I only had an empty pan to cart home. My kids used to get so involved with their friends that they'd inevitably forget to eat. Eventually, to pacify my own children, I had to make two batches—one for the potluck and one for the family. If you have any leftover dip, toss it with some cooked tube pasta, such as ziti, moistening the mixture with some vegan milk, if needed, and top with vegan shredded cheese, if desired. Bake at 350°F until heated through, about 20 minutes.

5 TABLESPOONS OLIVE OIL, DIVIDED

8 GARLIC CLOVES, FINELY CHOPPED

1 (10-OUNCE) PACKAGE FROZEN SPINACH, THAWED

1 (12-OUNCE) JAR ARTICHOKE HEARTS, RINSED AND DRAINED

1 CUP (8-OUNCES) SOFTENED VEGAN CREAM CHEESE

1/2 CUP VEGAN MAYONNAISE, STOREBOUGHT OR HOMEMADE (PAGE 31)

1 TABLESPOON FRESH LEMON JUICE

SEA SALT AND FRESH GROUND BLACK PEPPER

1/2 CUP PANKO BREADCRUMBS OR GLUTEN-FREE BREADCRUMBS (OPTIONAL)

———————

SERVES 8

QUICK & EASY
GLUTEN-FREE OPTION

Preheat the oven to 375°F. Heat 4 tablespoons of oil in a small saucepan over medium-low heat. Add the garlic and cook, stirring, until the garlic is golden brown, about 3 minutes. Reduce the heat if the garlic is browning too fast. Remove from the heat and set aside to cool.

Squeeze the excess moisture from the thawed spinach and transfer it to a food processor. Add the artichoke hearts, cream cheese, mayo, lemon juice, salt and black pepper to taste, and the cooled oil with the garlic. Pulse the food processor until the mixture is combined but not pureed, scraping the sides as needed. Season to taste with salt, black pepper, and more lemon juice, if needed.

Transfer the dip to a 9 x 9-inch baking dish. Sprinkle with the breadcrumbs, if using, and drizzle on the remaining 1 tablespoon of oil.

Bake the dip in the preheated oven until heated through and the crumbs are golden brown, about 20 minutes. Serve with slices of French bread or celery sticks.

Everyday Vegan Nachos

Almost too simple to call it a recipe, but too delicious not to include it, these nachos can be enjoyed as a snack, a side, or as meal in itself. Among the choice of toppings are several recipes in this book, such as the salsa on page 23 and the refried beans (page 200), but for quicker nachos you can substitute storebought salsa and warm some canned beans instead. The amount of ingredients needed depends on personal taste and how you will be serving the nachos.

TORTILLA CHIPS

CHEESE SAUCE (PAGE 27)

REFRIED BEANS WITH TOMATOES (PAGE 200) OR COOKED PINTO BEANS

SALSA FRESCA (PAGE 23) OR STOREBOUGHT SALSA

OPTIONAL TOPPINGS: SLICED BLACK OLIVES, SLICED SCALLIONS, DICED TOMATOES, SLICED JALAPEÑOS, VEGAN SOUR CREAM, GUACAMOLE OR DICED AVOCADO, SHRED-DED VEGAN CHEESE, MINCED ONION, MINCED CILANTRO, SHREDDED LETTUCE

QUICK & EASY

Preheat the oven to 350°F. Spread the tortilla chips in a single layer on a baking sheet and bake for 5 to 8 minutes to warm.

While the chips are warming, heat the cheese sauce and beans.

Transfer the warm chips to a plate or serving platter and top with the cheese sauce, beans, salsa, and add as many of the optional toppings as you like. Serve immediately.

Hungarian Paprika Potatoes

While this is an easy and quick weeknight meal, especially with the extra protein added, note that the grown-up variation, Hungarian March of the Grenadiers (page 152), is far superior. Use Hungarian paprika for the authentic punch. In fact, you should only use Hungarian paprika period, unless you are using the smoked kind. (Just the opinion of a Hungarian!) This is really great served with Hungarian Tomato Salad (page 113). The acid in the salad cuts through the richness of the potatoes. For a complete meal, cut two vegan sausage links into 1/2-inch pieces and add them to the potatoes near the end of cooking time to heat through.

1 TABLESPOON GRAPESEED OR SUNFLOWER OIL

1 TABLESPOON TOASTED SESAME OIL

1 LARGE ONION, COARSELY CHOPPED

2 GARLIC CLOVES, MINCED

1 TABLESPOON HUNGARIAN SWEET PAPRIKA

3 POUNDS GOLD OR RED POTATOES

2 CUPS WATER

2 RIPE ROMA TOMATOES, QUARTERED

1 MEDIUM GREEN OR RED BELL PEPPER, CORED, SEEDED, AND COARSELY CHOPPED

2 TEASPOONS SEA SALT

———————

SERVES 4

QUICK & EASY
GLUTEN-FREE
SOY-FREE

Heat the oils in a large saucepan over medium heat. Add the onion and garlic and cook, stirring, until golden, about 8 minutes. Remove the saucepan from the heat and stir in the paprika.

Peel the potatoes and slice them in half lengthwise. Slice each half into quarters lengthwise, about 1/2-inch thick.

Return the saucepan to the heat and stir in the potatoes, water, tomatoes, bell pepper, and salt. Bring to a boil, then reduce to a simmer. Cover and cook until the potatoes are fork-tender, about 20 minutes. Stir occasionally, but do not stir too much toward the end of the cooking time, since it will break up the potatoes. Adjust the seasoning with salt and black pepper. Set the potatoes aside for 5 minutes, to allow the sauce to thicken. Serve the potatoes ladled with the sauce.

Braised Brussels Sprouts

I love these cabbage-like vegetables. They are just like candy to me and I find myself walking by the skillet just to pop one in my mouth. These melt in your mouth and are a bit crispy on the cut side.

1 POUND BRUSSELS SPROUTS

2 TABLESPOONS OLIVE OIL

2 GARLIC CLOVES, CUT INTO 1/8-INCH SLICES

SEA SALT AND FRESH GROUND BLACK PEPPER

6 TABLESPOONS VEGETABLE BROTH

SPLASH OF APPLE CIDER VINEGAR (OPTIONAL)

SERVES 4

QUICK & EASY

GLUTEN-FREE

SOY-FREE

Trim the stem end of each sprout about 1/4 to 1/2 inch, removing a few of the outer leaves in the process. Remove any yellowed leaves, as needed. Cut each sprout in half through the stem and set aside.

Heat the oil in a large skillet over medium-low heat. Add the garlic and cook, stirring, until golden, about 3 minutes. Turn down the heat if the garlic is browning too fast. When the garlic is golden, remove it with a slotted spoon and set aside.

Increase the heat to medium. Arrange the sprouts in the skillet with the cut side down, placing as many as you can in the skillet. Season with salt and black pepper to taste. Cook until the sprouts are golden brown on the cut side, about 8 to 12 minutes, stirring a few times to caramelize as many on the cut side as possible.

Pour the broth over the sprouts, add the reserved garlic, cover the skillet with a lid, and cook the sprouts until they are tender and the broth has evaporated, about 5 minutes.

When the sprouts are tender, add a splash of vinegar, if desired. The vinegar will evaporate as soon as it hits the hot skillet. Stir the sprouts. Taste and adjust the seasoning with salt and pepper. Serve hot.

Garlicky Greens

Garlic and greens are a match made in nirvana. Some tough greens, such as kale and mustard greens, must be stemmed first, while other, more bitter greens, like collards and rapini, are best when simmered in a large pot of boiling water. Still others need no such preparation, like fresh spinach. Regardless of the greens, however, their bitterness pairs amazingly well with garlic and olive oil.

1 POUND GREENS, TOUGH STEMS REMOVED

2 TABLESPOONS OLIVE OIL

5 GARLIC CLOVES, FINELY CHOPPED

SEA SALT AND FRESH GROUND BLACK PEPPER

———

SERVES 4

QUICK & EASY

GLUTEN-FREE

SOY-FREE

If using tough greens, such as kale and collard greens, bring 2 quarts of water to boil in a large pot. Add 1/2 teaspoon salt. Stir in the greens and cook for 4 minutes, until just tender. Drain the greens in a colander and cool them quickly by spreading them on a baking sheet. Spinach and tender baby greens do not need this step.

Heat the oil over medium heat in a large skillet or large pot. Stir in the garlic. Stir and cook until the garlic is just beginning to turn golden brown, about 30 seconds.

Stir in the greens, previously steamed, if needed, and mix well with tongs. Season to taste with salt and black pepper, but take care not to over-season.

Cook the greens until they are heated through and cooked to your liking, covering the pot with a lid if needed. Serve hot.

Measuring Greens

Nothing is as loosely interpreted as how well to pack your greens for measuring. Whether you're working with cilantro leaves or lettuce, how tightly you pack the measuring cup will yield various results. Where indicated to pack well, please pack your measuring cup densely (although greens aren't brown sugar, so no need to crush them); pack the cup until you can't add anymore without damaging the greens. Otherwise, where there is no indication that the greens need to be packed, simply scoop and measure.

Cheesy Summer Squash Sauté

Hubby and I used to patronize a popular cafeteria in Texas that is famous for their Cheesy Summer Squash. During and after pregnancy with my youngest daughter, I took double and triple portions of the casserole in lieu of other offerings. Frankly, this was the only reason I loved going there. Naturally, it had to be made vegan. If you aren't a summer squash fan, substitute with other lightly steamed veggies: cauliflower, broccoli, hearty greens, etc.

1 CUP PLAIN UNSWEETENED VEGAN MILK, DIVIDED

3 TABLESPOONS DICED JARRED PIMIENTOS OR ROASTED RED PEPPERS

3 TABLESPOONS NUTRITIONAL YEAST FLAKES

4 TEASPOONS ARROWROOT STARCH OR 1 TABLESPOON CORNSTARCH

2 TABLESPOONS OLIVE OIL, DIVIDED

1/2 MEDIUM ONION, FINELY CHOPPED

2 GARLIC CLOVES, FINELY CHOPPED

1/2 TEASPOON FRESH OR DRIED THYME LEAVES

1 1/2 POUNDS YELLOW SQUASH OR ZUCCHINI, CUT INTO 1/4-INCH HALF-MOONS

SEA SALT AND FRESH GROUND BLACK PEPPER

SERVES 4

QUICK & EASY
GLUTEN-FREE
SOY-FREE

Combine 3/4 cup milk, pimientos, and nutritional yeast in a blender. Blend well until smooth. Set aside. Whisk together the remaining 1/4 cup milk and arrowroot in a small bowl. Set aside.

Heat 1 tablespoon of oil in a large skillet over medium heat. Add the onion, garlic, and thyme and cook, stirring, until the onions are beginning to brown, about 3 minutes.

Stir in the remaining 1 tablespoon oil and the squash. Cook until lightly browned, stirring occasionally, about 10 minutes.

Stir in the reserved milk and pimiento mixture. Bring to a boil, then reduce to a simmer and stir in the arrowroot mixture. Simmer only until thickened, about 30 seconds, and immediately remove the skillet from the heat. Season to taste with salt and black pepper.

Roasted Asparagus with Sesame Seeds

I love, love, love this side dish. Asparagus is best when not over-cooked and stringy, but crisp and lightly tender. The sesame seeds are complementary to the garlic and asparagus.

2 TABLESPOONS OLIVE OIL

2 GARLIC CLOVES, MINCED

1 POUND ASPARAGUS SPEARS, TRIMMED

2 TEASPOONS TOASTED SESAME SEEDS

SEA SALT AND FRESH GROUND BLACK PEPPER

———————

SERVES 4

QUICK & EASY
GLUTEN-FREE
SOY-FREE

Preheat the oven to 400°F. Heat the oil in a small sauce-pan over medium heat. Stir in the garlic and reduce the heat to low. Cook until the garlic is light golden brown, about 5 minutes. Strain and set aside.

Toss the asparagus spears with the drained oil, sesame seeds, and salt and black pepper to taste on a baking sheet. Bake for 5 minutes.

Sprinkle the asparagus with the reserved garlic, turn the spears with tongs, and continue to cook for another 5 minutes, or until tender but not stringy. Lessen the cooking time for thinner spears.

Sautéed Collard Ribbons

Feijoada (page 127) is frequently served with sautéed collard greens or kale. This completes the Brazilian experience.

2 BUNCHES COLLARD GREENS, TOUGH STEMS
    REMOVED

1 TABLESPOON OLIVE OIL

4 GARLIC CLOVES, MINCED

2 TEASPOONS SAVORY BROTH MIX (PAGE 19)

1 CUP WATER

SEA SALT AND FRESH GROUND BLACK PEPPER

———————

MAKES ABOUT 2 CUPS

QUICK & EASY

Roll up the collard leaves into a long log. With a sharp knife, shred the collards into very thin slices or ribbons. Set aside.

Heat the oil in a large skillet over medium heat. Stir in the garlic and cook until fragrant, about 30 seconds.

Stir in the collards, broth mix, and water. Simmer the collards until they are almost tender, about 4 minutes. Season to taste with salt and black pepper. Set aside and keep warm.

Refried Beans with Tomatoes

No Mexican or Tex-Mex dish should be served without refried beans, so it's a good thing this easy recipe takes only about 15 minutes to prepare.

1 TABLESPOON GRAPESEED OR SUNFLOWER
   OIL

1 MEDIUM RIPE TOMATO, CORED AND
   COARSELY CHOPPED

1/2 SMALL ONION, FINELY CHOPPED

2 GARLIC CLOVES, FINELY CHOPPED

1/2 TEASPOON GROUND CUMIN

1 (15.5-OUNCE) CAN PINTO BEANS, RINSED
   AND DRAINED

1/4 CUP WATER

SEA SALT AND FRESH GROUND BLACK PEPPER

MAKES 1 CUP

QUICK & EASY
GLUTEN-FREE
SOY-FREE

Heat the oil in a medium saucepan over medium heat. Add the tomato, onion, garlic, and cumin. Cook, stirring, until the tomato breaks down, about 5 minutes.

Add the beans. Cook, stirring, until the beans heat through, about 3 minutes. Coarsely mash the beans or, for a creamier texture, completely mash the beans with a potato masher or fork. Stir in the water, cover, and reduce the heat to medium-low. Cook the beans until they are thickened and the flavors have melded, about 10 minutes. Season to taste with salt and black pepper. Serve hot.

Dining Out Smart

Dining out can be a challenge for vegans, but these days, there is something satisfying to be had almost anywhere. The question really becomes how flexible you are.

If there is nothing obviously vegan available on the menu, don't hesitate to ask if they have vegan options. Many restaurants do make concessions, they just don't put it on the menu. As a last resort, you can always ask for a plate of steamed vegetables and a baked potato without butter or a salad with oil and vinegar. Ideal? Maybe not, but you won't starve.

If you are going someplace because you want to spend time with your family or friends, go for exactly that reason—to spend time with them, not with the food. If you can, try to steer them to a vegan-friendly restaurant or one that is willing to accommodate you. If possible, plan ahead and check out the restaurant menu online. You can also call the restaurant and ask questions such as:

- Do you have a vegetarian menu?

- Do you cook with butter, lard, or animal fat?

- Are your potatoes, rice, or beans made with beef or chicken stock or with meat?

- Do your vegetable sides contain beef or chicken stock or meat?

Often, it's easiest to get a vegan meal in an ethnic restaurant. For these venues, you may need to ask some focused inquiries:

- Asian: ask if a specific dish contains egg, fish sauce, shrimp, or oyster sauce.

- Mexican: ask if a specific dish contains pork, lard, or beef or chicken stock.

- Indian: ask if a specific dish contains cream or ghee, which is butter.

- Italian: ask if a specific dish contains anchovies, animal fat or stock, eggs, cheese, or other dairy. (Ask specifically about eggs and cheese in pastas and sauces.)

Finally, ask your server to help you. Ask them if it is possible to leave off certain ingredients. Explain your situation briefly and tell them what you need. Most servers will be happy to help as long as you have a pleasant attitude. It can also help if you tip well. Typically, vegan meals cost less than meat-based ones and the percentage for a possible tip goes down. As my mother used to say, if you can't tip well, take it to-go. But even then you ought to tip, even if it's not as much.

Sautéed Pesto Vegetables

Pesto is definitely my son's favorite way to eat anything—pasta, veggies, you name it; toss it in pesto and it's as good as gone. As with the other vegetable dishes, if you prefer other veggies, feel free to replace the crucifers or carrot.

2 CUPS BROCCOLI FLORETS

2 CUPS CAULIFLOWER FLORETS

1 CUP SLICED CARROT

6 TABLESPOONS PESTO SAUCE OR LOWER-FAT PESTO SAUCE (PAGE 153)

SALT AND FRESH GROUND BLACK PEPPER

———————

SERVES 4

QUICK & EASY

GLUTEN-FREE

SOY-FREE

Steam the vegetables in a steamer until tender, about 4 minutes.

Heat the pesto in a large skillet over medium heat. Cook, stirring, for 30 seconds.

Add the tender vegetables and cook, stirring, until the vegetables are lightly caramelized, about 3 minutes. Season with salt and black pepper to taste. Serve hot.

CHEF'S TIP: Substitute green beans, asparagus, summer squash, or zucchini for any of the vegetables in equal amounts.

Fried Vegan Omelet (page 208)

CHAPTER 10

Breakfast & Brunch

Many people tend to eat the same breakfast every day, such as oatmeal, toast, or smoothies. Some, however, enjoy rotating several heartier breakfast meals, like tofu scrambles, pancakes, and waffles. If you are the latter type of person, this chapter has some great ideas for you. You can always change things up a bit, especially on a lazy Sunday morning or Easter brunch, but for a typical day, these everyday vegan eats are great ways to start the day.

Breakfast should not be relegated to just the morning. If you ask my kids, they will tell you that Fluffy Buttermilk Pancakes and Classic-Style Benedict are not just for the break of day, thank you very much. Tex-Mex Migas make an excellent, quick lunch and Fried Vegan Omelet sandwiches are fantastic at supper time. This chapter ensures that the vegan cook has plenty to eat at breakfast or at any time of day. You'll also find a handy list of super-quick breakfast suggestions.

Morning Scrambles

This is a very quick breakfast. Don't forget to begin pressing the tofu before you start to cook; it speeds up the cooking time of the dish. Steaming the tofu at the end makes for a fluffy scramble. And don't be afraid to go wild! Add different ingedients to the scramble such as sautéed onion, sautéed mushroom, scallions, finely chopped vegan sausage, or finely chopped Bacon Tofu. While the black salt is optional, it really elevates the humble tofu to an eggy-tasting scramble.

1 TABLESPOON VEGAN BUTTER

1/4 SMALL ONION, FINELY CHOPPED

1/4 SMALL RED BELL PEPPER, FINELY CHOPPED

14-OUNCES FIRM TOFU, PRESSED FOR 10 MINUTES, PATTED DRY AND MASHED WELL

2 TABLESPOONS NUTRITIONAL YEAST FLAKES

1/8 TEASPOON GROUND TURMERIC

1/4 TEASPOON BLACK SALT (BELOW) OR SEA SALT

1/4 CUP WATER

1/4 TO 1/2 CUP VEGAN SHREDDED CHEESE (OPTIONAL)

1/8 TEASPOON PAPRIKA

FRESH GROUND BLACK PEPPER

SERVES 2 TO 4

QUICK & EASY
GLUTEN-FREE

Heat the butter in a large skillet over medium heat. Stir in the onion and bell pepper and cook, stirring, until the onions are soft, about 2 to 3 minutes.

Stir in the mashed tofu, nutritional yeast, turmeric, and salt. Cook, stirring, until the tofu is heated through, about 2 minutes.

Stir in the water, cover the skillet, and cook until the water evaporates, about 3 minutes.

Stir in the cheese, if using, and the paprika. Taste and adjust the seasoning using more salt or black salt, if needed. Cover the skillet again and cook until the cheese melts, about 1 minute. Serve hot.

Black Salt

Also known as kala namak, this pungent-smelling purplish rock salt is often used in Indian cuisine. In vegan food, it offers an eggy flavor and aroma. It cooks out when heated, so add the bulk of the black salt after the dish is done cooking. In addition, keep in mind that kala namak is salty, so balance the black salt and the sea salt (or table salt) thoughtfully. Black salt is readily available in Indian grocers or online. It is more expensive online, so try to find an Indian grocer before making an online purchase.

Fried Vegan Omelet

Omelets were a favorite breakfast of my husband during childhood. This is a wonderful replacement. Whether making a plain omelet, stuffed omelet, or sandwich version, this easy dish will please anyone. (See photo on page 204.)

14-OUNCES SOFT, FIRM, OR EXTRA-FIRM TOFU, PATTED DRY AND ROUGHLY CRUMBLED

1/4 CUP PLAIN UNSWEETENED VEGAN MILK

1/4 CUP UNBLEACHED ALL-PURPOSE FLOUR OR WHOLE WHEAT FLOUR

1/4 CUP NUTRITIONAL YEAST FLAKES

1 TEASPOON SEA SALT

1/4 TEASPOON GROUND TURMERIC

PINCH FRESH GROUND BLACK PEPPER

1 GARLIC CLOVE, ROUGHLY CHOPPED

OIL SPRAY OR OLIVE OIL, AS NEEDED

BLACK SALT (PAGE 206) (OPTIONAL)

OPTIONAL FILLINGS: VEGAN CHEESE, SAUTÉED SPINACH, MUSHROOMS, ONIONS OR PEPPERS

SERVES 4

QUICK & EASY

Blend the tofu, milk, flour, nutritional yeast, salt, turmeric, black pepper, and garlic in a blender or food processor into a smooth, thick batter, scraping down the sides as needed. Taste and adjust the seasoning, if needed, with salt and pepper.

Preheat a large non-stick skillet or well-seasoned cast iron skillet over medium heat. Spray the pan with oil or spread with a small amount of olive oil.

Pour 1/2 cup of the batter into the pan. Use a spatula to spread it to about 1/4-inch thick. If you accidentally scrape up some batter, just spread it back.

Cook the omelet until the surface looks dull and very dry, about 4 minutes. Lift up a corner and check if it has brown flecks all over the bottom side, including the center. Flip the omelet with a spatula when it is no longer sticking to the pan. Cook the other side the same way, about 2 minutes. Push down on the omelet with a spatula to cook the inside. Sprinkle with black salt, if using.

Optional fillings: If adding cheese, sprinkle the omelet with the cheese, fold in half, cover the pan, and cook on low until the cheese melts. If adding vegetables, repeat the same procedure, but cook the omelet only until the vegetables are heated through. Serve hot.

VARIATION: Fried Vegan Omelet Sandwich. Spread mayonnaise on toasted bread and add slices of tomato, slivers of red onion, and a plain or cheese omelet.

Quick Breakfast Recipes

Try any of these super-easy ideas for a quick and delicious way to start your day:

Strawberry Smoothie: Blend 1 sliced frozen banana, 1 cup frozen strawberries, 1 cup vegan milk, and sweetener to taste in a blender until smooth.

Nut Butter English Muffin: Toast an English muffin. Spread with nut butter. Top with slices of apples or bananas.

Breakfast Sandwich: Place leftover scrambles or Benedict tofu eggs on toasted bread with slices of tomato and vegan mayo.

Breakfast BLT: Place leftover Bacon Tofu on toasted English muffins with mayo, lettuce and tomato. If you have any leftover, throw on some scramble or omelet.

Breakfast Parfait: Layer vegan yogurt, granola, and fresh fruit in a cup or glass.

Strawberry Oatmeal: Make regular oatmeal. Top it with a dollop of vegan sour cream, strawberry (or other fruit), and sprinkling of brown sugar.

Hot Cereal with Apple Butter: Cook hot cereal or farina. Swirl in a few tablespoons of apple butter and sprinkle with toasted walnuts.

Breakfast Quinoa: Follow the directions for making quinoa on page 111, but replace the liquid with vegan milk and replace the garlic with 3 tablespoons of brown sugar. Cook as directed. Toss the cooked quinoa with fresh chopped fruit. Sprinkle with cinnamon.

Toast with Yogurt: You can spread toast of any kind with vegan yogurt, nut butter, apple butter, vegan cream cheese, or fruit preserve and sprinkle with nuts or add slices of fruit.

Oatmeal or Yogurt: Stir in a few tablespoons of fruit preserves or crushed pineapple. Add a few crushed nuts.

Breakfast Quesadillas: Lightly butter a flour tortilla, place in a warm skillet, add a few tablespoons of vegan cheese and slices of granny smith apple, and fold in half. Cook until golden brown; flip and cook on the other side.

Waffles: Cook a bunch of waffles, freeze them and use them as needed.

Oatmeal and Pumpkin: Make regular oatmeal. Stir in a few tablespoons of pumpkin puree and a shake of pumpkin pie spice; sweeten to taste.

Strawberry Cream Cheese Bagels: Mix 1 cup vegan cream cheese with 1 tablespoon strawberry fruit preserve. Serve with toasted bagels.

Tex-Mex Migas

Having grown up in Texas, a few miles from the Mexican border, my husband constantly reminisced about the beloved migas his mother used to make on Sunday mornings. He is quite pleased with this version of the traditionally egg-based dish. Turn these amped-up breakfast burritos into a feast: serve with Refried Beans (page 200) or Mexican Red Rice and Beans (page 158).

1 MEDIUM POBLANO CHILE

14-OUNCES SOFT, FIRM, OR EXTRA-FIRM TOFU, PATTED DRY AND MASHED WELL

2 TABLESPOONS NUTRITIONAL YEAST FLAKES

1/8 TEASPOON GROUND TURMERIC

3 TABLESPOONS GRAPESEED OR SUNFLOWER OIL, DIVIDED

4 (5-INCH) CORN TORTILLAS

1/2 SMALL ONION, FINELY CHOPPED

1/2 TEASPOON MILD CHILI POWDER

3/4 CUP SALSA FRESCA (PAGE 23)

BLACK SALT (PAGE 206), SEA SALT AND BLACK PEPPER

1/2 CUP SHREDDED VEGAN CHEESE (OPTIONAL)

FLOUR TORTILLAS, OR MORE CORN TORTILLAS, FOR SERVING (OPTIONAL)

VEGAN SOUR CREAM (OPTIONAL)

SERVES 4 TO 6

QUICK & EASY
GLUTEN-FREE OPTION

Heat a small dry skillet over medium-high heat. Add the poblano and cook until blackened on all sides, 4 minutes. Transfer to a bowl, cover tightly, and let it steam for 10 minutes. Peel the chile by rubbing the skin off. Remove the stem and seeds and cut the chile into 1/2-inch dice. Set aside.

Combine the mashed tofu, nutritional yeast, and turmeric in a medium bowl. Set aside.

Prepare a paper-towel lined plate. Heat 2 tablespoons of oil in a large skillet over medium heat. Fry each corn tortilla, one at a time, in the hot oil until crisp, about 1 minute, flipping after 30 seconds. Drain on paper towels. When cooled enough to handle, cut the tortillas into 1-inch squares. Set aside.

Heat 1 tablespoon of oil in the same large skillet. Add the onion and cook until softened and lightly browned, about 5 minutes. Stir in the chili powder and reserved pepper and tofu mixture. Cook, stirring, until the tofu is dry and getting golden, about 5 minutes.

Stir in the salsa, cover, and cook for another 2 minutes. Uncover and season to taste with black salt, sea salt, and black pepper. Stir in the reserved corn tortilla pieces and the cheese, if using. Cover and cook until the cheese melts. Uncover and cook the tofu, undisturbed, for another few minutes to develop a bit of a crust on the bottom. Serve the migas in warmed tortillas with more salsa and sour cream, if desired.

Classic-Style Benedict

Making Benedict is a monthly event at our house. It is a weekend brunch meal, but well worth the effort, and can be quick to make, especially if you have vegan bacon on hand. Like the egg-based version, this dish is rich and scrumptious and covered with Hollandaise sauce.

1/2 CUP VEGAN MAYONNAISE, STOREBOUGHT OR HOMEMADE (PAGE 31)

5 TABLESPOONS VEGAN BUTTER, DIVIDED

2 TABLESPOONS PLAIN UNSWEETENED VEGAN MILK

2 TEASPOONS FRESH LEMON JUICE

1 TEASPOON DIJON MUSTARD

1/2 TEASPOON GROUND TURMERIC, DIVIDED

1/4 TEASPOON SEA SALT

PINCH OF CAYENNE

FRESH GROUND BLACK PEPPER

14-OUNCES SOFT TOFU, PATTED DRY

3/4 CUP WATER

1/4 CUP NUTRITIONAL YEAST FLAKES

1/4 TEASPOON BLACK SALT (PAGE 206) (OPTIONAL)

6 ENGLISH MUFFINS, SPLIT AND TOASTED

12 SLICES BACON TOFU (PAGE 36) OR STOREBOUGHT VEGAN BACON

———————

SERVES 6

QUICK & EASY

For the Hollandaise sauce, combine the mayonnaise, 2 tablespoons butter, milk, lemon juice, mustard, 1/4 teaspoon turmeric, sea salt, cayenne, and black pepper to taste in a medium glass bowl. Whisk well to combine. Heat the sauce either in a microwave in 30 second intervals, whisking in between intervals, until hot, or place the bowl over a double boiler, whisking occasionally, until hot, about 10 minutes. Set the sauce aside but keep warm.

Cut the tofu block in half crosswise. Cut each half crosswise into 6 square slabs. Melt 1 tablespoon of the butter in a large skillet. Cook the tofu squares in the skillet until lightly browned, about 2 minutes per side. Remove from the heat, drain, and set aside.

Heat the water, nutritional yeast, black salt, and 1/4 teaspoon turmeric in a medium saucepan. Bring to a boil, reduce to a simmer, and add the browned tofu to the broth. Simmer for 5 minutes. Remove the tofu from the heat and set aside but keep warm.

Heat 1 tablespoon of butter in the large skillet previously used over medium heat. Cook the vegan bacon until heated through, about 30 seconds per side.

To assemble, butter each half of the toasted English muffins, arrange a slice of bacon on each half, transfer a piece of drained tofu onto each bacon slice, and spoon about 2 tablespoons of sauce on top. Serve hot.

Country Hash

Hash should have a crispy crust, creamy potatoes, flavorful herbs and spices, and plenty of kick. This hash will not disappoint. It's a far cry from the same-old tofu scramble you might be used to.

1 POUND RUSSET POTATOES, CUT INTO 1/2-INCH DICE

1 BAY LEAF

2 TABLESPOONS VEGAN BUTTER, DIVIDED

14-OUNCES SOFT OR FIRM TOFU, PRESSED FOR 10 MINUTES AND MASHED

2 TABLESPOONS NUTRITIONAL YEAST FLAKES

1/4 TEASPOON BLACK SALT (PAGE 206), OPTIONAL

1/8 TEASPOON GROUND TURMERIC

1 MEDIUM ONION, FINELY CHOPPED

2 GARLIC CLOVES, MINCED

2 TEASPOONS DRIED CHIVES

3/4 TEASPOON SEA SALT

1/4 TEASPOON FRESH OR DRIED THYME

1/4 TEASPOON DRIED OREGANO

1/8 TEASPOON FRESH OR DRIED DILL

1/8 TEASPOON GROUND CORIANDER

FRESH GROUND BLACK PEPPER

1 CUP CANNED BLACK-EYED PEAS, RINSED AND DRAINED

1/8 TEASPOON CAYENNE

GARNISH: 1 SCALLION, FINELY CHOPPED

SERVES 4

QUICK & EASY
GLUTEN-FREE

Place the potatoes and bay leaf in a medium saucepan with just enough water to cover and bring to a boil, then reduce to a simmer. Cook for 5 minutes, then drain and set aside. Remove and discard the bay leaf.

In a medium bowl, combine the mashed tofu, nutritional yeast, black salt, and turmeric. Set aside.

Heat 1 tablespoon of butter in a large skillet over medium heat. Stir in the onion, garlic, and chives. Cook, stirring, until softened, about 3 minutes.

Stir the drained potatoes into the onion mixture. Stir in the salt, thyme, oregano, dill, coriander, and black pepper, to taste. Cook until the potatoes are tender, stirring occasionally, about 10 minutes. When the potatoes begin to stick to the the pan, add 2 tablespoons of water to the pan and use a sturdy spatula to stir. This will help the potatoes cook as well as avoid having to add more butter each time. You may add up to 1/2 cup of water to the pan in increments.

When the potatoes are tender and nicely browned, stir in 1 tablespoon of butter, reserved tofu, and black-eyed peas. Season with cayenne, salt, and black pepper as needed. For a crispy crust, firmly press down on the mixture with the back of the spatula. Cook until a light crust develops on the bottom, about 2 minutes. Flip portions of the hash, press down with a spatula again, and cook in the same way for a few minutes. Repeat as needed. Serve garnished with scallions.

Chef's Tip: If you are using canned beans, freeze the remaining legumes in an airtight container for future use.

Southern Biscuits and Gravy

Biscuits and gravy are a southern breakfast staple. This creamy gravy, with your choice of vegan protein, over flaky biscuits is a great way to serve leftover biscuits, if you have any, or you can just make a fresh batch. This gravy also pairs very well with the Garlicky Greens (page 196), with or without biscuits.

1 1/2 CUPS WATER

1 1/2 TABLESPOONS SAVORY BROTH MIX (PAGE 19)

1/4 CUP GRAPESEED OR SUNFLOWER OIL

1 SMALL ONION, FINELY CHOPPED

3 GARLIC CLOVES, MINCED

1/2 TEASPOON FRESH OR DRIED THYME LEAVES

1/4 TEASPOON FENNEL SEEDS

1 1/2 CUPS MARINATED TOFU (PAGE 34), TENDER SOY CURLS (PAGE 35), 4 SIMPLE SEITAN CUTLETS (PAGE 40), OR THREE LINKS STOREBOUGHT VEGAN SAUSAGE, FINELY CHOPPED

1/4 CUP UNBLEACHED ALL-PURPOSE FLOUR

1 1/2 CUPS PLAIN UNSWEETENED VEGAN MILK

SEA SALT AND FRESH GROUND BLACK PEPPER

2 TABLESPOONS FINELY CHOPPED FRESH SAGE, OR TO TASTE (OPTIONAL)

8 FLAKY BUTTERMILK HERB BISCUITS (PAGE 239)

SERVES 4

QUICK & EASY

Combine the water and broth mix in a measuring cup or small bowl. Set aside.

Heat the oil in a large skillet over medium heat. Stir in the onions, garlic, thyme, and fennel seeds. Cook, stirring, until the onions begin to brown, about 4 minutes.

Stir in the chopped protein and cook, stirring, until golden brown, about 5 minutes. Stir in the flour and cook, stirring, for 1 minute. Stir in the reserved prepared broth, whisking to avoid lumps. Stir in the milk. Bring the gravy to a boil, reduce to simmer, and simmer until thickened, about 5 minutes. Season the gravy to taste with salt and black pepper. Stir in the sage, if using. Serve the gravy over warmed split biscuits.

Oat Flour

Grind rolled oats into flour by blending the oats in a dry blender jar or personal blender until finely ground. If needing a certain amount, grind a little more than you need. For example, grind 1/2 cup plus 1 tablespoon of rolled oats to yield about 1/2 cup of oat flour.

Fluffy Buttermilk Pancakes

Fluffy, buttery, hearty pancakes love to soak up the sweet maple syrup you pour over them. These pancakes are easy and quick to make; ready for a meal anytime—morning, noon, or midnight.

1 3/4 CUPS PLAIN UNSWEETENED VEGAN MILK

3 TABLESPOONS VEGAN BUTTER, MELTED OR GRAPESEED OR SUNFLOWER OIL

2 TABLESPOONS APPLE CIDER VINEGAR

1 TEASPOON PURE VANILLA EXTRACT

3 TABLESPOONS PACKED BROWN SUGAR

2 TABLESPOONS FLAX SEED MEAL

3/4 CUP OAT FLOUR

3/4 CUP WHOLE WHEAT FLOUR

1/3 CUP UNBLEACHED ALL-PURPOSE FLOUR

1/4 CUP FINELY CHOPPED TOASTED WALNUTS

1 TEASPOON DOUBLE-ACTING BAKING POW-DER

1/2 TEASPOONS BAKING SODA

———————

SERVES 4

QUICK & EASY

CHEF'S TIP: The skillet will heat up in between batches. In order to avoid cooking the pancakes too fast, and risk burning them on the outside, remove the skillet from the heat when you add the second and each subsequent round of pancake batter. Just those few seconds off the heat will cool your skillet enough to continue to cook the pancakes evenly.

Combine the milk, butter, vinegar, vanilla, sugar and flax meal in a medium bowl. Mix well and set aside.

Combine the flours and nuts in a separate medium bowl. Sift in the baking powder and soda. Mix well with a whisk.

Add the flour mixture to the milk mixture. Using a whisk, gently mix the batter until there are no big lumps. A few small lumps are fine. Allow the batter to sit while you preheat the skillet, about 3 minutes.

Heat a large skillet or griddle over medium heat. Add a few drops of water to the skillet; when it sizzles the skillet is heated.

Spray the skillet with oil or spread it with a 1/2 teaspoon of neutral-tasting oil. Reduce the heat to medium-low. This will cook the inside of the pancake without burning the outside. The total time to cook the pancakes throughout is around 3 minutes. Adjust the temperature of the skillet until a pancake takes about that long to cook without burning the outside.

Add the pancake batter to the skillet in 1/4 cup portions. Cook as many pancakes as will comfortably fit in the skillet without touching. When the pancakes are bubbling and the edges are dry, about 2 minutes, flip the pancakes gently so they do not deflate. Cook the pancakes on the other side until golden brown, about 1 minute.

Repeat until all the pancakes are cooked. Serve warm with vegan butter, maple syrup, jam, or sliced fruit.

French Toast with Apple and Candied Nut Topping

This recipe makes French toast that tastes just like its egg-based counterpart. The quick trip to the oven ensures that the toast is creamy on the inside and crunchy on the outside. The decadent apple and candied nut topping is completely optional, making this an easy everyday meal. Whether you choose to make the topping or not, serve the French toast with maple syrup or warm Caramel Sauce (page 224). To make this dish soy free, use a soy-free vegan butter.

2 CUPS PLAIN, UNSWEETENED VEGAN MILK

1/4 CUP PLUS 2 TABLESPOONS FLAX SEED MEAL

1/4 CUP ARROWROOT STARCH

1 TEASPOON GROUND CINNAMON, DIVIDED

1/4 TEASPOON SEA SALT

1 TABLESPOON VEGAN BUTTER, PLUS MORE FOR SAUTÉING

2 TABLESPOONS PACKED BROWN SUGAR

1/4 CUP CHOPPED RAW PECANS OR WALNUTS

2 MEDIUM APPLES, ANY KIND, PEELED AND CUT INTO 1/2-INCH DICE

1/4 TEASPOON FRESHLY GRATED NUTMEG

10 OUNCES STALE FRENCH BREAD, CUT INTO 3/4-INCH SLICES OR 8 SLICES OF BREAD OR GLUTEN-FREE BREAD

SERVES 4 TO 6

QUICK & EASY
GLUTEN-FREE OPTION
SOY-FREE OPTION

Combine the milk, flax meal, arrowroot, 1/2 teaspoon cinnamon, and salt in a shallow baking dish. Mix with a whisk and set aside to thicken for 10 minutes.

Melt 1 tablespoon butter in a medium saucepan over medium heat. Add the sugar, nuts, and pinch of salt. Cook, stirring, for 3 minutes to melt the sugar and coat the nuts. Remove the nuts to a work surface to cool. Add the apples, 1/2 teaspoon cinnamon, and nutmeg to the same saucepan. Cook the apples until tender, 5 to 7 minutes. Set aside, but keep warm. When the nuts are cool enough to handle, coarsely chop them and add them to the cooked apples.

Melt enough butter in a large skillet or electric griddle over medium heat to coat the bottom of the skillet. Stir the reserved batter and soak as many bread slices as will fit in your skillet. Soak the bread in the batter long enough to absorb some of the mixture; the more stale the bread the longer they can soak. Preheat the oven to 400°F.

Remove the bread from the batter, allowing excess batter to drip off, and transfer to the heated skillet. Cook until golden brown on the bottom, about 1 minute. Flip and cook the other side until golden, 1 minute. Transfer to a platter and set aside until all the bread is cooked, then transfer the bread to a greased baking sheet. Bake the toast until crispy on the outside, about 8 to 10 minutes. Serve with the topping.

Flaky Buttermilk Herb Biscuits (page 239)

CHAPTER 11

Desserts & Bakery

In our family, baked goods and sweets are a must. Some of my favorite sweets in this chapter are the Chocolate Chip Cookies and Fudge Brownies, partly because they remind me of my childhood and partly because they will remind my children of theirs. Since a good bakery is not limited to sweets, the Corn Muffins (which are moist and full of corn flavor) and Flaky Buttermilk Herb Biscuits (which are actually flaky) will have you convinced that a vegan bakery is delightfully delicious. Since I don't bake often, I insist that anything I do bake is spot-on in flavors and results. Baking takes time, and in this book there is only room for fantastic recipes.

Fudge Brownies

These rich and decadent brownies are easy to prepare but make sure not to over- or under-cook them. Some crumbs should still be clinging to the test toothpick when the brownies are ready.

2/3 CUP UNBLEACHED ALL-PURPOSE FLOUR

1/4 CUP UNSWEETENED COCOA POWDER

1/2 TEASPOON DOUBLE-ACTING BAKING POW-DER

1/4 TEASPOON SEA SALT

1/3 CUP (2 OUNCES) SEMI-SWEET CHOCOLATE CHIPS

1/4 CUP GRAPESEED OR SUNFLOWER OIL

2 TABLESPOONS MASHED RIPE BANANA

2 TEASPOON PURE VANILLA EXTRACT

2/3 CUP NATURAL SUGAR

1/3 CUP PLAIN UNSWEETENED VEGAN MILK

1 TABLESPOON FLAX SEED MEAL

1/3 CUP SEMI-SWEET CHOCOLATE CHIPS (OP-TIONAL)

1/3 CUP FINELY CHOPPED TOASTED NUTS (OP-TIONAL)

CARAMEL SAUCE (PAGE 224), AS NEEDED (OP-TIONAL)

MAKES 12 SMALL BROWNIES

Preheat the oven to 325°F. Line the bottom of an 8-inch square baking dish with a long strip of parchment paper, folding the paper as needed. The paper should hang out of the top of the pan; when the brownies are baked you then lift up on the two opposite edges of the paper to cleanly remove the brownie from the pan. Alternatively, generously oil the pan and set aside.

In a bowl, sift together the flour, cocoa, and baking powder. Stir in the salt and set aside.

Melt the chocolate chips and oil in a small bowl in the microwave in 30-second intervals until soft. Alternatively, melt the chips and oil in a double boiler. Stir the chips and oil until combined.

Using a blender or electric hand mixer, blend the melted chips and oil, banana, vanilla, sugar, milk, and flax meal until combined. Stir the flour mixture into the wet mixture. Fold in the chocolate chips, if using. Transfer the batter to the prepared baking pan. Sprinkle with the nuts, if using.

Bake until a toothpick inserted in the middle of the pan comes out with a few moist crumbs attached but no wet batter, 20 to 45 minutes, depending on the kind of pan you use. Glass baking dishes need longer baking time. If your toothpick comes out completely dry, the brownie has over-baked, but is still tasty. Cool in the pan on a wire rack for 30 minutes. Remove the brownies by pulling up on the parchment paper overhang. Cut into squares. Drizzle with Caramel Sauce, if desired.

Caramel Sauce Over Vanilla Ice Cream

In addition to being a delicious topping for ice cream, the caramel sauce can also be used to top pancakes, French toast, brownies, and cake. Make this dish soy free by using soy-free vegan butter and ice cream.

2 TABLESPOONS VEGAN BUTTER

1 CUP NATURAL SUGAR

1/2 CUP PLAIN UNSWEETENED VEGAN MILK

1 TEASPOON PURE VANILLA EXTRACT

VEGAN VANILLA ICE CREAM, TO SERVE

––––––––––

SERVES 4

QUICK & EASY

GLUTEN-FREE

SOY-FREE OPTION

Melt the butter in a medium saucepan over medium heat. Add the sugar all at once and do not stir. Cook the sugar until it starts to melt, about 3 minutes. When some of the sugar has melted, stir gently to prevent it from burning as it melts further, breaking up any large chunks with a wooden spoon. Completely melt the sugar (some pieces of sugar floating in the liquid is okay), about 5 more minutes, stirring frequently. It should be a light caramel color.

Remove the pan from the heat, carefully add the milk and stir. The mixture will foam and bubble. Return the pan to the heat and stir with a sturdy wooden spoon until the hardened sugar dissolves; this can take up to 5 minutes, and the mixture will again start to foam as it boils.

Remove from the heat, stir in the vanilla, cool slightly, and strain the sauce to remove any un-melted sugar lumps, if desired. The sauce will thicken as it cools.

Serve warm over the ice cream. If not using right away, the sauce can be stored in an airtight container in the refrigerator for 4 weeks. To thin the cooled sauce, reheat it over low heat.

Apple Crumble

This crumble is very easy to throw together and is just sweet enough without being over the top, making it an ideal everyday dessert.

5 MEDIUM APPLES (ANY KIND)

3 TABLESPOONS MAPLE SYRUP

1 TEASPOON ARROWROOT STARCH

1/2 TEASPOON LEMON ZEST

1/2 TEASPOON FINELY GRATED GINGER

1/2 CUP OLD-FASHIONED ROLLED OATS, DIVIDED

1 CUP WHOLE RAW PECANS OR WALNUTS

1/4 CUP PACKED BROWN SUGAR

1/2 CUP COLD VEGAN BUTTER, CUT INTO PIECES

2 TEASPOONS PURE VANILLA EXTRACT

1/2 TEASPOON GROUND CINNAMON

1/4 TEASPOON FRESH GROUND NUTMEG

CARAMEL SAUCE (PAGE 224) OR VEGAN ICE CREAM (OPTIONAL)

SERVES 4 TO 6

GLUTEN-FREE
SOY-FREE OPTION

Preheat the oven to 400°F. Peel the apples. Core them and cut them into about 1/2-inch pieces. Combine the apples, maple syrup, arrowroot, zest and ginger in a large bowl and mix well with a large spoon. Transfer the apple mixture to a 9-inch square glass baking dish. Bake the apples for 10 minutes.

Place 1/4 cup of the oats in a food processor and process into flour. Add the remaining 1/4 cup oats, nuts, sugar, butter, vanilla, cinnamon, and nutmeg to the food processor. Pulse the mixture about 10 times and set aside.

After the apples have baked for 10 minutes, carefully remove the baking dish from the oven and place it on a heat-resistant surface. Reduce the oven temperature to 375°F.

Evenly arrange the topping mixture over the apples. Return the baking dish to the oven and continue to bake the crumble until the apples are tender, about 30 minutes. Cool the crumble for 10 minutes before serving with optional caramel sauce or vegan ice cream.

Chocolate Chip Cookies

These cookies are crisp on the outside and chewy on the inside. Full of just the right amount of chocolate chips to actually be able to taste the cookie, these are like the ones mom used to make.

1 1/2 CUPS UNBLEACHED ALL-PURPOSE FLOUR

3/4 TEASPOONS BAKING SODA

1/4 TEASPOON SEA SALT

1/2 CUP (1 STICK) VEGAN BUTTER

2 TABLESPOONS APPLESAUCE

1/3 CUP PACKED BROWN SUGAR

1/2 CUP NATURAL SUGAR

1 TABLESPOON PURE VANILLA EXTRACT

2 TABLESPOONS PLAIN UNSWEETENED VEGAN MILK

1/2 CUP VEGAN SEMI-SWEET CHOCOLATE CHIPS

1/4 TO 1/2 CUP FINELY CHOPPED TOASTED NUTS (OPTIONAL)

MAKES 18 COOKIES

QUICK & EASY

Preheat oven to 375°F. Line two baking sheets with silicone baking mats or parchment paper.

Combine the flour, baking soda, and salt in a large bowl. Stir well and set aside. Melt the butter in the microwave or on the stovetop.

In a medium bowl, combine the melted butter, applesauce, sugars, vanilla, and milk. Whisk vigorously for 20 seconds.

Stir the dry mixture into the wet mixture until just combined. (Do not overmix.) Fold in the chocolate chips and the optional nuts.

Drop heaping tablespoons of dough 2 inches apart onto the prepared baking sheets.

Bake for 6 minutes, rotate the baking sheets, and continue to bake for 5 to 6 minutes, or until the cookies are browning around the edges. Cool on the baking sheet for 5 minutes, then transfer to a wire rack to cool completely.

Desserts Without Eggs?

A common misconception in the baking world is that eggs are necessary for successful baking. The fact is, there are lots of natural plant-based binders that can achieve fantastic results, such as mashed bananas, ground flaxseeds mixed with water, applesauce, and many others.

Whether you want to make cookies, cakes, or other desserts, they can all be made vegan. Since baking is more of a science than an art, substituting vegan binders, leaveners, or emulsifiers can be a trial-and-error process. The good news is there are lots of great tried-and-true recipes in this chapter for your favorite baked goods.

Apricot and Raisin Rugelach

These rugelach cookies are light and crisp with an apricot and nut filling. The dough is made with vegan cream cheese and vegan butter and, therefore, needs an overnight chill to firm up. They require a little planning, but the reward is melt-in-your-mouth perfection.

8 TABLESPOONS (1 STICK) VEGAN BUTTER, CUT INTO CUBES

1/2 CUP VEGAN CREAM CHEESE

2 TABLESPOONS NATURAL SUGAR

1 TEASPOON PURE VANILLA EXTRACT

1/4 TEASPOON SEA SALT, PLUS A PINCH

1 2/3 CUP UNBLEACHED ALL-PURPOSE FLOUR, PLUS MORE FOR ROLLING

1/2 CUP RAW WALNUTS OR PECANS, FINELY MINCED OR GROUND

1/4 CUP RAISINS

2 TABLESPOONS BROWN SUGAR

1 TEASPOON GROUND CINNAMON

6 TABLESPOONS APRICOT PRESERVES, DIVIDED

MAKES 24 COOKIES

Combine the butter, cream cheese, sugar, vanilla, and 1/4 teaspoon salt in a food processor. Process to cream the butter and cream cheese. Add the flour and pulse just to combine the dough into a ball.

Divide the dough into two pieces, shape them into disks, and wrap them in plastic wrap. Chill the dough overnight to firm up. Preheat the oven to 375°F. Line two baking sheets with parchment paper.

Combine the ground walnuts, raisins, brown sugar, cinnamon, and a pinch of salt in a small bowl. Mix well and set aside.

Roll each dough disk into a circle about 1/8-inch thick on a lightly floured surface. The dough will be delicate. Spread 3 tablespoons of apricot preserves over the surface of the dough with an off-set spatula or the back of a spoon. Sprinkle half of the filling over the preserves. Slice the dough into quarter wedges using a pizza cutter or knife, as if you were cutting a pizza pie. Cut each quarter wedge into three wedges, for a total of 12 wedges of cookie dough. Roll each wedge of dough into a crescent, starting at the wide edge and ending at the pointed end.

Transfer each cookie, pointed side down, to the prepared baking sheet. Bake for 20 minutes or until lightly browned, rotating the baking sheets half-way through. Cool on the baking sheet for 3 minutes before moving the cookies to a wire rack to cool completely. Store in an airtight container for up to a week.

Fruit Cobbler

This is an easy dessert to have on the table by the time dinner is eaten. Put it in the oven before you sit down to the meal and enjoy it within an hour. Use your choice of blueberries, cherries, peaches, apples, or blackberries for the fruit in this cobbler. It's best served warm with vegan ice cream.

Topping:

2 CUPS UNBLEACHED ALL-PURPOSE FLOUR

1 TABLESPOON DOUBLE-ACTING BAKING POWDER

1/2 TEASPOON SEA SALT

1/4 CUP PLUS 1 TABLESPOON NATURAL SUGAR, DIVIDED

1/4 CUP GRAPESEED OR SUNFLOWER OIL

1/2 CUP PLAIN UNSWEETENED VEGAN MILK

Filling:

6 CUPS FROZEN FRUIT, WELL THAWED AND WELL DRAINED

1/2 TO 3/4 CUP NATURAL SUGAR

1/4 CUP ARROWROOT STARCH

1/4 TEASPOON SEA SALT

ZEST OF 1 LEMON

SERVES 6 TO 8

Topping: Combine the flour, baking powder, salt, and 1/4 cup sugar in a food processor. Pulse to mix the ingredients. Add the oil and pulse to combine. Add the milk and process the dough until it comes together into a ball. Alternatively, use your hands to gently knead it into a ball. Place the dough in an airtight container and refrigerate for at least 30 minutes. If the dough is chilled for longer than 1 hour, bring it to room temperature for 15 minutes before rolling. Preheat the oven to 375°F about 15 minutes before baking the cobbler.

Filling: Combine the fruit, sugar, arrowroot, salt, and zest in a medium bowl. Use 1/2 cup sugar if the fruit is very sweet and more sugar if the fruit is tart. Mix well to combine. Transfer to a deep 2-quart baking dish. Bake for 15 minutes, stirring the fruit after 7 minutes.

Remove the dough from the refrigerator and roll it out on a lightly floured work surface. The dough should be rolled out to be slightly smaller than the baking dish.

Carefully remove the baking dish from the oven and transfer the rolled dough onto the hot fruit filling; use caution. If it is too difficult to move the entire dough to the hot dish, cut the dough into manageable shapes to transfer the dough. Arrange the dough pieces in a single layer over the fruit filling. Sprinkle with 1 tablespoon of sugar. Return the cobbler to the oven and continue to bake it until the topping is golden brown and the fruit filling is tender and bubbling, about 30 more minutes. Cool on a wire cooling rack for 20 minutes before serving.

Carrot Cake with Cream Cheese Frosting

My family adores carrot cake, but unfortunately, many carrot cakes are either too dense, too oily, too spiced, or too sweet. This recipe is balanced perfectly. The cake is delicious with or without the frosting.

Cake:

1/2 CUP APPLESAUCE

1/2 CUP GRAPESEED OR SUNFLOWER OIL

1/3 CUP PLAIN UNSWEETENED VEGAN MILK

1/4 CUP PACKED BROWN SUGAR

1/4 CUP NATURAL SUGAR

1 TEASPOON PURE VANILLA EXTRACT

1 1/2 CUPS COARSELY SHREDDED CARROTS

1 1/4 CUPS UNBLEACHED ALL-PURPOSE FLOUR

1/4 TEASPOON SEA SALT

3/4 TEASPOON GROUND CINNAMON

1/4 TEASPOON FRESH GROUND NUTMEG

1/4 TEASPOON CARDAMOM OR ALLSPICE

3/4 TEASPOON DOUBLE-ACTING BAKING POWDER

1/2 TEASPOON BAKING SODA

Frosting:

1/4 CUP VEGAN BUTTER

1/4 CUP VEGAN CREAM CHEESE

1/2 CUP SIFTED POWDERED SUGAR

1/4 TEASPOON PURE VANILLA EXTRACT

1/4 CUP TOASTED AND COARSELY CHOPPED WALNUTS OR PECANS

———

SERVES 8

Preheat the oven to 350°F. Lightly grease a 8- or 9-inch square baking dish.

Cake: Combine the applesauce, oil, milk, sugars, and vanilla in a medium bowl. Whisk well to combine. Add the carrots, mix gently, and set aside.

Combine the flour, salt, cinnamon, nutmeg, and cardamom in a separate large bowl. Sift in the baking powder and baking soda. Stir well to combine.

Transfer the dry mixture to the wet mixture. Using a sturdy wooden spoon or spatula, mix gently just to combine. Transfer the batter to the prepared baking pan.

Bake until a toothpick inserted into the center of the cake comes out clean, about 25 to 35 minutes. Remove the cake from the oven and cool completely on a wire rack.

Frosting: combine the butter and cream cheese in a medium bowl. Use a sturdy whisk or hand mixer to beat them until fluffy. Add the powdered sugar and vanilla and continue to mix until well blended.

When the cake is completely cool, run a knife around the edges of the pan and invert the cake onto a plate. Flip the cake over onto a separate plate. Frost the cake with an off-set spatula or regular spatula, sprinkle with the nuts, and serve.

Blueberry Scones

Scones are a relative of biscuits. They are tender, flaky, and light. These scones have the added benefits of blueberries and lemon. The glaze is completely optional, but even just a little bit is delightful; it adds a sweet, lemony zing and takes no time to prepare. They are best when eaten warm out of the oven.

3 CUPS UNBLEACHED ALL-PURPOSE FLOUR

1 TABLESPOON DOUBLE-ACTING BAKING POWDER

1/2 TEASPOON PLUS A PINCH SEA SALT

6 TABLESPOONS VEGAN BUTTER

1/4 CUP NATURAL SUGAR

ZEST OF 1 LEMON

1 CUP PLAIN OR VANILLA VEGAN MILK

1 1/2 TEASPOONS APPLE CIDER VINEGAR

3/4 CUP THAWED AND WELL-DRAINED FROZEN BLUEBERRIES

1 CUP CONFECTIONERS' SUGAR, SIFTED

1 1/2 TABLESPOONS FRESH LEMON JUICE

MAKES 8 SCONES

QUICK & EASY

Sift Your Sugar First

If you are making the glaze, which my daughter would encourage you to do, be sure to sift your confectioners' sugar before using. It saves tons of frustration! Most, and especially organic, confectioners' sugar has lumps that are nearly impossible to whisk out. It's easier to sift and crush the pebbles of sugar while they are dry.

Preheat the oven to 400°F. Lightly oil a baking sheet or line it with parchment paper.

Mix the flour, baking powder, and salt in a medium bowl. Add the butter. With a pastry knife or your fingers, cut the butter into the flour until it is the size of peas. Stir in the sugar and zest. Chill the bowl of flour in the freezer for 10 minutes.

Mix the milk, vinegar, and blueberries in a small bowl. Chill the milk mixture in the freezer while the flour is chilling.

Add the milk mixture to the flour mixture. Using a large spoon, gently mix the milk and flour until just combined; the dough will seem dry. Turn the dough out onto a lightly floured surface. Knead gently to combine and form into a 1-inch thick rectangle. (Kneading with a heavy hand will burst the blueberries and create a wet dough.) At this point the dough will be sticky.

Cut the dough into 8 equal pieces (triangles are traditional) and transfer them to the prepared baking sheet, about 1 inch apart. Bake until they are light golden brown on top, 15 to 18 minutes.

Combine the confectioners' sugar, lemon juice, and a pinch of salt in a medium bowl. Mix with a sturdy whisk or electric hand mixer until the glaze is smooth. Add a teaspoon of lemon juice or water if it is too thick. Cool the scones on a baking rack for 5 minutes before spreading each scone with glaze. They can be frozen for three months in an airtight container.

Banana-Walnut Loaf

This delicious banana-walnut loaf is a great way to use up those ripe bananas you have stashed in the freezer. Use soy-free vegan milk to make this loaf soy free.

2 CUPS UNBLEACHED ALL-PURPOSE FLOUR

1 CUP TOASTED WALNUTS, COARSELY CHOPPED

1/2 CUP NATURAL SUGAR

1 TABLESPOON DOUBLE-ACTING BAKING POWDER

1/2 TEASPOON SEA SALT

7 TABLESPOONS PLAIN OR VANILLA VEGAN MILK

1 TEASPOON APPLE CIDER VINEGAR

1 1/2 CUPS FROZEN RIPE BANANAS, THAWED AND WELL MASHED (4 TO 6 BANANAS)

1/3 CUP GRAPESEED OR SUNFLOWER OIL

1 TEASPOON PURE VANILLA EXTRACT

MAKES 1 LOAF

SOY-FREE OPTION

Freezing Bananas

Peel and cut ripe or over-ripe bananas into 1-inch slices. Store them in an airtight container in the freezer. When the bananas are needed, remove and thaw the amount needed. Use all the liquid from the thawed bananas in this recipe.

Preheat the oven to 350°F. Prepare a 9 x 5-inch loaf pan by lightly greasing it and dusting it with flour, emptying the pan of excess flour.

Combine the flour, walnuts, sugar, baking powder, and salt in a medium bowl. Mix well.

Combine the milk and vinegar in a separate medium bowl. Add the mashed bananas, oil, and vanilla. Mix well with a spatula.

Fold the flour mixture into the banana mixture, taking care not to over-work the batter. Fold only until the flour is incorporated into the liquid.

Transfer the batter to the prepared loaf pan and bake until a toothpick inserted into the bread comes out clean, about 1 hour. Remove the bread from the loaf pan immediately after it is baked and allow it to cool on a wire rack for at least 10 minutes before cutting.

VARIATION: Banana-Chocolate Chip Mini-Muffins. Omit the walnuts. Add 2/3 cup vegan semi-sweet chocolate chips to the banana mixture before combining it with the flour mixture. Scoop the batter, 2 tablespoons at a time, into mini muffin tins. Bake in the preheated 350°F oven until a toothpick inserted into the muffins comes out clean and the tops of the muffins are golden, about 35 minutes. Makes 12 mini muffins.

Corn Muffins

These cornbread muffins do not crumble. They are light and buttery and taste delightfully of corn, as any cornbread should. Serve these for breakfast with maple syrup or with Chipotle Chili (page 63), slathered with a little vegan butter. These are equally good sweet or savory. If desired, you can substitute whole wheat pastry flour for the unbleached all-purpose flour. Use soy-free vegan butter and milk to make these muffins soy free.

3 TABLESPOONS VEGAN BUTTER, AS NEEDED

1 CUP FRESH OR FROZEN CORN KERNELS, THAWED IF FROZEN

1 CUP PLAIN UNSWEETENED VEGAN MILK

1 TABLESPOON APPLE CIDER VINEGAR

3 TABLESPOONS PACKED BROWN SUGAR

2 TABLESPOONS APPLESAUCE

1 CUP UNBLEACHED ALL-PURPOSE FLOUR

3/4 CUP MEDIUM-GRIND CORNMEAL

1 TEASPOON SEA SALT

2 TEASPOONS DOUBLE-ACTING BAKING POWDER

1/4 TEASPOON BAKING SODA

MAKES 10 MUFFINS

QUICK & EASY
SOY-FREE OPTION

Preheat the oven to 400°F. Prepare a 12-muffin tin by generously greasing 10 of the tins with butter.

Combine the thawed corn, milk, vinegar, sugar, and applesauce in a blender. Blend for 10 seconds to break up the corn kernels. Set aside.

In a medium bowl, combine the flour, cornmeal, and salt. Sift in the baking powder and baking soda. Whisk to combine.

Make a well in the middle of the flour mixture and add the milk mixture. Fold together gently to combine; do not overwork the batter.

Transfer 1/4 cup batter to each of the 10 buttered muffin tins. Bake until they are light golden brown and a toothpick inserted in the center of the muffin in the middle tin comes out clean, about 15 minutes.

Cool the muffin tin on a wire rack for 5 minutes. Remove the muffins to the rack and continue to cool them for 5 more minutes before serving.

Flaky Buttermilk Herb Biscuits

These biscuits bake up big and beautiful! They have all the layers that you've come to expect from good-quality biscuits. The fact that they're vegan is just a bonus.

1 1/4 CUPS PLAIN UNSWEETENED VEGAN MILK

2 TEASPOONS APPLE CIDER VINEGAR

3 3/4 CUPS UNBLEACHED ALL-PURPOSE FLOUR, PLUS MORE FOR ROLLING

2 TABLESPOONS DOUBLE-ACTING BAKING POWDER

1 TEASPOON SEA SALT

1 1/2 STICKS (12 TABLESPOONS) COLD VEGAN BUTTER, CUT INTO 1/2-INCH CUBES

1/2 CUP MINCED PARSLEY LEAVES

1 TABLESPOON DRIED CHIVES

MAKES 10 TO 12 BISCUITS

Preheat oven to 450°F. Mix the milk and vinegar in a small bowl. Set it aside for 3 minutes to thicken.

Mix the flour, baking powder, and salt in a large bowl. Add the butter. Using a pastry knife or your fingers, cut the butter into the flour until the butter is about the size of peas. Create a well in the center of the flour mixture and pour in the milk mixture all at once. Add the parsley and chives. Gently combine the flour and milk with your hand just until the milk is absorbed into the flour. Handle carefully to avoid tough biscuits.

Turn the dough out onto a well-floured surface and knead it 6 to 8 times or until the dough comes together. Add more flour to the dough if it is too sticky, adding just enough flour to prevent a lot of sticking, but not too much to achieve a light, flaky biscuit.

Roll the dough out into a rough rectangle about 1/2-inch thick. Fold the dough in half and then in half again. Roll it out again into a rough rectangle about 1/2-inch thick, adding more flour as needed. Repeat the folding and rolling 4 more times, for a total of folding it 5 times. If the dough becomes too difficult to roll, allow it to relax for 5 minutes before proceeding.

Roll the dough into a rough rectangle about 1/2-inch thick one final time. Cut it into about 10 (3-inch) rounds using a floured biscuit cutter, or a floured drinking glass. Place the biscuits on a lightly oiled baking sheet. Bake for 5 minutes, then reduce the temperature to 425°F. Continue to bake until golden brown, about 15 to 20 minutes. Transfer to a wire rack to cool for 5 minutes before serving.

Soft Pretzels

It's surprising just how easy pretzels are to make at home, not to mention how much fun! Watching the pretzels darken to a golden shiny brown is kitchen magic. Pass the mustard!

1 1/2 CUPS WARM WATER

2 TABLESPOONS GRAPESEED OR SUNFLOWER OIL

1 TABLESPOON MAPLE SYRUP

2 1/4 TEASPOON ACTIVE DRY YEAST

4 1/2 CUPS UNBLEACHED ALL-PURPOSE FLOUR

1 TEASPOON SEA SALT

4 CUPS WATER, FOR BOILING

1/2 CUP BAKING SODA

1/2 TEASPOON KOSHER SALT

2 TABLESPOONS VEGAN BUTTER, MELTED

MAKES 10 PRETZELS

VARIATION: Sweet Cinnamon Pretzels. To make sweet cinnamon pretzels, omit the kosher salt. Sprinkle the baked pretzels with 2 tablespoons sugar mixed with 1/2 teaspoon cinnamon after the pretzels are buttered. Serve as is or dip them in your favorite icing.

Combine the warm water, oil, maple syrup, and yeast in a small bowl. Stir and set aside for 5 minutes.

Combine the flour and salt in a food processor or a stand mixer fitted with a dough hook. Pulse to combine.Add the yeast mixture. Process until well combined and kneaded, 1 minute in a food processor or 4 minutes in a stand mixer. Knead the dough until it comes together and is shiny. If it is too sticky, add another 1/4 cup of flour. It should be a soft, tacky dough. Alternatively, knead the dough by hand.

Oil a large bowl with 1 tablespoon of oil. Transfer the dough to the oiled bowl, cover with plastic wrap, and set in a warm place to double in size, about 1 hour. Preheat the oven to 425°F.

Heat 4 cups of water and the baking soda in a large pot. Bring to a simmer while you form the pretzels. Lightly oil 2 baking sheets. Transfer the dough to an unfloured work surface. Divide the dough into 10 equal portions. Roll each portion into a 20-inch long rope. Fold the ends over into a pretzel shape and transfer the formed pretzel dough to the oiled baking sheet. Repeat with all portions of dough.

Transfer 2 raw pretzels to the baking soda water. Cook for 20 seconds then remove with a slotted spoon, allowing excess water to drip off. Place the pretzels back onto the oiled baking sheet. Repeat until all the pretzels have been dipped into the baking soda water. Sprinkle the pretzels with kosher salt. Bake until golden brown, 7 to 10 minutes. Remove from the oven and brush the pretzels with melted butter while still hot.

RESOURCES

Online Shopping

Sometimes it's easier to locate an ingredient or two online than in stores. When that happens, I turn to these online retailers.

www.amazon.com
www.bluemountainorganics.com
www.bobsredmill.com
www.butlerfoods.com (Soy Curls)
www.foodfightgrocery.com
www.healthy-eating.com
www.vitacost.com
www.veganstore.com
www.veganessentials.com

Online News and Support

American Vegan Society: www.americanvegan.org
Compassion Over Killing: www.cok.net
Farm Sanctuary: www.farmsanctuary.org
Mercy for Animals: www.mercyforanimals.org
North American Vegetarian Society: www.navs-online.org
PETA (People for the Ethical Treatment of Animals): www.peta.org
Post Punk Kitchen: www.ppk.com
The Vegan Society: www.vegansociety.com
The Vegetarian Resource Group: www.vrg.org
Vegan.com: www.vegan.com
Vegan-friendly alcohol: www.barnivore.com
Vegan-friendly restaurants: www.happycow.net
Vegsource: www.vegsource.com

Online Nutrition Resources

Vegan Outreach: www.veganoutreach.com
Physicians Committee for Responsible Medicine: www.pcrm.org
No Meat Athlete: www.nomeatathlete.com
Hidden Animal Ingredients: www.happycow.net/health-animal-ingredients.html
Jack Norris, R.D.: www.jacknorrisrd.com
Virginia Messina, R.D.: www.theveganrd.com
Vegan Health by Vegan Outreach: www.veganhealth.org

Apps

Application software, or apps, help the user perform certain tasks efficiently and quickly. There are now apps that scan the bar code of products to determine whether they are vegan or not. There are apps that contain lists of animal ingredients and even one that translates your vegan food needs into different languages to help when you are traveling internationally. Below are some useful ones.

To determine if a product is vegan:
Is It Vegan? and VegScan

List of animal derived ingredients:
Animal-Free

List of cruelty free products:
Cruelty-Free and BNB (Be Nice to Bunnies)

Finding vegan recipes:
Vegan Recipe Finder

Beer, wine, and spirits:
Vegan Is Easy

Vegan and vegetarian restaurant finder:
Happy Cow

Educational Films on DVD

Blackfish
Earthlings
Food, Inc.
Forks Over Knives
Vegucated

Kitchen Tools & Equipment

Where kitchen equipment is concerned, a few things are not vital but make life easier, and then there are gadgets that seem over-the-top. However, there are several kitchen tools that you simply can't work well without. Here, I have assembled a list of the tools and equipment that I use in my kitchen and which are essential to making meals as quickly and easily as possible.

Aluminum foil: The best way to keep a pot or casserole dish tightly covered for baking is by using foil. If the food will be touching the foil, it is best to first cover the dish with parchment and then with the foil.

Baking sheets: You should have at least two that are small enough to fit in your oven. Ones with raised edges are best for multi-tasking.

Bowls, glass and stainless steel: Glass bowls are great for storing things and rising dough, but for mixing ingredients, the lighter-weight stainless steel bowls are more efficient. A variety of sizes is best.

Box Grater: Sturdy because it is shaped like a box, with a fine grater on one side and a coarse grater on the other.

Cake pans: 2 deep round metal pans and one or two 8-inch square metal pans.

Casserole dishes: Useful sizes are a deep 3-quart dish, a shallow 2-quart dish, and a 9 x 13-inch baking dish for lasagna and seitan.

Cheesecloth and twine: Useful for tying up a seitan roast to keep its form.

Citrus reamer: I have a wooden reamer that I use with a strainer. Using a reamer actually extracts more juice than just squeezing the citrus by hand.

Colander: Used for draining pasta, rinsing beans, and draining boiled potatoes.

Dry measuring cups and spoons: Choose measuring spoons that fit inside your spice jars to save time and frustration, and have more than one set on hand if you can.

Fine mesh strainer, large and small: To sift flour, rinse quinoa, sift confectioners' sugar, and strain citrus juice of seeds.

Food processor: Better than a blender for use with solid or dry ingredients or mixtures that don't turn over easily. It's also capable of slicing and grating, if applicable blades are provided. Dough-making is a snap in a food processor.

Grill spatula/pancake turner: A stainless steel spatula with a 4 to 6 inch flat turner, useful for cast iron skillets or stainless steel skillets. Not to be used on nonstick pans.

High-speed blender: High-speed blenders, such as Vitamix and Blendtec, are great for making very smooth sauces and mixtures, but they are costly. Once you're ready to spring for one, they are well worth the price.

Ice cream scoop: I have a smaller scoop (2 tablespoon capacity) for scooping cookie dough and measuring batter into mini-muffin tins, and a bigger ice cream size scooper to measure portions for burgers or batter for regular muffins tins. These make measuring and portioning ingredients much faster.

Immersion blender: Otherwise known as a stick blender, it can be immersed in the liquid (such as soups and sauces) in order to blend them. It is also usable in a wide-mouth Mason jar.

Kitchen scale (optional): I love my kitchen scale. I have a digital scale that I use every time I make seitan to measure the flour. I also use it to weigh produce and divide ingredients into equal portions.

Knives: I have an 8-inch chef knife and a 3 1/2 inch paring knife. There are some great knives at reasonable process, so just buy the best you can afford. It's important to keep your knives sharp as it will makes your work easier, faster, and safer. You are more likely to cut yourself with a dull knife.

Liquid measuring cups: I love to have 2-cup measuring cups and a few quarter-cup measuring cups. The smaller cups are very handy for measuring tablespoons of liquid.

Mandoline: Slicing potatoes, cucumbers, or other vegetables paper thin is made very quick and easy using a mandoline slicer. Make sure to learn how to use the guard efficiently.

Mason jars: Quart-size wide-mouth jars are great for making dressing and mayo and they fit most stick blenders.

Microplane zester: Used for zesting citrus, grinding whole nutmeg, and grating ginger.

Muffin tins: Standard 12-muffin tin pan and a 24-mini-muffin tin pan are great.

Nut milk bag: Can be used to strain yogurt or nut milk.

Offset spatula: A 4 1/2-inch bent spatula used for spreading frosting on cakes, spreading batter into pans, spreading pizza sauce on dough, and countless other uses.

Oven thermometer: Spend the $5 and get one. Most ovens are off by at least 10°F, which can make a big difference when it comes to baked goods and cooking seitan.

Pastry or basting brush: A brush with a 6-inch handle is ideal for brushing butter onto pretzels and basting your seitan roast to perfection.

Pastry scraper: This very handy tool is used to loosen dough stuck onto the work surface, scoop veggies into pots, or even cut seitan or dough into proper portions. Also known as a bench scraper.

Peeler: my favorite peeler is a straight-edge one, with the blade parallel to the handle, as that of a knife. It is important that the peeler remove enough of the vegetable peel that a second pass with the tool is not required.

Personal blender: These are useful in making small amounts of sauces, blending small amounts of liquids, as a seed and nut grinder, and, of course, making smoothies.

Pizza stone: A flat stone or ceramic slab that heats up and pulls moisture away from the dough to help achieve a crispy crust. A pizza pan does not absorb moisture or distribute heat like a pizza stone does.

Plastic wrap: The best way to keep heat inside of a bowl, such as for rising dough, is by covering the bowl with plastic wrap.

Potato masher: Mashers are not just for potatoes. Actually, they shouldn't be used for potatoes at all; you should use a potato ricer for potatoes and use your potato masher for mashing beans, bananas, and tofu.

Potato ricer: Great for mashed potatoes, a larger one is best, one that will fit a regular sized potato. Once you cut the cooked potato in half, place the cut side of the potato against the ricer, squeeze down to press with the handle and the potato emerges on the other side, while the skins stay behind in the machine. It is also great to use for squeezing the water out of cooked greens.

Pots and pans: Large, medium, and small pots with lids are needed for cooking. If they are oven safe, that's an added bonus.

Rolling pin: Standard rolling pins range from 17 to 20 inches long, but if you can find one that is around 10 inches long, it will make rolling small items or seitan cutlets much easier.

Salad spinner: Nothing beats a salad spinner for drying greens and herbs. Choose one with a solid base instead of one with holes.

Sharpening stone or knife sharpener: Needed to keep knives sharp.

Silicone baking mat or parchment paper: Silicone baking mats prevent baked goods from sticking without the need for oil or parchment paper. Nevertheless, parchment paper comes in handy, too.

Silicone spatulas in multiple sizes: These are high-heat resistant utensils that can be used in hot liquids on the stove without melting.
Skillet: Stainless steel skillets are great, but you have to use more oil to keep food from sticking, and the pans cannot be seasoned. Cast iron skillets can become semi-non-stick with the help of seasoning. Learn how to season your skillet using high heat and oil. The oil will "burn" onto the cast iron, creating a patina, which makes the skillet almost non-stick. Commercially made non-stick skillets are coated with a material that prevents food from sticking.

Steamer basket: Silicone or metal baskets that fit into a large pot, instantly transforming a pot into a steamer for vegetables.

Tofu Xpress or flour sack towel: I wrap tofu in lint-free kitchen towels called flour sack towels and set it aside to absorb excess moisture. Another way to press tofu is the Tofu Xpress, a plastic box with a plastic top that is pressed down with the help of a sturdy spring.

Whisks, large and small: Two whisks in different sizes are ideal.

Wooden cutting boards in various sizes: I prefer the feel of wood to plastic boards, but that is subjective. Do not use glass cutting boards; they are no friends of your knives.

Wooden spoons and spatulas: Select sturdy items that are high-heat resistant.

Acknowledgments

Many thanks are due to my incredibly creative and supportive testers. I am extremely grateful for your hard work, your patience, your taste buds, and your critiques. Looking back through the recipes, I see your individual imprints and how you have made the recipes all the better. Huge thanks to Dorian Farrow, who was an internet friend from the very beginning, Kelly and Mac Cavalier, Liz Wyman, Jenna Patton, Russell Patton, Claire Desroches, Anna B. Holt, and the boys, Megan Clarke, GiGi Anber Tasse and Larry, Rebecca Ross, Jael Baldwin, Ruchama Burrell, and Nichole Kraft. There are no words to properly convey my gratitude.

On the home front, I couldn't have done any of this without my darling husband, David Dever, who now hopes he can retire. And I am incredibly blessed to have three of the most amazing children, Mikel, Catriona, and Katelyn who might not like everything I cook, but, nonetheless, try everything.

A special thanks to cookbook authors Robin Robertson and Tamasin Noyes for their support and encouragement.

And deep gratitude to Jon Robertson and the staff at Vegan Heritage Press. It is incredible how much work goes into publishing a book and your guidance kept me moving in the right direction. Thank you for all your talent and hard work.

About the Author

Photo by Katelyn Dever

Zsu Dever is the author of *Everyday Vegan Eats.* Also known online as Vegan Aide, she has been involved in the restaurant business most of her life. She hails from a long line of culinary professionals and restaurateurs. She is the author of the blog Zsu's Vegan Pantry. Zsu is passionate about teaching new vegans and vegetarians how to succeed with their newly chosen diet and become lifelong vegans. She is a homeschooling mother of three teenagers and resides in San Diego, CA.

Website: www.zsusveganpantry.com
Facebook: https://www.facebook.com/zsuzsanna.dever
Facebook: https://www.facebook.com/ZsusVeganPantry
Facebook: https://www.facebook.com/EverydayVeganEats
Twitter: https://twitter.com/ZsuDever
Pinterest: http://www.pinterest.com/zsudever/
Instagram: http://instagram.com/zsus_vegan_pantry

Index